CRACKING JOKES:

Studies of Sick Humor Cycles & Stereotypes

Alan Dundes

TEN SPEED PRESS

Credits & Permissions

"The Dead Baby Joke Cycle" (Chapter 1) first appeared in *Western Folklore* 38 (1979): 145–57, and is reprinted by permission of the California Folklore Society.

"Game of the Name: A Quadriplegic Sick Joke Cycle" (Chapter 2) first appeared in *Names* 3 (1985): 289–92 and is reprinted by permission of the American Name Society.

"Auschwitz Jokes" (Chapter 3) first appeared in *Western Folklore* 42 (1983): 249–60, and is reprinted by permission of the California Folklore Society.

"On Elephantasy and Elephanticide" (Chapter 4) first appeared in the *Psychoanalytic Review* 56 (1969): 225–41, and is reprinted by permission of the Guilford Press.

"Jokes and Covert Language Attitudes: The Curious Case of the Wide-Mouth Frog" (Chapter 5) first appeared in *Language in Society* 6 (1977): 141–47, and is reprinted by permission of Cambridge University Press.

"The J.A.P. and the J.A.M. in American Jokelore" (Chapter 6) first appeared in the *Journal of American Folklore* 98 (1985): 456–75 and is reprinted by permission of the American Folklore Society.

"97 Reasons Why Cucumbers Are Better Than Men" (Chapter 7) appears for the first time in this volume.

"Slurs International: Folk Comparisons of Ethnicity and National Character" (Chapter 8) first appeared in *Southern Folklore Quarterly* 39 (1975): 15–38, and is reprinted by permission.

"A Study of Ethnic Slurs: The Jew and the Polack in the United States" (Chapter 9) first appeared in the *Journal of American Folklore* 84 (1971): 186–203, and is reprinted by permission of the American Folklore Society.

"Polish Pope Jokes" (Chapter 10) first appeared in the *Journal of American Folklore* 92 (1979): 219–22, and is reprinted by permission of the American Folklore Society.

"Many Hands Make Light Work or Caught in the Act of Screwing in Light Bulbs" (Chapter 11) first appeared in *Western Folklore* 40 (1981): 261–66, and is reprinted by permission of the California Folklore Society.

"Misunderstanding Humor: An American Stereotype of the Englishman" (Chapter 12) first appeared in *International Folklore Review* 2 (1982): 10–15, and is reprinted by permission of Dr. Venetia Newall, editor.

"Laughter Behind the Iron Curtain: A Sample of Rumanian Political Jokes" (Chapter 13) first appeared in the *Ukrainian Quarterly* 27 (1971): 50–59, and is reprinted by permission.

1☺

TEN SPEED PRESS
P. O. Box 7123
Berkeley, California 94707

Book Design by Nancy Austin
Cover Design by Brent Beck
Composition by Classic Typography

Library of Congress Cataloging-in-Publication Data
Dundes, Alan.
    Cracking jokes.
    Bibliography: p.
    1. Wit and humor — Psychological aspects.   2. Stereo-
types (Psychology)   I. Title.
PN6149.P5D85   1987   809.7   86-23068
ISBN 0–89815–188–0 (paper), ISBN 0–89815–206–2 (cloth)

Manufactured in the United States of America
1 2 3 4 5 — 90 89 88 87 86

CONTENTS

Preface   v

PART I: SICK HUMOR CYCLES

Chapter 1   The Dead Baby Joke Cycle   3

Chapter 2   Game of the Name: A Quadriplegic Sick Joke Cycle   15

Chapter 3   Auschwitz Jokes *(with Thomas Hauschild)*   19
            Postscript: More on Auschwitz Jokes
            (with Uli Linke)   29

PART II: STEREOTYPES

Chapter 4   On Elephantasy and Elephanticide: The Effect
            of Time and Place *(with Roger D. Abrahams)*   41

Chapter 5   The Curious Case of the Wide-Mouth Frog:
            Jokes and Covert Language Attitudes   55

Chapter 6   The Jewish American Princess and the
            Jewish American Mother in American Jokelore   62

Chapter 7   97 Reasons Why Cucumbers Are Better Than Men   82

Chapter 8   Slurs International: Folk Comparisons of
            Ethnicity and National Character   96

Chapter 9   The Jew and the Polack in the United States:
            A Study of Ethnic Slurs   115

Chapter 10 Polish Pope Jokes   139

Chapter 11 Many Hands Make Light Work, or
            Caught in the Act of Screwing in Light Bulbs   143

Chapter 12 Misunderstanding Humor:
            An American Stereotype of the Englishman   150

Chapter 13 Laughter Behind the Iron Curtain:
            A Sample of Rumanian Political Jokes   159

PREFACE

All my life, I have loved jokes. I cannot remember a time when I did not enjoy hearing someone tell a joke well. From grade school on, I became avidly interested in jokes, frequently repeating favorites to anyone who would listen to me. I recall with nostalgia how my father, despite his fatigue after a day of work sixty miles from home, would often share a "new" joke he had heard during the day. Nearly forty years later, I can still retell some of the jokes he told.

During my high school years, I eagerly devoured the few compilations of published jokes available in local libraries. I learned dirty jokes at adolescent outings, parties, and summer camp. At that time, I simply enjoyed the jokes, without a thought that I might ever want to study them seriously.

In college, as an English major, I learned to appreciate humor in more literary terms. Comedy was something that any student of classical writers or of Shakespeare had to take into consideration. Eventually I discovered Freud's essay, *Wit and Humor in the Unconscious*. I marvelled at the lucidity of his writing, even in translation from the German, and at the truly remarkable insights contained in his brilliant analysis of the jokes he presented.

After graduating from college, I served in the Navy for two years, where I heard hundreds upon hundreds of jokes. Often, during a dull four-hour watch, the men on duty with me would swap stories to help while away the time. I participated for pleasure; it never occurred to me to take notes on these jokes or to record them.

Only in graduate school at Indiana University, in the doctoral program in folklore, did I finally discover that jokes were a standard folklore genre and that it was perfectly all right to investigate them. In a course in American folklore taught by the late Professor Richard M. Dorson, we were required to make a collection of folklore, and were permitted to use ourselves as informants. My own considerable repertoire of jokes, I discovered, was enough to fulfill this assignment. I was astonished to learn that the great Finnish folklorist Antti Aarne had included the category "Jokes and Anecdotes" in his pioneering tale type index, the *Verzeichnis der Märchentypen.*[1] I soon realized that some of the jokes I had heard in childhood were merely American versions of international tale types, with analogues in Europe, the Near East, and even Asia. Still later, I delved into Gershon Legman's massive scholarly treatment of dirty jokes.[2] Legman's unique combination of erudition and analysis made a lasting impression on me.

Of course, jokes are only one genre of folklore. I have spent many years studying other genres as well: myths, proverbs, riddles, legends, superstitions, and so on. I find all folklore challenging, and I never cease to be grateful that I became a professional folklorist.

Since 1963 I have taught an introductory course in the forms of folklore in the Anthropology Department at the University of California, Berkeley. Following the example of my mentor, Richard Dorson, I asked students to make collections by gathering folklore from their friends, their families, and themselves. This enabled them to understand the power and meaning of folklore more than they possibly could have simply from reading books or listening to my lectures. These students' collections include a great variety of folklore genres. One might consist entirely of fiddle tunes or guitar strums; others might be a mixture of proverbs, riddles, and gestures. Every class has some students who especially like jokes and they frequently turn in some of their favorite specimens. These folklore collections keep me in touch with various joke cycles that come into being. The combined personal networks of all the students in my folklore classes every year almost ensure that every new joke cycle will come to my attention.

From this never-ending source, I have sought to keep tabs on a number of distinct joke cycles during the past two decades. The American penchant for novelty tends to prohibit any cycle from lasting too long. Any given cycle seems to be gradually or abruptly replaced by another. For example, no one tells 1940s "Little Moron Jokes" in the 1980s. Elephant jokes, once all the rage in the 1960s, have virtually disappeared from the scene, having yielded to such cycles as Polack jokes or dead baby jokes or light bulb jokes. Unless such joke cycles are documented while they are current, they may be lost to posterity forever. Oral tradition can disappear without a trace if no one bothers to record it. I stress that these joke cycles are *oral*. Occasionally they may be found in written form, as in mass-produced books aimed at a commercial popular market. But for the most part, joke cycles come into vogue and are told everywhere in the country for a time, after which the novelty wears off and the flurry of joketelling on that subject ebbs as suddenly as it began.

In hearing elephant jokes or dead baby jokes, you cannot help but be struck by the *content* of these jokes. The activities of the elephant protagonist are so apparently absurd and the details of the dead baby jokes so gruesome and grotesque that it seems hopeless to ask what such jokes might mean. Certainly, the vast majority of people who transmit and enjoy these jokes seems to have little idea of the possible meaning(s) behind them. It is deemed sufficient to memorize enough of the latest joke cycle craze in order to participate in a group joke-swapping session. This is certainly the case among teenagers, who worry (perhaps unduly) about not being in the "know" about such matters. Yet if you asked these teenagers what dead baby jokes might mean, they might respond, "They're just *gross!* They don't mean anything." Adults might well share this view.

As a folklorist, I have come to believe that no piece of folklore continues to be transmitted *unless* it means something — even if neither the speaker nor the audience can articulate what that meaning might be. In fact, it usually is essential that the joke's meaning *not* be crystal clear. If people knew what they were communicating when they told jokes, the jokes would cease to be effective as socially sanctioned outlets for expressing taboo ideas and subjects. Where there is anxiety, there will be jokes to express that anxiety. A society with political repression will generate an abundance of political jokes. Indeed, the more repressive the regime, the more numerous the political jokes.

In the United States, we have relatively few *orally* transmitted political jokes. Why? Because we have a relatively free press. It's easy to hear or read editorials lambasting political figures on a daily basis; we have little need for oral political jokes. It is in countries without free press that a multitude of political jokes can be found. In the United States, subjects such as sexuality and racism — which cannot always be discussed openly — tend to become the hidden subjects of joke cycles.

In the essays reprinted in this volume, I have tried to analyze various jokes, usually those that appear in an extended series or cycle. Over the years, it's been interesting to see possible cycles begin but end almost immediately. For example, during the presidency of Lyndon B. Johnson, one of his aides, Walter Jenkins, was arrested in a Washington, D.C. men's room for involvement in a homosexual act. Homosexuality — then certainly a taboo topic — probably accounted for a small series of jokes that appeared within weeks (if not days) of the incident.

Now we know why all the lights at the White House are turned out (al-
luding to an economy measure introduced by President Johnson);
What was the first thing LBJ said upon hearing the news about Jenkins?
I'll never turn my back on Walter Jenkins (referring to former President
Harry S. Truman's famous remark about Alger Hiss, a former State
Department official accused of being a Communist). Did you hear
about the new sign on the White House lawn? All trespassers will be
violated. But this incipient cycle died almost as soon as it started, and
the creative force that produced it turned to other matters. Similarly,
in 1985, when a newborn baby Fae, suffering from a heart deficiency,
was given the heart of a baboon in a hospital in Loma Linda, California, a small rash of Baby Fae jokes began to circulate. What's the
fastest thing in the world? A baboon going through Loma Linda. What's
Baby Fae doing now? She's picking lice off the other babies in the nur-
sery. What will Baby Fae do about the scar when she grows up? No
problem, the hair will cover it. No doubt the poor infant's death put
an early damper on such jokes; but the fact remains that the thought
of an animal donor providing a transplant for a human captured the
nation's imagination. Neither the Jenkins jokes nor the Baby Fae jokes
ever achieved full cycle-status. They are but brief, faded instances of
how one person's tragedy may become a point of projection or catharsis
for the fears and anxieties of others. Remember, people joke about only
what is most serious. That is why there are so many jokes about death
or ethnic stereotypes. Even the end of the world can be grist for the
joke mill.

"Did you hear the World War III knock-knock joke?"
"No."
"Knock, Knock."
"Who's there?"
(Silence!)

Don't be deceived by the facade of humor. The expression, "laughing
to keep from crying," has a good deal of merit.

Some readers may find some of the jokes discussed in this volume
offensive. Even I did. In fact, initially I had some difficulty getting
a few of my essays published. The political jokes from Rumania could
not possibly be published there. There is even a political joke on that
very point: Did you hear about the new joketelling contest in Bucharest? No. Yes, the first prize, fifteen years! When I tried to publish
the essay, "Laughter Behind the Iron Curtain," in the United States,

I encountered problems as well. The editor of *East European Quarterly*, an obvious publishing outlet for the piece (I thought), informed me that although these jokes were certainly traditional (authentic), he felt he had to worry about the East European subscribers to his journal. Publishing such an essay, he argued, might cause difficulties in the countries behind the Iron Curtain. The subscriptions might be cancelled as a protest. Hoping that I would "understand the sensitive nature of such an editorial decision," he regretfully declined to publish the essay. So there is self-censorship here as well. Publishing such political jokes is not forbidden, just inconvenient. Only when I found an emigré journal, the *Ukrainian Quarterly*, could I get that paper published.

Another example of censorship occurred with respect to my study of the Jew and the Pole in jokes, reprinted here. I originally submitted it to Hungarian colleagues who had requested me to write something for a *festschrift* (a volume of essays to celebrate a colleague's sixtieth birthday or retirement) to honor Gyula Ortutay, one of this century's leading Hungarian folklorists. The essay (as you will see) compares the stereotypes of Jews and Poles as expressed in ethnic slur jokes. For some months, I heard nothing from Hungary. Then from an indirect source (not the editors of the *festschrift*) I was told that my paper was causing the editors real difficulties. After a second note from yet another indirect source, I decided to write the editors, whom I had certainly not intended to embarrass, for clarification. They quickly answered by saying that I would have to make some revisions before they could publish my paper. They explained that there was a state law in Hungary prohibiting the ridiculing of national groups, making it impossible for me to include any jokes about the Poles. They proposed that my essay would be acceptable if I simply deleted all the texts about the Poles. This took me aback—it was hard to see how a paper comparing the Jew and the Pole in jokes could possibly survive the deletion of all the jokes about Poles. Also, I was struck (though not entirely surprised) by the fact that my jokes about Jews could remain intact. Evidently, the Hungarian state law in question did not object to jokes about Jews! I responded by saying that I could not delete all the jokes about Poles, if the integrity of the paper were to be maintained, and suggested that the editors put a disclaimer on the paper to the effect that the views expressed were mine and not theirs. Otherwise, they should return the paper to me. They did return the paper— to their great relief, no doubt. It is fairly unusual to be rejected from a *festschrift* volume to which one had been formally invited to submit a paper. (A *festschrift* invitation is regarded in the academy as virtually a certain, foolproof publication.) I mention this incident only to show just how sensitive jokes can be.

Fascinating though the jokes in this volume are, the commentaries are equally valuable. For my aim, in folklore in general and in jokelore in particular, is to analyze and interpret the material. You may or may not agree with my interpretation of the jokes presented, but what matters is that you think about the possible meaning(s) of these and other jokes. There are dozens and dozens of anthologies of jokes, but few if any make the slightest attempt to analyze the jokes they include. On the other side of the spectrum are the treatises devoted to the subject of humor or the nature of comedy; but these, which are often highly philosophical or psychological, rarely include or discuss the kinds of joke cycles presented here.[3] With few exceptions,[4] specific humor cycles are never even mentioned, much less analyzed.

In a sense, then, *Cracking Jokes* attempts to fill the gap between the popular anthologies of jokes that are presented *without analysis*, and the many abstract treatises on humor that offer the other extreme of analysis *without texts*. Both the jokes and analyses are necessary.

Several years ago, someone responded to a newspaper story about my research by sending me a letter addressed simply to "The Joke Professor, University of California, Berkeley." That was understandable; the writer had simply forgotten my name. What surprised me, however, was that the letter was delivered! I suppose the epithet wouldn't be a bad one really. Still, I would prefer to be a professor of jokes rather than a joke professor. The essays in *Cracking Jokes* should explain that preference.

Alan Dundes
Berkeley, California

PART ONE:

Sick Humor Cycles

CHAPTER 1

The Dead Baby Joke Cycle

Dead baby jokes are not for the squeamish or the faint of heart. They are told mostly by American adolescents of both sexes with the intent to shock or disgust listeners. "Oh how gross!" is a common (and evidently desired) response to a dead baby joke. Informants who were teenagers during the 1960s and 1970s indicate that dead baby jokes were often used in a "gross out," in which each participant tries to outdo previous joketellers in recounting unsavory or crude jokes.

Dead baby jokes are a form of sick humor, and it cannot be denied that there is a sick streak — and a longstanding one at that — in American humor. Perhaps it is partly a reaction to the traditional failure of Americans to discuss disease and death openly. Folklorist Louise Pound once amassed a considerable number of popular euphemisms for death and dying, although she declined to comment on the possible sociological significance of why there was such a large corpus of conventional circumlocutions.[1] The higher the incidence of euphemisms that scrupulously avoid direct mention of a subject, the greater the anxiety about that subject. Even today, many Americans prefer not to say that an individual is dead or has died. They are more comfortable saying that so-and-so has "passed away" or "passed on" or "is no longer with us" or "is no longer living." If someone is no longer living, he is dead! Yet saying "no longer living" is somehow less blunt than saying "dead." In written discourse, the adjective "late" is often used to communicate politely the status of death, as in paying a scholarly tribute to the late Professor Such-and-such. However, it is by no means altogether clear how long after an individual's death it is appropriate to use this term. If a person has been dead for twenty years, is he still "late"? Maybe "late" is a shortened form of "late lamented," in which case "late" should cease to be used once the customary period of mourning or lamenting has ended.

Folklore provides a socially sanctioned outlet for the discussion of the forbidden and taboo. American idealism proclaims the Christian principle of "love thy neighbor" and celebrates such political rhetoric as "all men are created equal." Yet not all Americans really love their neighbors or believe in equality. Accordingly, American ethnic humor permits the expression of hate and the indulgence in the articulation of inequality. If Americans worship health and refuse to deal with disease—even after being struck by it—then American folklore might well (as in so many analogous instances) treat in fantasy what is avoided in reality.

It is not easy to pinpoint the beginnings of sick humor in America. However, surely one of the earliest and most influential sick humor cycles was the series of "Little Willie" quatrains. These date from the turn of the century and lasted well into the 1930s. Some believe that this cycle was inspired by a minor English poet, Harry Graham, who specialized in light verse and amusing doggerel. In 1899 he published *Ruthless Rhymes for Heartless Homes*. One such rhyme ran as follows:

> Billy, in one of his nice new sashes,
> Fell in the fire and was burnt to ashes;
> Now, although the room grows chilly,
> I haven't the heart to poke poor Billy.[2]

In time, the folk transformed Billy into Willie. In one of the Little Willies published in 1936, we find this version.

> Little Willie, in bows and sashes
> Fell in the fire and got burned to ashes.
> In the winter, when the weather is chilly,
> No one likes to poke up Willie.[3]

In any event, the Little Willie series involved much murder and mayhem. Typically, Willie killed off parents and siblings:

> Willie poisoned his father's tea;
> Father died in agony.
> Mother came, and looked quite vexed:
> "Really, Will," she said, "what next?"

> Little Willie hung his sister;
> She was dead before we missed her.
> Willie's always up to tricks.
> Ain't he cute? He's only six.[4]

Supposedly, the ghoulish quality and popularity of Little Willies led to the creation of the folk metaphor, "to give someone 'the Willies,'" which continues in oral tradition to the present day.[5]

In light of our consideration of dead baby jokes, the occasional Little Willies that mention babies are especially interesting. Actually, Harry Graham also included one or two references to infanticide. An 1899 rhyme entitled "Calculating Clara" went like this:

> O'er the rugged mountain's brow
> Clara threw the twins she nursed,
> And remarked, "I wonder now
> Which will reach the bottom first?"[6]

And a rhyme in the 1930 sequel, *More Ruthless Rhymes for Heartless Homes*, begins with a motivation for the action. The rhyme *"l'enfant glacé"* runs:

> When Baby's cries grew hard to bear
> I popped him in the Frigidaire.
> I never would have done so if
> I'd known that he'd be frozen stiff.
> My wife said: "George I'm so unhappé!
> Our darling's now completely *frappé*!"[7]

Several of the Little Willies are in the same vein:

> Willie, with a thirst for gore,
> Nailed the baby to the door.
> Mother said, with humor quaint,
> "Willie dear, don't spoil the paint."[8]

> Willie split the baby's head
> To see if brains were gray or red.
> Mother, troubled, said to father,
> "Children are an awful bother!"[9]

The last line of the latter quatrain may well contain a clue to the psychological rationale underlying the wish to kill babies.

Sometimes it was a girl rather than a little boy who disposed of a baby sibling rival:

> Baby sat on the window-seat;
> Mary pushed her into the street.
> Baby was spilt all over the area
> And mamma held up her forefinger at Mary.[10]

Here is another version:

> Baby sat on the window-seat.
> Mary pushed Baby into the street.
> Baby's brains splattered the 'arey,'
> And mother smiled "Tchk, tchk!" at Mary.[11]

Incidentally, the variations in these versions attest to the traditional nature of the Little Willies. Although Little Willies were popular in print, they also circulated orally.

The Little Willies cycle was followed by other sick humor series, such as Little Audrey.[12] Surely the best known of these are the sick or cruel jokes. Brian Sutton-Smith published a selection of 155 cruel jokes collected between September and December of 1958 in his article, "Shut Up and Keep Diggin': The Cruel Joke Series" and his compilation was supplemented by Roger Abrahams in his follow-up essay, "Ghastly Commands: The Cruel Joke Revisited."[13]

In the 1970s, sick humor has been manifested in a number of forms. There are, for example, sick Jesus jokes. Do you know why Jesus can't eat M & Ms? Because they fall through the holes in his hands.[14] A more common format for sick humor is provided by the good news/bad news opposition. Representative texts might include the following:

> A governor of a southern state goes for a long-overdue physical examination. Concerned about his health, the governor calls the doctor the next day and asks for a report. The doctor says he has good news and bad news.
> "Well," the governor says, "what's the good news?"
> "The good news is that you have six months to live."
> "The good news is I have six months to live? What's the bad news?"
> "The bad news is you have sickle-cell anemia."[15]

Actually, a number of the sick humor good news/bad news jokes are centered around conversations with doctors:

> A man goes for a check-up. The doctor examines him and says, "I have bad news and worse news."
> "What's the bad news?"
> "The bad news is you have one month to live."
> "Oh my god, what's the worse news?"
> "It's February."

> A man is in a hospital for a hernia operation. A nurse enters the operating room and drops a tray of instruments.

This causes the surgeon to make a slip and he accidentally cuts off the patient's testicles. When the man wakes up, he asks how he is. The doctor tells him he has bad news and good news. The bad news is that he cut off both testicles; the good news is there was no cancer.

A man who had to have a leg amputated woke up in the hospital. He asked his doctor how he was. The doctor said, "I have bad news and good news. The bad news is we took off the wrong leg. The good news is the other leg is getting better."

A man who was in an automobile accident wakes up in a hospital bed and asks the doctor how he is. "Well, I have bad news and good news."

"What's the bad news?"

"The bad news is that we had to amputate both your legs. The good news is that there's a man in the next bed who wants to buy your shoes."

A few good news/bad news jokes have dead baby content:

A doctor comes in to the maternity ward and tells a woman who just gave birth to a baby, "I have good news and bad news."

"What's the good news?"

"The good news is that your baby's alive and it's a giant eye."

"Oh my god, doctor, then what's the bad news?"

"The bad news is: It's blind."

This is similar to another sick joke involving a doctor in a maternity ward:

A doctor enters the maternity ward with a baby and he slings it around several times and finally throws it against the wall. It goes Splat! The mother screams, "Oh doctor, oh doctor, that was my baby."

The doctor replies, "Don't worry. It was dead anyway."[16]

Another recent sick joke involving a baby requires a knowledge of football ritual:

A fire breaks out in Houston. The firemen arrive and they see a black woman with her baby up on the balcony of the thirtieth floor of an apartment building. A fireman steps forward and tells the woman to drop her baby to him.

She is afraid to do so. She says, "I ain't gonna drop my baby to no white man." She refuses to drop the baby. The flames grow higher and higher. Finally, a black man steps out of the huge crowd that has gathered. He yells, "Throw down your baby, I'm Billy 'Whiteshoes' Johnson, the great pass catching football player. I'll catch your baby." He convinces her and she throws down her baby. Billy "Whiteshoes" Johnson circles around and makes a great one-handed catch of the baby. The crowd goes wild and cheers and cheers. Then doing a little dance (as if in the endzone), Billy "Whiteshoes" Johnson takes the baby and spikes it (dashes it to the ground as is done with the football upon scoring a touchdown).

None of these jokes is really part of the dead baby joke cycle. For one thing, dead baby jokes are in riddle form, beginning with a "what" question. The only reference to dead babies in Sutton-Smith's 1960 article is in the form of a folk simile rather than a riddle: **You're about as funny as a carload of dead babies.**[17] Abrahams calls the form "sick proverbial comparison" and gives as his first example, **As funny as a barrel of chopped-up babies on Mother's Day.**[18] The nature of the dead baby joke form will become abundantly clear from the following examples.

Probably the most common dead baby joke is:

What's red and sits in a corner?
A baby chewing (teething on, eating, sucking on) razor
    blades.

A text that may occur together with the above joke is:

What's green and sits in a corner?
Same baby two weeks later.

The "What's red?" formula is found in other, less common, dead baby jokes:

What's red and swings?
A baby on a meathook.

What's red and green, red and green?
A baby going through a lawn mower.

What's red and white, red and white, pink, pink, pink?
Baby in a blender.

Other colors are reported. For example, a very popular dead baby joke uses blue instead of red:

> What is blue and sits in a corner?
> A baby in a plastic bag. (A baby in a baggie.)

As with red, the blue text may also be followed by a related joke:

> What's blue and kicks? A baby in a plastic bag.
> What's blue and stiff? Same baby three days later.

Not all the dead baby jokes depend on color:

> What's harder to unload, a truck full of bowling balls (or
> bricks) or a truck full of dead babies?
> A truck full of bowling balls because you can't use a pitch-
> fork.

This common joke also has a sequel:

> What's more disgusting than a truckload of dead babies?
> A truckload of dead babies with one live one eating his
> way out.

The following text relates to this imagery pattern of a necrophagous nightmare:

> What's worse to be buried under: bowling balls or dead
> babies?
> Bowling balls—you can't eat your way out.

> or

> What's the difference between a bowling ball and a baby?
> You can't eat a bowling ball.

The cannibalistic theme continues:

> How do you make a dead baby float?
> Two scoops dead baby and one pint of root beer.[19]

Sometimes the dead babies are mutilated rather than eaten:

> What's more fun than nailing a dead baby to a wall (tree)?
> Ripping it off again.

Another example of body mutilation is an updated parody of an old riddle:

> How did the dead baby cross the road?
> He was stapled to a chicken.

There are other examples of dead baby jokes, e.g., **What is baby powder used for? Blowing up babies. What is baby oil used for? Frying babies.** But these are less common than those cited above. Still, sometimes the exceptional text may provide an important clue for those concerned with trying to discover underlying meanings. Thus, **What's red and goes round and round? A baby in a garbage disposal** may be of interest. Another text, **What's the difference between a baby and a spoon? You can't get a spoon down a garbage disposal,** confirms the association. Babies are like garbage—recall the texts in which they are placed in plastic bags—and the abiding concern seems to be with disposal. The issue literally seems to be how to get rid of babies.

Yet the meaning of the dead baby joke cycle is elusive. There are a number of possibilities, and they are not necessarily mutually exclusive. The joke cycle appears to have begun in the early 1960s and it has continued to flourish up until the late 1980s. The visual reporting of the Vietnam war, with its unending pictures of carnage and death, may have had something to do with the popularity of the cycle. Like gallows humor, the dead baby joke cycle tries to make light of the worst kind of human atrocity.

Another plausible interpretation might turn on the growing fear of technology. As Western cultures become more and more mechanized, there is concern lest man be mastered by, rather than master of, machines. Certainly, a large percentage of the dead baby jokes explicitly describe babies being ground up by a variety of modern "conveniences," such as lawnmowers, blenders, razor blades, and garbage disposals. Is the joke cycle warning of the possible or probable fate of modern man? Are we doomed to be destroyed by uncaring machines that we ourselves have created, allegedly to make life easier and more pleasurable?

There may also be an undercurrent of racism in the cycle. The repeated references to colors (red, blue, and so on) suggest that it is specifically "colored" babies who are—in terms of folkloristic wishful thinking—being killed off. Even supposedly liberal northern communities in the United States, including the white children in such communities, have opposed integration. The dead baby jokes are particularly popular with junior and senior high school students. This would explain why an elephant joke was selected to be converted into a dead baby joke (**How to make a dead baby float?**), since the elephant joke cycle may have been a socially sanctioned subterfuge to express white hostility and aggression against blacks.[20] It may be noteworthy that one variant of the "baby in a blender" joke (which also depends on color) is: What is green and goes two hundred and fifty miles an hour? A frog in a blender. If a red or colored object (in the dead baby joke cycle) is symbolic of a frog, and if a frog (such as a wide-mouth frog) is symbolic of a black, then the cycle may well represent white protest against the perceived unwelcome intrusion of hundreds of colored babies.[21]

But the most obvious interpretation of the cycle seems to be a protest against babies in general. The attempt to legalize abortion and the increased availability of improved contraceptives (e.g., the pill) have brought the debate about the purpose of sexual activity into the public arena, where even teenagers can participate. There is, of course, the element of sibling rivalry—any child's fear of being displaced by a younger sibling—which we can clearly see in the turn-of-the-century Little Willies. However, sibling rivalry alone would not account for the popularity and growth of the dead baby joke cycle in the 1960s and 1970s. Sibling rivalry has been a factor in human societies from the beginning of human existence; the dead baby joke cycle in its present form has flourished for only two or three decades.

The highly publicized improved means of contraception and the initiation of sex-education classes in the public schools have made teenagers more aware of the dangers of pregnancy. Women's liberation ideology may also have contributed by insisting that women's place was not necessarily in the home and that motherhood was not the only career open to women. More and more, babies were perceived as a perfidious male plot to keep women subjugated. "Keep 'em barefoot, pregnant, and in the kitchen" is a folk dictum expressing this male chauvinistic point of view. For women to be liberated, they need to keep from getting pregnant; or, if they become pregnant, they may wish to consider abortion as a means of retaining their newly found freedom.

But a price is paid for contraception and abortion. That price includes the guilt of preventing the creation of, or destroying, a potential human being. Planned Parenthood does try to separate sexuality from procreation, but that does not alter the essential biological fact that any heterosexual act of intercourse can, in theory, produce a new being. It is possible that one way of fighting the fear or gilding the guilt is to tell gross dead baby jokes, as if to dehumanize babies and thus destroy them through modern technology (including contraceptive devices). The razor blade may be analogous to the sharp instrument used (unwisely) in nonmedical abortions; the baby trapped in a plastic baggie is perhaps the fantastic realization of a potential being trapped in a condom or stopped by a diaphragm, or a newborn left to die. Whether the means is a pitchfork or a garbage disposal unit, the baby is to be thrown away forever.

Sometimes what is thrown away forever may come back to haunt the guilty party. In a joke that depends very much upon convulsive gestures and stuttering speech for its impact, this is precisely what happens:

> A greatly misshapen, bent-over man with twisted, gnarled limbs clambers up a long flight of stairs and knocks on the door of an apartment. The door is opened by a kindly, apple-cheeked, gray-haired woman. The man says, "E-E-Ex-cuse m-m-me, a-a-are y-y-you, M-M-Mrs. Sm-Sm-Smith?"
>
> The woman replies, "Why, yes I am."
>
> "D-D-Did y-y-you u-u-used t-t-to l-l-live in M-M-Mil-waukee?"
>
> "Why, yes I did."
>
> "I-I-In 1932, d-d-did y-y-you h-h-have a m-m-miscar-riage?"
>
> "Why, yes I did, but how on earth did you know?"
>
> "M-M-Mother!" (said with arms outstretched to embrace the woman).[22]

Folklore is always a reflection of the age in which it flourishes. Whether we like it or not, the dead baby joke cycle is a reflection of American culture in the 1960s and 1970s. If we do not like the image, we should not blame the mirror. If anything is sick, it is the society that produces sick humor. Eliminating the humor—even if such censorship were possible, which it definitely is not—would not solve the problems that led to the generation of the folklore in the first place. Our concern, therefore, should not be with dead baby jokes so much as with dead babies. We need to prevent wars that modern technology has modified to the terrifying point that human beings, including babies, can be instantly converted into garbage. We need to see that machines work for us, not against us; that machines improve the quality of life, not end it. We need to oppose racism and allow babies of whatever color an opportunity to lead full, productive lives. And finally, we need to work toward solving the difficult problem of balancing the rights of individuals with the rights of the children of those individuals. Parents should not sacrifice *their* lives for their children, nor sacrifice their *children's* lives for their own selfish, self-centered interests. To the extent that greater longevity and lesser infant mortality have made overpopulation a real danger in the modern world, planned parenthood is probably necessary. If so, then Americans (and other peoples of the world, as well) will have to come to terms with limiting human population growth. Surely contraception is infinitely preferable to abortion, but in either case the dead baby configuration is going to have to be dealt with in reality. It is no joke; it is a serious matter of the greatest importance.[23]

But as Americans become more and more self-indulgent, it becomes increasingly difficult to find the proper balance. The higher incidence of divorce and of so-called broken homes reflects the growing tendency for individual Americans to seek personal self-fulfillment at the expense of their children, their babies. A recent joke parodies parents who defer their own needs because of their children:

> Two octogenarians are in divorce court. She's 81; he's 84. The judge inquires why, at their age, do they wish to get a divorce? The woman explains, "We haven't gotten along for years."
>
> "If that's the case," says the judge, "why did you wait until now?"
>
> "Oh," says the woman, "we both decided that we would wait to get a divorce until all our children were dead."

This is not a dead baby joke, but its content is related. The audience expects the woman to say that the couple decided to wait until the children were grown up, finished with college, self-supporting, and so on. The point is that the younger generation does not want to wait until their children grow up and die before pleasing themselves. Better to kill off the babies right at the start, the dead baby joke cycle would seem to argue.[24]

The cycle provides a means for adolescents and young teenagers to try to relieve their anxiety about impending parenthood. The transition from child to parent, accomplished biologically by producing a baby, is a traumatic one in most societies, and American society is no exception. American culture prolongs childhood, as it is. Adulthood, by cultural definition (at age 21 or age 18 or whatever the age of drinking, driving, voting, or marrying without parental consent may be in a particular state) occurs long after the onset of puberty, when individuals are physically and physiologically capable of conceiving and bearing children. Avoiding or disposing of unwanted babies — at least in dead baby joke fantasy terms — is thus a means of wishful thinking, a means of remaining a child. Parenthood means responsibility; childhood (in theory) allows irresponsibility. An adult must legally be responsible for a child. The difference between the biological ability to have babies and the cultural norms for when marriage and procreation should ideally take place creates stress. Adolescents could have babies and do have sexual drives, but, in theory, society insists that they postpone such activities. With sex education in the public schools and the greater availability of contraceptive devices, the gap between biology and culture has perhaps narrowed, but the guilt cannot so easily be removed. Having sexual relations without wishing to have babies — or even the very knowledge of the fact that abortion clinics are a part of modern society — has provided a source of anxiety that is clearly a factor in the generation and transmission of dead baby jokes.[25]

CHAPTER 2

The Game of the Name: A Quadriplegic Sick Joke Cycle

Misfortunes (preferably someone else's) have been a source of laughter for centuries, and have continued to provide a solid basis for humor. Indeed, the graver the misfortune, the more humans may need to laugh in response. In the cool light of reason, it seems heartlessly cruel to laugh at mutilation or maiming, but the recorded evidence reveals that laughter is an important defense mechanism, enabling individuals to deal with matters they could not otherwise easily face. What has been termed "gallows humor" suggests that even victims of attempted genocide managed to keep their joke-making facilities until the bitter end.[1]

Such humor goes back to antiquity, as Homer's striking description of Thersites, in the second book of the Iliad attests.[2] He was "the ugliest man who came beneath Ilion. He was bandy-legged and went lame of one foot, with shoulders stooped and drawn together over his chest." After Thersites criticized Agamemnon for instigating a war for his own personal vengeance, Odysseus quickly rebutted him and physically hit him. "So he spoke and dashed the sceptre against his back and shoulders, and he doubled over, and a round tear dropped from him, and a bloody welt stood up between his shoulders. . . ." The response of those assembled is of interest: "Sorry though the men were they laughed over him happily."[3] This mixture of pity and laughter is not unique. Whipping a hunchback was a cruel act, but it was also a cause of laughter.

A morbid curiosity about monsters and freaks can be easily documented.[4] In part, the history of fairs and circuses — with their sideshows

of bearded ladies, two-headed calves, Siamese twins, and the like—
demonstrates the fascination with deformity. But whereas formerly
people with such afflictions were often to be found working in a side-
show, today various handicapped individuals are making a concerted
effort to participate in as normal a life as possible. No longer banished
to institutions providing care, individuals aided by the rapid advances
of technology (motorized wheelchairs for example), are courageously
taking part in everyday society. Wheelchair access to public buildings
is becoming more and more common. Special parking places are re-
served for vehicles of the physically disabled. So whether people are
victims of birth defects or were injured through war or accident, they
may be seen by the general public.

Etiquette dictates that we not refer to another person's disability.
Physical infirmity, like death, either is not mentioned at all or is alluded
to only indirectly, through accepted euphemisms. This taboo against
speaking frankly about physical handicaps is probably one reason why
there are jokes about the handicapped. The joke typically provides a
socially sanctioned outlet for talking about what normally cannot be
discussed openly. You might think that quadriplegics are an unlikely
subject for humor; but the fact is, jokes about them are told. In the
early 1980s, a whole new cycle of sick jokes circulated, most of which
shared the initial question: **What do you call a man with no arms and
legs who . . . ?** This cycle is the subject of this present chapter.

There have been sick joke cycles in American humor since at least
the beginning of the twentieth century. Little Willies were popular
in the first decades of the century.[5] Later joke cycles in the same vein
include the so-called sick or cruel jokes of the 1960s, the dead baby
jokes of the 1970s, and the Helen Keller jokes of the 1960s–1980s.[6]
The fact that jokes could be told about a truly exceptional woman who,
despite being blind, deaf, and dumb, was able to live a rich and fruit-
ful life, attests to America's penchant for sick humor. If Helen Keller
can inspire a joke cycle, it should really be no surprise to learn that
quadriplegics have spurred a similar series of jokes. Some are in standard riddling question format: **What is the hardest part of the vegetable
to eat? The wheelchair.** Others can be traced back to the 1960s at least.
One of the classic jokes about the disabled is:

> **"Can we play baseball with Billy?"**
> **"No, you know he has no arms or legs."**
> **"We know, but we want to use him for 3rd base."[7]**

The quadriplegic cycle seems to have emerged in 1982 and 1983. Here are some representative texts:

What do you call a man with no arms or legs . . .
—in a swimming pool?
  Bob.

—on your doorstep?
  Matt.

—stuffed in your mailbox?
  Bill.

—in a pile of leaves?
  Russell.

—in a hot tub?
  Stew.

—lying on hot pavement?
  Flip.

—waterskiing?
  Skip.

—in a hole?
  Phil.

—nailed to a wall?
  Art.

—in the meat display case?
  Chuck.

—on a barbecue?
  Frank.

Although most of these jokes involve puns on men's names, a few refer to women's names.

What do you call a woman with no arms or legs . . .
—on a grill?
  Patty.

—on a beach?
  Sandy.

What do you call a woman with one leg shorter than the
    other?
Eileen.

> What is a Japanese woman with one leg shorter than the
>   other?
> Irene.[8]

Occasionally animals are described rather than humans.

> What do you call a cow with three legs?
> Lean beef.

> What do you call a cow with no legs?
> Ground beef.

Except for the few animal examples, all the jokes involve puns on personal names. Whether it is "Phil" in a hole or a meat "Patty" on a grill, the technique is the same.[9]

It is interesting that most of the names used in this joke cycle are either nicknames or standard shortenings of formal names: Art for Arthur, Matt for Matthew, Phil for Philip, Stew for Stewart, Bill for William, Rob for Robert, and Chuck for Charles. What we have here is a play on *familiarity*. Only if one is a close friend or associate of Robert can one properly use the more familiar Bob. The familiar nickname contrasts with the unfamiliar referent: a man without arms and legs. It is not easy for individuals who have all four limbs to speak of or refer to paraplegics. It is not that quadriplegics don't have a sense of humor or enjoy jokes, but rather that nonquadriplegics tend to be embarrassed in their presence. No doubt there is more than a hint of guilt for having four sound limbs.

As the disabled rights group becomes ever more vocal, insisting (rightly) on ramp access to streets and public buildings, and with the remarkable advances in medicine and technology that permit quadriplegics to be much more independent than possible before, quadriplegics are likely to be even more visible to the public consciousness. No one likes to be reminded of human fragility and frailty. Even those who are, in theory, favorably disposed to quadriplegics' struggle to live as normal a life as possible may feel annoyance at having to accommodate such individuals. Someone has to pay for the cost of making public transportation and street corner curbs accessible for the handicapped. But it is taboo to express true feelings of guilt, revulsion, pity, or annoyance. I believe this curious joke cycle is an attempt to recognize and articulate the public's discomfiture in the presence of armless, legless, or otherwise disabled individuals.

CHAPTER 3

Auschwitz Jokes

(with Thomas Hauschild)

Nothing is so sacred, so taboo, or so disgusting that it cannot be the subject of humor. Indeed, it is precisely those topics culturally defined as sacred, taboo, or disgusting that tend to provide the principal grist for humor mills. In a history of world atrocities, of which there are far too many instances, it would be hard to think of any example more gruesome than the methodical murder of millions of Jews in Nazi Germany. The sordid, unspeakably cruel, and vicious details of the extermination of Jews in such concentration camps as Dachau, Buchenwald, and Auschwitz have been amply documented many times over.[1] In reading the accounts written by survivors, it is hard to imagine that any humor could possibly arise from the mass gassing of thousands of individuals.

The phenomenon known as "gallows humor"[2] generally refers to jokes made about and by the *victims* of oppression. Such jokes are told by those supposedly about to be hanged, not by the hangmen. In situations involving great anxiety, it is not uncommon for participants to tell jokes to relieve the tension. In time of war, for example, some individuals facing death are able to joke about it. These jokes may be a form of bravado—a kind of necessary defense mechanism—designed to articulate genuine fears and at the same time partly allay terror through humor.

The aggressive tendency in jokes has been obvious at least since Freud's pioneering study, *Wit and Humor in the Unconscious*, appeared in 1905. Jokes told about the members of one particular ethnic, national, or religious group may offer a socially sanctioned outlet for the expression of aggression toward that group. Even when members of the group in question tell jokes about their own group, it still may be a matter of aggression. The

19

concept of self-hate may explain why Catholics tell anti-clerical jokes or why Jews tell anti-Semitic jokes.[3]

Yet there are some anti-Semitic jokes that Jews would rarely if ever tell. It is one thing for a Jew to poke fun at the alleged proclivities of Jewish women, either the Jewish mother or the Jewish wife — for example, **How do you cure a Jewish nymphomaniac? Marry her. What's Jewish foreplay? Twenty minutes of begging.** It would be quite another matter for a Jew to tell jokes about World War II concentration camps. Nevertheless, such jokes do exist, though they are not ordinarily told by Jews. There are traditional jokes about the plight and fate of Jews in World War II, which are current in the 1980s in West Germany. This type of sick humor, which many will no doubt find to be in extremely bad taste, might be said to constitute a form of "executioner's humor" rather than "gallows humor." Whether these "Auschwitz jokes" are considered funny or not is not an issue. This material exists and should be recorded. Jokes are always an important barometer of the attitudes of a group. The jokes must fill some psychic need for those who tell them and those who listen to them. They demonstrate that anti-Semitism is not dead in Germany — if documentation were needed to prove that point.

Anti-Semitism is not confined to West Germany. One can find it throughout Europe, North and South America, and elsewhere. Several of the jokes we report from Western Germany, for example, have also been collected in England, Sweden, and the United States. The implication is that to the extent that anti-Semitism is international, the jokes expressing such prejudice are equally international. However, we do not believe there are parallels for all the Auschwitz jokes we shall report from modern West Germany.

Here is a text collected from an informant from Mainz in 1982:

(1) *Wie viele Juden passen in einen Volkswagen?*
How many Jews will fit in a Volkswagen?
506, sechs auf die Sitze und 500 in die Aschenbecher.
506, six in the seats and 500 in the ashtrays.[4]

This joke is quite similar to the following text collected in Berkeley, California, in 1980:

How many Jews can you fit in a Volkswagen?
Fourteen. Two in front, two in the back, ten in the ashtray.

The Jew-ashes equation turns out to be an all-too-common theme in Auschwitz jokes.

(2) *Wussten Sie schon, dass an der Olympiade 1936 in Berlin 50,000 Juden teilgenommen haben?*
Did you know that 50,000 Jews took part in the 1936 Olympic Games at Berlin?
Nein.
No.
Ja doch, auf der Aschenbahn! [als Asche]
But yes, on the cinder track! [as ashes]

Although historically inaccurate, the implication is that the ashes of Jewish people's remains made the red-colored (blood?) track. The joke alludes to Hitler's attempts to keep Jewish athletes from participating in the Olympics. The Nazis were embarrassed when a half-Jewish fencer won a gold medal (for Germany) and when Jesse Owen, the celebrated black track star, won his medals for the United States.

(3) *Zum Abschluss der Olympiade in München hält Hitler folgende Rede: "Ich danke dem deutschen Volk, das die herrlichen Bauten errichtete, welche diese Olympiade ermöglichten. Und ich danke dem jüdischen Volk für die Erfindung der Aschenbahn."*
At the conclusion of the Olympic Games, Hitler spoke in Munich as follows: "I thank the German people who made possible the Olympic Games by providing these wonderful buildings. And I thank the Jewish people for the invention of the cinder track."

The joke refers to the postwar, pro-Semitic argument that the German people received so many inventions and intellectual contributions from the Jewish minority—for instance, quantum physics and psychoanalysis. Hitler's "respect" for these inventions is rendered metaphorically as "Jews are only good for burning." A shorter variant collected from a fourteen-year-old informant in Tübingen makes a clearer reference to burning:

Wozu hat man die Juden 1936 bei der Olympiade gebraucht?
What were the Jews used for in connection with the 1936 Olympics?
Für die Aschenbahn und fürs olympische Feuer.
For the cindertrack and for the Olympic flame.[5]

Burning is just as common a theme as ashes. It is, after all, essentially the same theme.

(4) *Kennst du die jüdische Hitparade?*
Do you know the Jewish Hit Parade?

Nein.
No.
Die geht so: Platz 1 "Hey Jude"; *Platz* 2 "In the Ghetto";
    Platz 3 "I'm on Fire."
It is: Place #1. "Hey Jude" [Hey Jew]; Place #2. "In the
    Ghetto"; Place #3. "I'm on Fire."

This joke is obviously of modern vintage, since the record titles
refer to recordings made by the Beatles, Elvis Presley, and others. A
variant of this joke that circulated in Sweden in the early 1970s asks,
Which tune is Number 1 on the German hit parade? 'Hey Jude' with the
Gas Chamber Choir.[6]

(5) *Was ist der Unterschied zwischen einer Tonne Koks und
        1000 Juden?*
     What is the difference between a ton of coal and a thou-
        sand Jews?
     Die Juden brennen länger.
     Jews burn longer.

(6) *Warum fahren die Juden mehr so gerne nach Italien in
        Urlaub?*
     Why don't Jews like to go to Italy anymore for their holi-
        days?
     Weil sie dann über den Brenner müssen.
     Because they have to go over the Brenner [Pass].

Brenner is the German word for burner, as in a gas burner.
Auschwitz jokes reveal other elements of the Holocaust as well.

(7) *Ein Kind spielt mit einem Stück Kernseife. Da sagt die Oma:
        "Willst du wohl die Finger von Anne Frank lassen?!"*
     A child plays with a cake of soap. [*Kernseife* is a type of
        soap that is raw and unscented.] Granny says, "Keep
        your fingers off Anne Frank."

The Germans did experiment with transforming Jewish corpses
into soap, a metaphorical reductio ad absurdum to convert "dirty" Jews
into an agent of cleanliness. (This parallels the attempt to make Germany *Judenrein*, clean of Jews, which has been linked with Germany's
anal-erotic national character.)[7] The poignant *Diary of Anne Frank* had
a dramatic effect on many contemporary Germans who refused to
believe right-wing assertions that the diary was a fake. The joke seems
to suggest that the child should not play with Anne Frank. In other
words, the dead should be allowed to rest in peace. Perhaps there is

also an implication that the younger generation should not play with the products of Nazi Germany — even though the joke cycle itself does represent a form of play with such products.

The condensation (by boiling the body) of Anne Frank into a bar of soap suggests one of the principal themes of these jokes: the reduction (literally) of masses of Jews. After the war, Germans were confronted with the grim picture of the Holocaust, either through reports in the press or forced visits to concentration camps. Such images do not appear in these jokes. Instead there is only the "condensed" Jew who fits into the ash tray or who is reduced into a piece of soap. There is irony insofar as Granny, like most Germans, favors cleanliness; but in this instance she orders the child *not* to touch the soap. She is the "clean" Granny — the representative of the Nazi generation who killed and condensed Jews — wishing to repress all that "dirty" part of history.

(8) Two [Jewish] children are sitting on top of a roof near a chimney. A passerby asks, "What are you doing there?" "We are waiting for our parents."[8]

(9) A Jew is walking down the street carrying a gas container with a pipe connecting it to his mouth. A passerby asks, "What are you doing?" "I'm addicted."

This may allude to a conventional German idiom that shows the "smallness" of an adversary: *"Den rauch ich in der Pfeife"* ("I will smoke him in my pipe"). In any case, guilt is resolved through an insidious form of projection: the Jews wanted to be gassed; they like it! The same device appears in the next two texts. By repressing and projecting, the joketeller and his audience can pretend that it is not "our" guilt; the Jews wanted such treatment.

(10) Why did so many Jews go to Auschwitz? The fare was free.

(11) *Was ist der Traum eines Juden?* What is a Jew's dream? *Ein Fensterplatz im Hochofen.* A window-seat in a high oven.[9]

A new scapegoat has been added to the German repertoire: the Turk. The influx of Turkish migrant workers in Germany and elsewhere in Europe has inspired an extensive cycle of anti-Turkish jokes.[10] However, the Turk does not replace the Jew as the butt of jokes. Note how the same joke treats Jews and Turks:

(12) *Ein Türke und ein Jude springen vom Haus. Wer ist schneller unten?*
      A Turk and a Jew fall from a house. Who falls down faster?
      Der Türke ist aus Scheisse, der Jude aus Asche, also ist der Türke schneller.
      The Turk is shit, the Jew is ashes, so the Turk lands first.

In this parody of Galileo's experiment at the Tower of Pisa, the Turk is ahead of the Jew because the Jew has already been destroyed. The point is that the Turk is yet to be exterminated. The Turks, like so many immigrants to a country before them, are invariably asked to do the most menial or *dirty* work. The depiction of an undesirable in terms of feces reflects a more general scatological tendency in German culture. A similar anti–Turkish sentiment shows up in the following text:

(13) *Ein Deutscher, ein Türke und ein Jude stehen vor der Entbindungsstation des Krankenhauses und warten darauf, ihre neugeborenen Kinder sehen zu können. Da kommt die Krankenschwester heraus und gesteht, dass sie die drei Kinder verwechselt hat und nicht mehr weiss, welches Baby zu welchem Vater gehört. Der Deutsche sagt: "Lassen Sie mich mal fünf Minuten allein mit denen." Er geht rein und kommt nach ein paar Minuten wieder heraus und verteilt mit grosser Bestimmtheit die Kinder: "Das ist deins, das gehört mir . . . ," usw. Die Krankenschwester will unbedingt wissen, wie er das gemacht hat. Erst sagt der Deutsche: "Das kann ich nicht sagen," aber sie drängt immer weiter und so erzählt er schliesslich: "Ich bin reingegangen, habe den Arm gehoben und 'Heil Hitler' gerufen. Meiner ist sofort stramm gestanden und hat wiedergegrüsst. Der Jude hat sich in die Windeln geschissen und der Türke hat es weggeputzt."*
      A German, a Jew, and a Turk are waiting in the clinic to see their new-born babies. A nurse comes and tells them that their children have been mixed up and they do not know which baby belongs to which father. The German says: "Let me be in there undisturbed for five minutes." He goes in and comes back a couple of minutes later and with great certainty says: "This is your child, this is mine . . . ," etc. The nurse wants to know how he has done this. At first, the German says: "That I cannot say." But she presses him further and finally he tells: "I went in, raised my arm and

> shouted, 'Heil Hitler.' Immediately, my son lifted his arm
> and returned the same greeting. The Jew shit in his swad-
> dling clothes and the Turk cleaned it up."

The mixing up of the children may reflect the German's continuing concern with racial purity. No "good German" would want to have a child with tainted blood, such as Jewish or Turkish blood. The German's reluctance to tell the nurse how he succeeded in identifying the racial stock of each baby suggests that he realizes that racist ideology is unpopular. Still, in the end he does admit that he uses the Hitler salute to distinguish the true German from the inferior races. The joke implies that the Jewish baby is so frightened by seeing the dreaded Nazi salute that he "shits in his pants," a common metaphor in German folklore. The modern twist is that the Turk, low man in terms of social status, is identified by his cleaning up after the "dirty" Jew.

(14)   *In KZ Dachau spielen die Türken gegen die Juden Fussball.*
       Wer gewinnt?
       In the Dachau concentration camp, the Turks and the Jews
       play soccer. Who wins?
       Die Juden—Sie haben Heimvorteil.
       The Jews—They have the home field advantage.

It is surely significant that the German hatred of Turkish migrant workers is expressed in jokes that also include Jews; as if when the Germans want to hate any group, they do so in comparison with their longstanding hatred of the Jews. This is certainly explicit in the following question:

(15)   *Was unterscheidet die Türken von den Juden?*
       What is the difference between Turks and Jews?
       Die Juden haben es schon hinter sich, die Türken haben
       es noch vor sich.
       The Jews have behind them what the Turks have now be-
       fore them [mass murder].[11]

These jokes suggest that German anti-Semitism is alive and well. These texts show little evidence of remorse. Only the reference to leaving Anne Frank alone hints at any compassion for all the millions of victims of Nazi death camps. The unchanging consistency of anti-Semitism is manifested in a joke that finds Hitler in hell:

(16)   *Hitler hat jahrzehntelang in der Hölle geschmort, zur*
       Busse für seine Taten. Schliesslich ist er gereinigt und

kommt in den Himmel. Gott fragt ihn: "Nun, Adolf, was würdest du tun, wenn du jetzt wieder auf die Erde zurück könntest?" Hitler darauf: "Na, Juden vergasen!" Verärgert schickt Gott ihn für weitere drei Jahre in die Hölle—Als er zurückkommt, stellt Gott ihm wieder dieselbe Frage: "Was würdest du tun?" "Juden vergasen." Wieder geht er für drei Jahre in die Hölle. Als er zurückkommt fragt Gott das dritte Mal: "Was würdest du jetzt tun, wenn du auf die Erde zurückkönntest, Adolf?" Hitler hat sich die ganze Sache überlegt und sagt: "Ich würde schöne Autobahnen bauen. . . ." Da fragt Gott zurück: "Und wohin würdest du die Bahnen bauen?" Hitler: "Vor allem eine, von Prag direkt nach Auschwitz."

Hitler has been burning in hell for dozens of years for all his sins. Finally he is cleansed and he enters heaven. God asks him: "What would you do if you could return to earth, Adolf?" Hitler answers: "I would gas Jews!" Angrily, God sends him back to hell for three more years. When Hitler returns to heaven, God asks him again the same question: "What would you do?" However, Hitler says: "Gas the Jews." Again Hitler is sent back to hell for three years. When he comes back, God asks him a third time: "What would you do if you could return to earth?" Hitler has thought over the whole thing and says: "I would build some beautiful highways. . . ." God asks then: "To what places would you build these highways?" Answers Hitler: "Directly from Prague to Auschwitz."

This joke was heard in Bavaria from a bus driver who told it to amuse tourists on his bus. The joke contains a common argument, namely that Hitler was right in some of the things he did, such as building good highways (something surely of importance to a professional bus driver!). The highways were, in fact, built largely to facilitate the transportation of German war machinery. The joke also shows the virulence of Hitler's anti-Semitism (and perhaps German anti-Semitism generally)—not even the horrors of hell could change it. For the Holocaust was a hell, and that hell has not wiped out all traces of anti-Semitism in contemporary Germany. The joke's initial premise—that Hitler had suffered enough in hell to cleanse himself, and thus to be allowed possible entrance into heaven—is itself worthy of notice. The question is whether there is enough penance in the world to allow a Hitler to go to heaven. Of course, the joke clearly states that Hitler was not at all affected by his stay in hell—he remained the vicious anti-Semite he was in life. This conclusion may be a good sign for modern Germany — the recognition of the evils of anti-Semitism — on the other hand, the very existence of the Auschwitz joke cycle may not be much of a harbinger of healthier attitudes. It is somewhat alarming to realize that an idiom such as *bis zur Vergassung* (to be gassed, to be at the point of gasification) is in common use in contemporary Germany. It refers to someone carrying out an action to the point of extinction or utter futility.[12]

Jews in Germany were treated not as humans but as a dirty problem to be solved or eliminated. Jokes also dehumanize and may be used to make light of a serious problem. Auschwitz is a problem for the conscience of modern Germany, which is no doubt why Auschwitz jokes exist and circulate. It is not easy to make light of Auschwitz and the travesty of human decency that occurred there. At least the Auschwitz joke cycle indicates that Germans, or at any rate some Germans, are admitting that the tragic events of Auschwitz did happen. For many years during and after the war, countless "good" Germans claimed either they knew nothing of the atrocities of the death camps or that they never happened at all — that they were the fabrications of Allied propaganda campaigns. In this context, the Auschwitz jokes at least seem to be an admission that the horrors of the death camps are a reality that must be faced. But the reality is so ghastly, so terrible, so frightful that it is difficult to confront — surely another reason why these jokes are told. They allow both joketeller and audience to admit that Auschwitz is a part of German history. (It is ironic that the name Auschwitz includes *Au* ["ow," as in pain], *schwitz* [sweat], and *witz* [joke]). While it may be a healthy sign for Germans to admit the historical reality of Auschwitz, it is also disturbing to think that the recognition of the grim reality has not ended centuries of anti-Semitic sentiments in Germany.

Just how old and widespread these Auschwitz jokes are in Germany is difficult to determine. We can testify that they are not easy to collect; and to date, German folklorists have not reported them. Still, a revealing couplet from a poem entitled "Auschwitz" by Ulrich Otto Berger, published in 1966, suggests that these jokes have been around for some years:

> *Der Volksmund weiss heute zu erzählen*
> *mehr als einen Witz über Auschwitz.*
> The folk speech of today knows how to tell
> more than one joke about Auschwitz.[13]

Even when modern jokes are about Turks, Auschwitz may function as a metaphor for total annihilation.

(17) *Ein mit Türken vollbesetzer Zug fährt in Istanbul ab—und
      kommt in Frankfurt leer an. Warum?*
      A train full of Turks leaves Istanbul—and comes to Frankfurt empty. Why?
      Er fuhr über Auschwitz.
      It went via Auschwitz.[14]

As long as such jokes are told, the evil of Auschwitz will remain in the consciousness of Germans. Auschwitz jokes may seem a sorry and inadequate memorial for all the poor, wretched souls who perished at Auschwitz; but when one realizes that comedy and tragedy are two sides of the same coin, we can perhaps understand why some contemporary Germans might need to resort to the mechanism of humor, albeit sick humor, to try to come to terms with the unimaginable and unthinkable horrors that occurred at Auschwitz.

POSTSCRIPT:

More on Auschwitz Jokes

(with Uli Linke)

Most students of sick humor cycles were probably unaware that Auschwitz jokes were circulating in post-World War II Germany until the 1983 publication of "Auschwitz Jokes" in *Western Folklore*.[15] These jokes are so repugnant and distasteful that some people have questioned whether they should have been published at all.[16] A Jewish graduate student in folklore at UCLA sent a letter of protest to the editor; another angry response from a U.C. Berkeley student appeared in the campus newspaper, *The Daily Californian*, suggesting that it would be better if scholars ignored such "sick" jokes.[17]

The answer, of course, is that censorship, whether imposed from without or self-imposed, is unthinkable in an academic environment of free inquiry and expression. Auschwitz jokes exist and continue to be told in contemporary West Germany—whether or not a sample is published in an American folklore journal. The authors of the article in question did not make up the jokes, they merely reported them. Folklorists, in our view, have an obligation to record and report folklore accurately, no matter whom it might offend. One might even go so far as to argue that if someone had observed and called attention to the degree of anti-Semitism in Germany *before* the Holocaust, lives might conceivably have been saved. In any case, if anti-Semitism does flourish in Germany or anywhere else in the world, Jewish scholars should be among the first to seek to document and attack such continued bigotry. Instead, *Jewish Social Studies* rejected the original article without review, and several hate-mail letters were sent to the article's American co-author. One can't help wondering when some Jews will finally learn

29

that pretending anti-Semitism doesn't exist provides no help in a world unfortunately filled with intolerance and discrimination.

Once more, we must state that anti-Semitism is alive and well in Germany. According to a 1982 survey, fewer than 25 percent of all West Germans have abandoned the traditional pattern of prejudice—a frightening statistic, if true.[18] Visual evidence of the seemingly endless anti-Semitic sentiments manifests in the form of wall graffiti—drawings of swastikas or gallows displaying a dangling victim bearing the Star of David.[19] Such drawings are analogs of the vicious jokes that advocate mass murder and seek to make light of the death-camp reality. And "occasionally the prejudice goes from verbal violence to physical. . . . The violence has chilling resonance in West Germany, where small neo-Nazi groups have seized the racial issue and made it their own."[20] It is sad to think how easy it still is to document the persistence of German anti-Semitism, and it is alarming to realize that such prejudice feeds in part on a fantastic refusal to admit that the methodical murder of millions of Jews in Nazi Germany ever occurred.

With the construction of the death camps, the Nazis created a world so horrible that it became difficult to confront. For many years after the war, countless Germans pleaded ignorance or claimed that the atrocities never happened at all. While this hesitation to face the historical facts might be understood as an attempt to escape or resolve the problem of guilt, such a repression of memories seems to have left Germans unable to feel compassion for the tormented victims or to grieve for the dead.[21] The denial of the past continues, although with the modern twist of mockery:

> In 1978, at a demonstration of right-wing extremists in Hamburg, the participants gathered, dressed in black leather suits, wearing "donkey"-masks over their faces, carrying large signs strapped to their bodies which read: *"Ich Esel glaube immer noch, dass in deutschen KZs Juden vergast wurden"* (What an ass I am for still believing that Jews were gassed in German concentration camps!)[22]

In German folk speech, as in English, an "ass" or "donkey" refers to a stupid, naive, dim-witted fool. Here the expression is used to ridicule those who have come to accept the atrocities of the death camps as historical fact. We find a similar response to such a direct confrontation with the past in the following incident, which evidently occurred in connection with the premiere of the German film *"Die Erben"* ("The

Inheritors") in 1982, a semi-historical docudrama about anti-Semitism in post-war Germany.

Just as the showing of the film at Hannover's "Hollywood"-theater had come to its conclusion, a gang, dressed in black, marched in. Twenty toughs, headed by the previously convicted Michael Kühnen, planted themselves in the front rows, and when in the panel discussion, mention was made of six million murdered Jews, they burst into roaring laughter.[23]

We see here no sign of remorse, regret, or sorrow. The response in both these instances consists of mockery and laughter. It is tempting to argue that these actions reflect the thinking of only a relatively small set of neo-Nazi groups. However, the views expressed by these actions are, we suggest, by no means confined to such extremist groups — the exact same sentiments are articulated in jokes about Auschwitz. Treating Auschwitz as a joke is as horrible and insensitive as the extremist demonstrations cited above. The difference is that many more individuals tell and listen to Auschwitz jokes in private than participate in public demonstrations.

To the corpus of Auschwitz joke texts included earlier in the chapter, we should like to add the following examples:[24]

(18) *Wie heisst ein jüdisches Feriendorf mit zwei Buchstaben?*
What is the name of a Jewish vacation resort with two letters?
KZ. (Konzentrationslager)
CC. (concentration camp)

Here the reality of the death camps is rendered metaphorically into a resort. The nuances hint at a place of rest, relaxation, and enjoyment; but a second text, which often is told after the first one, reveals the true nature of this "last resort":

(19) *Wie betritt der Jude das Feriendorf?*
How does the Jew enter the vacation resort?
Durchs Tor.
Through the gate.
Wie verlässt er es?
How does he leave it?
Durch den Schornstein!
Through the chimney!

(20) *Was ist der Unterschied zwischen dem Weihnachtsmann und dem Juden?*

> What is the difference between Santa Claus and the Jew?
> *Der Weihnachtsmann kommt von oben durch den Schorn-*
> *stein.*
> Santa Claus comes down through the chimney from above.

This German text can be compared with sick American jokes involving Santa Claus, such as What is the difference between Santa Claus and God? There is a Santa Claus, or Why can't Santa Claus have any children? Because he comes only once a year and then it's down a chimney. Somehow, jokes about sex and the nonexistence of God seem less "sick" (if one can make such an ethnocentric value judgment) than burning Jews in ovens who therefore go up through the chimney from below!

We move from jokes about chimneys to texts involving ovens and burning. It still seems incredible that the incineration of human victims could possibly serve as a common theme for jokes.

(21)   *Ein Bus voller Juden fährt 1972 nach München die*
         Olympischen Spiele anzuschauen. In München sind aber
         alle Hotels belegt. Sie müssen in ihrem Bus von Hotel zu
         Hotel fahren, um zu fragen ob noch was frei ist. Der Leiter
         der Gruppe geht in ein Hotel rein und fragt en Portier:
         "Haben Sie Platz für einhundert Juden?" "Nein," kommt die
         Antwort, "wir haben auf Ölheizung umgestellt."
         A bus full of Jews drives to Munich in 1972 to watch
         the Olympic games. But in Munich all the hotels are oc-
         cupied. The group has to drive in their bus from hotel to
         hotel to ask whether there are still vacancies. The tour-
         guide walks into a hotel and asks the doorman: "Do you
         have room for one-hundred Jews?" "No," comes the an-
         swer, "we have switched to oil-heating."

The reference to the 1972 Olympics rather than to the more commonly mentioned 1936 Berlin games may have been stimulated by the PLO terrorist murder of Jewish athletes at the 1972 games in Munich.

(22a) *Was ist der Unterschied zwischen einem Kleinen und*
         einem grossen Juden?
         What is the difference between a short Jew and a tall Jew?
         Grosser Jude brennt länger!
         A tall Jew burns longer.[25]

And a variant:

(22b) *Was ist der Unterschied zwischen einem dicken und einem*
         dünnen Juden?

What is the difference between a fat and a thin Jew?
Brennt länger.
[The fat Jew] burns longer.

The reduction of masses of Jews into ashes is a theme that's repeated in this 1982 text from Hannover:

(23) *Wieviele Juden braucht man für die Olympischen Spiele 1936?*
How many Jews does one need for the Olympic games of 1936?
30,006. Sechs für das Olympische Feuer und 30,000 für die Aschenbahn. . . .
30,006. Six for the Olympic flame and 30,000 for the cinder-track.[26]

Another version of the same joke contains an even more explicit reference to how the corpses were used:

(24) *Wieviele Juden braucht man zum Bau eines Stadiums?*
How many Jews does one need for the construction of a stadium?
12,000. 10,000 für die Aschenbahn, 1,000 zum bauen, 500 für die Abtrittmatten und 500 für die Seife.
12,000. 10,000 for the cinder-track, 1,000 for the labor, 500 for the door mats and 500 for the soap.

Recurrent are images of the "condensed" Jew who fits into an ashtray, who is reduced into the form of a door mat (a convenient metaphor for a people oppressed by the goose-stepping boots of the German military) or a piece of soap.[27]

Auschwitz jokes are also recounted in countries of the Eastern Block. Although such texts draw on similar images, such as the equation of Jews and soap, they appear to convey a slightly different message than those told in West Germany. Historically, anti-Semitism has also flourished in Poland, and many of the death camps were actually located in German-occupied Poland. Auschwitz is the German name for what was the Polish town of Oswiecim. A Polish text from 1981 illustrates:[28]

(25) Do you know why there is a shortage of soap?
Because the authorities are trying to turn the soap back into Jews.

This text at least hints at some possibility of remorse. The extreme shortages of essential goods in Poland are a frequent subject of political jokes. In this instance, the soap shortage is "explained" by the fantasied efforts of the government to ritually undo the heinous crime of turn-ing Jewish corpses into soap. Since the infamous experimental efforts to manufacture soap from human fat took place at the Danzig Anatomic Institute during 1943 and 1944, it makes sense that the Poles have soap jokes in their national consciousness and memory. This Polish text, at least, suggests that the process should be reversed. Contrast this with the following variant, collected in Munich in 1982 from a thirty-year-old East German informant:

(26) *Was ist eine (deutsche) Wiedergutmachungsmaschine?*
What is a (German) retribution [literally: "make-it-all-well-again"] machine?
Man tut Seife oben rein und unten kommen Juden raus.
One puts soap in at the top and Jews come out below.

Although this explicit desire to restore and bring back the dead to life might imply some regret for the Nazi atrocities, traces of anti-Semitism still remain. Soap is on top while the Jews are at the bottom. Moreover, the oppositional structure contrasts the "clean" soap with the Jews who, by tradition, are considered dirty. The elimination of the dirty Jew occurs in another text:

(27) *Zwei Typen sitzen im Gefängnis. "Was hast du denn gemacht?" sagt der eine zum andern. "Ja, ich hab an die Grenze geschrieben 'Juden raus!' — Und du?" "Ich hab ge-schrieben 'Juden rein!' — aber an die Gaskammer."*
Two guys sit in prison. "What did you do?" says one to the other. "Well, I wrote on the border, 'Out with the Jews!'— and you?" "I wrote 'In with the Jews'— but on the gas chamber!"

Here we certainly have a play on *"Juden rein"* (Jews in) and *"Juden-rein"* (clean of Jews): One of the announced Nazi goals was to make Germany *"Judenrein,"* that is, "clean of Jews." This theme may also be expressed in other modern Auschwitz jokes.

(28) *Was ist eine jüdische Sauna?*
What is a Jewish sauna?
Aus-schwitz.
Auschwitz.

This joke text contains a pun on the word Auschwitz by breaking it down into *Aus* (out) and *schwitz* (sweat). The German phrase *"aus-schwitzen"* (sweat it out) denotes a state of distress, anguish, and even fear, which here alludes to the emotional experience of the death–camp victims. The association is partially obscured by the imagery of the "sauna," in which sweating is produced intentionally to cleanse the body from impurities. In this context, the principal metaphor is one of total annihilation, which succeeds in ridding Germany of "Jewish impurities."

The fact that the sauna is normally a place for pleasure calls attention to an important characteristic of these Auschwitz jokes. The whole problem of guilt for the Germans is solved through an insidious form of projection.[29] The Jews are depicted as masochists; they enjoy being victimized. Auschwitz is a sauna; concentration camps are vacation resorts. This technique of "blaming the victim" is demonstrated by the following text:

(29) *Was ist eine Jude mit einer Gasflasche unter dem Arm?*
What is a Jew with a gas-container under his arm?
Ein Süchtiger.
An addict.
Mit zwei Gasflaschen unter dem Arm?
With two gas-containers under his arm?
Ein dealer.
A (drug) dealer.

The implication is that Jews wanted to be gassed: They became addicts and a few became so mercenary that they even supplied gas to users. This may or may not allude to the conventional *Lachgas* (laughing gas) used as an anesthetic, so named because of the reaction of laughter and exhilaration that inhaling it may produce. In any event, the joketeller and his or her audience can pretend that the gas intended to kill Jews was never deadly; to the contrary, because of its pleasant effects, Jews came to like it. The defense of projection allows Germans to fantasize that the gasification of Jews is not their fault; Jews really wanted such treatment — some even aided others in obtaining gas. The Jews themselves are to blame.

Most Auschwitz jokes are concerned solely with the total destruction of the Jews. There is little or no attempt to conceal the virulent anti-Semitism. There isn't even a hint of self-reproach or compassion.

(30) A German officer speaks to Jewish prisoners: "I have some good news and some bad news for you. First the good news. Half of you are going to Auschwitz and half of you are going to Buchenwald. Now for the bad news: This half" (indicates the torso midsection upwards) "goes to Auschwitz, and this half" (points to the lower body) "goes to Buchenwald."[30]

Cutting bodies in half may be a not-so-oblique reference to the dreadful "scientific" medical experiments in which hapless Jews were forced into being unwilling guinea pigs.

Children were among the many victims of Auschwitz. The following text reminds us of this fact.

(31) *Ein Wärter und ein kleines (jüdisches) Kind in Auschwitz:*
Wärter: Und wie alt bist du?
Kind: Vier. Morgen werde ich fünf.
Wärter: Uh-uh (bewegt Kopf und Finger verneinend).
A guard and a small (Jewish) child at Auschwitz:
Guard: And how old are you?
Child: Four. Tomorrow I'll turn five.
Guard: Uh-uh. (moves his head and finger to indicate a
negative response)

Sometimes the jokes make a special point of excluding any sympathy for the real victims of the death camps.

(32) *"Mensch, mein Vater ist im KZ umgekommen!"*
"Du, Fritzchen, das tut mir echt leid."
"Nicht wie du denkst, er ist besoffen vom Wachturm ge-
fallen."
"Man, my father died in a concentration camp."
"Fritzie, I am truly sorry about that."
"It's not what you think. He fell from the watch-tower drunk."

The following text, collected in 1983 in Giessen, acknowledges Auschwitz as a death camp but misdirects the attention of the joke-teller's audience away from the suffering of the *human* victims.[31]

(33) *Welche Gruppe hat die grössten Verluste in Auschwitz*
erlitten?
Which group suffered the greatest losses at Auschwitz?
Die Flöhe!
The fleas!

The disgraceful living conditions of the inmates of the death camps have been amply documented by the numerous survivors' accounts and even by some photographs and film footage. It is not completely clear whether the above joke refers to the enormous number of fleas presumably burned to death along with the humans they inhabited, or whether one is supposed to imagine that the parasitic fleas survived as they were forcibly separated from their "hosts" who were incinerated or gassed. Either way, the attempted displacement is a shocking one.

What is one to make of these Auschwitz jokes? It is clearly an effort to deal with a painful, embarrassing, and guilt-producing subject for contemporary Germans. We do not suggest that *all* Germans know or tell these jokes, but traditional jokes are, by their very nature, a collective phenomenon. These jokes are circulating in West Germany. Young Germans do not like to feel guilty for what they think are the sins of their parents or grandparents. On the other hand, the enormity of the genocide has created what may be a permanent scar on the German national conscience. Crime may ultimately hurt the criminal as well as the victim. In this case, we would argue that telling Auschwitz jokes may provide some sort of necessary catharsis for the guilt feelings caused by recognizing the historical reality of Auschwitz and the other death camps. Jokes are told about only what is most serious. Most comedy treats tragedy lightly. While murdering Jews in fantasy (jokes) is obviously preferable to murdering them in death camps, fantasy can be dangerous if it reflects an unhealthy state of mind.

This is why we felt impelled to further document the existence of Auschwitz jokes. There is even a tendency to continue the long-standing anti-Semitic tradition of opposing "good" Christianity to "evil" Judaism in these jokes.

(34) *Was ist der Unterschied zwischen Kreuzigung und Be-*
scheidung?
What is the difference between the crucifixion and cir-
cumcision?
Bei der Kreuzigung kann man den ganzen Juden weg-
werfen.
In a crucifixion, one can throw away the whole Jew.

Evoking pro-Christian/anti-Semitic sentiments cannot absolve the Germans of responsibility for their actions, past or present. True anti-Semitism was, and is, not confined to Germany; but the excesses of inhumanity and torture that occurred at Auschwitz must be acknowledged. While there is no way to undo the ritual murder of six million Jews, contemporary Germans should make a conscious effort to stamp out anti-Semitism and all the associated notions of super race and racial purity. That is within their power. In theory, telling jokes about Auschwitz might be a step toward acknowledging the reality of the death camps; but it may be nothing more than the same kind of bigotry that led to Auschwitz in the first place.

For those who find Auschwitz jokes offensive (we include ourselves in that group), we ask: Do you really think it would be better not to report on the popularity of such jokes? Do you honestly think that evil, left to its own devices, will somehow disappear? World history suggests otherwise. Prejudice, stereotyping, gross inhumanity, and even ethnic genocide do not seem to be on the wane. Folklorists with a sense of social responsibility have an obligation to do what they can to fight injustice.

Folklore does not create society; it only mirrors it. If the mirror image is unattractive, does it serve any purpose to break the mirror? The ugly reality of society is what needs to be altered, not the folklore that reflects that reality.

Of course, this analogy is not perfect. It's not possible to stop folklore from forming and circulating. Auschwitz jokes exist; they are told in West Germany whether or not we report them. To the extent that folklore is not merely a passive reflector of society but a molder of attitudes, we admittedly are taking a risk in reporting these sick jokes. But it is not our intent to encourage anti-Semitism—quite the contrary! We are reporting these jokes not because we think they are amusing or funny, but because we believe that *all* aspects of the human experience must be documented, even those that most reflect the darker side of humanity. Unless or until the causes and extent of prejudice are recognized, that prejudice will persist. To the degree that folklore is a factor in the formation and perpetuation of prejudice, it must be held up to the light of reason. Perhaps one day, Auschwitz jokes, or jokes like them, will no longer be told.

PART TWO:

Stereotypes

CHAPTER 4

On Elephantasy
and Elephanticide:
The Effect of Time and Place

(with Roger D. Abrahams)

The literature on the theory of humor and wit and related subjects is vast and includes works by some of the greatest minds in Western history: Aristotle, Bergson, Freud, Meredith, and others more recent. In their analyses, these philosophical or psychological commentators have attempted to find out why people are amused, by concentrating on two aspects of the humor problem: The structure of devices that make people laugh and what laughter does to individuals.[1] Nevertheless, few have attempted to discern the effect of time and place on the creation and dissemination of jokes and other witticisms. Obviously, the "sense of humor" of one era or region differs from that of others, but little of substance has been written to explain these differences. The effect of time and place on humorous devices becomes especially important in analyzing joke cycles, for the jokes often achieve a spontaneous popularity and a widespread diffusion in a relatively short time. (See the chapter on light-bulb jokes for a discussion of why *they* became popular when they did.) Why and how does this phenomenon occur? The question remains unanswered. In an attempt to take one step toward this answer, we will investigate the latent content of a joke cycle that was popular in the United States during the 1960s — the elephant riddles — and relate it to certain important psychological and social factors in the lives of those who have transmitted these bits of jokelore.[2]

This investigation seems especially appropriate, for the elephant series is a relatively recent one and its notoriety may have surpassed even that of the "knock-knock," "little moron," or "sick joke" cycles. The elephant riddle, as with all these cycles, uses a childish type of humor. It involves the simple, highly repetitive form of the conundrum, deriving a great deal of its humor from the restricted form and subject matter. Furthermore, the world presented in these jokes is whimsically topsy-turvy, based on the premise that elephants can climb trees and do all sorts of other wonderful acrobatic tricks (such as jump down from trees, climb into refrigerators and Volkswagens, fly, and so on).

The elephant jokes are patently childish and nonsensical, emphasizing the basically regressive nature of wit, as suggested by Freud and his followers.[3] Wit, according to Freud, is only one form of the comic; and the comic itself is a regressive means of achieving a temporary sense of freedom from superego or societal restraint: "Under the influence of the comic, we return to the happiness of childhood. We can throw off the fetters of logical thought and revel in long-forgotten freedom."[4] But adults cannot resort to most forms of childhood humor except under extreme conditions of anxiety or during licentious occasions (such as those provided by stage performances or celebrations), for to talk nonsense or to act absurdly suggests a lack of maturity. Although everyone seems to need this kind of release from repression, the mere process of growing older makes it increasingly difficult to obtain.

One element of emotional maturity is the ability to accept restrictions on pleasure-seeking (id) drives and to redirect the energies into secondary gratifications (sublimation). These energies must find some secondary outlet. One most effective substitute gratification is wit, especially as an aggressive expression. The word-play of wit develops from childhood aggressive play activities; but while the formal devices of wit are the same in both childish and mature humor (puns, poetic devices, *non sequiturs*, balanced phrasing, etc.), in adult life their expression is more complex, the aggressions more veiled, and the results more ambiguous. Wit thus functions as a channel back to childhood, becoming an aggressive form of expression that is acceptable because of these increasingly complex formal devices.[5] Jokes perform a defensive function, denying the reality principle—for the moment—in favor of an infantile word-play and "nonsense" world in which dangerous expressions of aggression can be projected into harmless situations, thereby causing the jokes to serve the pleasure principle. Jokes thus can function as a steam valve, allowing the defense of aggressive expression against something that is causing a threat (and thus creating anxiety) by regressing to childish expressions of wit.

Regression is relative, however. It seems to vary in direct relation to the amount of anxiety present. Certain expressions hark back further in our experience than usual and tend to indicate feelings of abnormal anxieties — anxieties that are, in fact closer to infantile fears. Indeed, wit is anxiety-producing by its very nature. It asserts itself in an aggressive — often, a contest — situation in which anxiety is a natural concomitant. Wit allows certain topics to emerge that are otherwise taboo. However, under some circumstances, because of historical events in specific areas (for instance, war or depression), anxiety may become all-pervasive. In such cases, jokes arise to counterfeit the threatening situation, to cast it into harmless form, and thus to provide a release of anxiety. The more threatening the situation, the more harmless and infantile the created world must become. Such periods provide the perfect breeding ground not only for childish expressions of wit, but also for joke cycles, which — by the sheer number of witticisms that emerge because they suggest so many possible forms and subjects — allow the joketellers to multiply their ego gains.

Regression occurs because the childhood world was a more permissive one; assuming the mask of a child lets a person get away with aggressive expressions that the adult role denies. The aggressor must insist that he or she is harmless in order to get away with an attack. When an antagonist is especially powerful (therefore producing the most intense anxieties in the contest situation), there is a natural tendency for the individual to regress totally to the childish stance in order to be able to fight back at all.[6]

This regression is not simply a matter of defense, however. In childhood, the individual has achieved certain basic triumphs, such as the mastery of motor activity or language, to which he or she returns not only for defensive weapons but also for the simple pleasure of re-enacting these earlier victories. Joke telling brings about a feeling of safety in the already mastered infantile world. Thus, conflict is asserted in the aggressive nature of a joke, yet denied in its regressive use of childish forms and techniques. Or, to put it oxymoronically, the joke becomes a *harmless aggression* — an aggression that hurts no one, but that provides a transitory gain for the joker's ego.

The deceptive harmlessness of the joke is, of course, apparent in its nonactive aspect (the aggression is spoken, not enacted). Even the spoken aggression may be further ameliorated by being couched in symbolic terms. The apparently nonsensical world that features a tree-climbing elephant, for instance, lets us sidestep certain societal restrictions that would be imposed in more overt expressions of the themes and attitudes found in these jokes. The veil of nonsense is so opaque that it effectively conceals the serious nature of the underlying rationale of the humor. This is as it should be—or rather, as it always is. The release, the safety-valve function of oral humor, would be less effective if people knew what they were saying or laughing at. This veiling from consciousness is one way of duping society into casually accepting the underlay of the jokes. To escape from the psychological pressures of the human condition, we must translate or transmute reality into an unrecognizable form. That these forms should be those first used by children simply indicates that under certain conditions we continue to fight the same battles as adults, and with the same weapons.

What is the nature of the reality for which the elephant jokes are a sanctioned means of combat and escape? What early anxieties have been retriggered that necessitate the reactivation of such childish forms of defense and release? To cast light on the problem, we will first discuss the latent meanings disguised in this joke cycle and then attempt to show what made them arise when and where they did.

★   ★   ★

Like so many other joke cycles in American folklore, the elephant jokes contain a considerable amount of sexual content. However, in some of the jokes the content is latent and probably is not completely comprehended by the joketeller. In the elephant joke cycle, the elephant is the epitome of sexual power. His immensity (especially that of his phallus) and his alleged ability to procreate even under the most trying conditions are recurrent themes. The big, apparently clumsy, yet tremendously powerful and surprisingly adept elephant is in some ways a modern-day successor to the giant or ogre antagonist in folktales who poses a serious threat to the well-being of the hero. As Jack has to cut down the giant's stalk, and as Odysseus must put out Polyphemus' eye, so the modern American has to emasculate his nemesis, the omnipotent elephant.

This suggests that there are at least two distinct types of elephant jokes. In one the animal is the intimate elephant with huge parts, capable of acting as a sexual aggressor (often with other animals). The sexual superiority is signaled not only by his large organ but also by the ability to perform intercourse with impossible partners in impossible situations. The other type represents a defense against the superphallic elephant. These contain diverse techniques for keeping the elephant away and castrating him. In the first type, it is the elephant who is the protagonist: The elephant is somewhere, has something, or is performing some act. In the second type the elephant is the antagonist or victim: someone does something to or for the elephant.

Associating the elephant with phallic grandeur goes back considerably further than the present elephant joke cycle in American oral tradition. For example, American black folklore has an epic toast that concerns a fight between a lion and an elephant. In the struggle the elephant is portrayed as being obviously sexually superior to the lion.[7] A widely current joke (which, incidentally, found its way into Tennessee Williams' first draft of *Cat on a Hot Tin Roof*) tells of a man and his wife who take their young son to a zoo. They visit the elephant house, where the son notices that the bull elephant has an erection. The son asks his mother, "Mommy, what is that?" She quickly replies, "That's nothing, son," whereupon the father comments, "She's just spoiled." In other jokes, the human protagonist does not compare so favorably. A piece of folk poetry dating from the 1930s in northern California construction camps goes as follows:

> I took my gal to the circus
> The circus for to see
> When she saw the elephant's trunk
> She wouldn't go home with me.

The phallic reference is made abundantly clear by the next verse:

> I took my gal to the ballgame
> The ballgame for to see
> When the umpire yelled, "Four balls"
> She wouldn't go home with me.

The symbolic significance of the elephant's trunk is clear. It is the shape and mobility of the trunk that contributes a great deal to the elephant's image. In a typical risqué cartoon, an elephant stands outside a tent, beside which a car is parked. On the back of the car is a placard saying "Just Married." The elephant is shown inserting his trunk in between the two flaps of the tent. The caption reads, "Great Heavens, Paul!"[8]

The following representative elephant joke texts should illustrate the phallic and the castrative aspects of the cycle.

★   ★   ★

First the elephant becomes intimate. He may appear in bed or in the bathtub.

> How can you tell if there is an elephant in bed with you?
> He has buttons on his pajamas this big. (spreading hands apart about a foot)
>
> How do you know if an elephant is in the bathtub with you?
> By the faint smell of peanuts on his breath.

The true nature of the danger caused by the intimate elephant is made clear.

> How do you know when an elephant's in bed with you?
> Nine months later you have a problem.

Elephantine anatomy is frequently depicted in sexual terms.

> Why does an elephant have four feet?
> It's better than six inches.
>
> Did you hear about the man who got a job in Africa circumcising elephants?
> Well, the pay wasn't much, but the tips were tremendous.[9]
>
> Do you know how to make an elephant fly?
> You start with a zipper about 20 inches long.
>
> Do you know why elephants have long trunks?
> So they can French (kiss) giraffes.

That the elephant is especially interested in amorous affairs is explicit.

> How do elephants make love in the water?
> They take their trunks down.
>
> How does the elephant find his tail in the dark?
> Delightful.

The alleged sexual prowess of the elephant is demonstrated in a variety of ways. It may be a comment on the size of his seminal discharge, or it may be more obliquely stated by a reference to the lengthy period of the female's pregnancy—its duration presumably a result of the male's superior genital power.

What's big and gray and comes in quarts?
An elephant.[10]

How do you tell if a woman has been raped by an
    elephant?
She's pregnant for two years.

Even a prostitute, symbolizing unlimited sexual capacity, can easily
be impregnated by the elephant.

What do you get when you cross an elephant and a
    prostitute?
A three-quarter-ton pickup.

Perhaps the greatest tribute to the elephant's genital superiority is his apparent ability to indulge in intercourse with impossible sexual partners.

Why did the elephant marry the mosquito?
Because he had to.

Not only can the elephant impregnate any animal, small or large, but
he is also able to execute difficult sexual agressive attacks on his victims. In the early jokes, the elephant could climb trees. As Freud noted
long ago, flying or climbing in defiance of the laws of gravity can be
a symbolic form of erection.[11] The symbolic interpretation is reinforced
by the elephant's manifest motive in climbing the trees. Invariably he
wishes to jump down on top of some unwary passing victim (for example, mice, crocodiles, beavers, cheetahs, etc.).[12] In some elephant
jokes, the overt sexual aggression is directed against other animals.

Why do elephants climb trees?
To rape squirrels.

Why do elephants wear springs on their feet?
So they can rape flying monkeys.

What is the most fearsome sound to a flying monkey?
Boing, Boing.

In some phallic elephant jokes, the elephant's physical abilities are contrasted with the weaknesses of humans. Whereas the elephant can do
anything, the humans can do nothing. In some cases, the human weak-
ness is explicitly said to be sexual failure.

Can you get four elephants in a Volkswagen?
Hell, no—it's damn near impossible to get a little pussy
    in one.

> What is harder than getting a pregnant elephant in a
>   Volkswagen?
> Getting an elephant pregnant in a Volkswagen.

It should also be noted that the elephant's superiority is not limited
to the genital area. The elephant excels in all of the various body functions. One example is his anal power.

> What is the difference between a saloon and an elephant
>   fart?
> One's a bar-room; the other is more of a BarOOOMM!

> How can you tell an elephant has been using your bath-
>   room?
> You can't flush.

> How do you housebreak an elephant?
> You get fourteen copies of *The New York Times* — Sunday
>   edition.

★   ★   ★

In all the above examples, the elephant is giant animality
unleashed. The elephant, in the Paul Bunyan tradition, does everything
on a very large scale. This makes the second type of elephant joke,
in which the mighty beast is humbled and humiliated, strikingly different. The elephant may well be a representation of the infantile view
of the father figure, whose size, strength, sexual appetite, and ability,
seem (from a child's perspective) enormous. Like the father, the elephant
is found in intimate bedroom and bathroom (both genital and anal)
situations. But although he is familiar in the home, he is to be feared.
His actions are interpreted in terms of violence and rape. He is like
the giant in the world of folktales. And, as in the folktale, some way
must be found for the smaller observer to usurp the place of the omnipotent elephant, to cut him down to size and rob him of his defeat-
ing powers.

Several devices are used to conquer the elephant. One, based upon
the initial extraordinary phallic characteristics of the elephant, is castration — sometimes symbolic, sometimes literal.

> How do you keep an elephant from charging?
> Take away his credit card.

> How do you keep an elephant from stampeding?
> Cut his 'tam peter off.

> What did the elephant say when the alligator bit off his
>   trunk?
> Very funny. (nasalized)[13]

A more elaborate way of eliminating the elephant is to hunt and cap-
ture him.

> How do you catch an elephant?
> First you get a sign that says "No elehants allowed."
> Then a pair of binoculars, a milk bottle, and a pair of twee-
> zers. You put up the sign that says "No elehants allowed,"
> and all the elephants in the area gather around and laugh
> because elephants is spelled wrong. And then more ele-
> phants come and then more and more. They all tell their
> friends about this sign that's spelled wrong. Pretty soon
> you have a whole mob of laughing elephants, so you take
> the binoculars and turn 'em around the wrong way so
> that the elephants are real small and then you take the
> tweezers and pick 'em up and put 'em in the milk bottle.

This text suggests a child opposing an adult. The elephant is the
adult who knows how to spell; the hunter is the child who is laughed
at by the elephant for being unable to spell. But the child/hunter only
feigns ignorance in order to be able to trap the adult/elephant.[14] The
fact that the elephant laughs at the apparent ineptness of the hunter
in making a schoolboy spelling error and that the elephant tells his
friends (much as parents tell their friends of their children's errors,
sometimes in front of the children) makes the final revenge all the
sweeter. The magical technique of reducing the elephant's size by looking through the "wrong" end of the binoculars is very clever. The idea
that the child would like to look at life in a way that would reverse the
relative size differential between himself and adults (to make adults—
especially his parents—small enough to be manipulated with tweezers)
is an important one in the elephant joke cycle. The cycle provides a
means of reversing reality so that the small becomes great, and the
great becomes small. To reduce the great elephant in size is to bring
about detumescence in the giant rival. An alternative way of annihilat-
ing the elephant may reveal this goal more clearly.

> How do you kill a blue elephant?
> Shoot it with a blue elephant gun.
>
> How do you kill a pink elephant?
> You grab it by the balls (or trunk) and squeeze like hell

until it turns blue and then you kill it with a blue elephant gun.

The most drastic means of taking away the elephant's masculinity
is to transform him into a female. Whereas at the beginning of the
cycle the elephant wore tennis shoes that were usually too tight, causing wrinkles, later on he wore ballet slippers.[15] More and more, the
elephant began to do effeminate things, such as painting his toenails
or floating on his back (thereby assuming a passive or female position). Even though the pronoun referring to the elephant is masculine,
the activities are definitely feminine. In some texts, the plural "their"
is used to make the gender conveniently ambiguous. In a few instances,
feminine pronouns were used, revealing that the elephant had changed
sex completely.

> Why do elephants paint their toenails red?
> To hide in cherry trees.

> Have you ever seen an elephant in a cherry tree?
> See. It works, doesn't it? (In masculine versions, testicles
>   rather than toenails are painted.)

> Why did the elephant put straw on her head?
> She wanted to see if blondes had more fun.

> How do you give an elephant a shower?
> All you need is a few girls, some cake, cookies, and
>   perhaps a little tea.

In this text, the phallic elephant is completely humbled. Shorn of his
supermasculinity, he is a bride-to-be. No longer the dominant male,
now he is a potential victim of other dominant males. Through castration and feminization, the elephant's genital superiority is eliminated.
"He" becomes "she."

        ★   ★   ★

Looking at the elephant cycle in terms of the family
romance reveals both facets of the standard ambivalence towards the
father-figure. On one hand, there is the fascination with and envy of
his physical parts and powers; on the other hand, there is the Oedipal
success story, which requires that this archetypal rival be emasculated
and his position of power usurped. As in fairy tales, where the hero
who is initially fascinated by the minutiae of the giant's intimate life
must ultimately slay the giant, thereby asserting his hitherto untested

masculinity, so also in the elephant jokes the narrator/joker must triumph over the elephant.

Ultimately, this triumph is motivated by the desire to magically usurp the power of authority and assert it toward the mother (or, more typically in fiction and real life, a mother-substitute). But the ambiguous attraction–rejection of the giant elephant signifies more than just a fictive fulfillment of the Oedipal wish. The elephant's powers provide more than a threat; they also suggest a model, an ego ideal. As such, the elephant's actions represent fulfillment of sexual desire. His powers are to be emulated and usurped. His actions are described totally in id terms. The ambiguous interest in and fear of the elephant are conditioned by both the wish to implement sexual desires and the fear of reprisal (castration) for doing so. The giant-figure represents the possibility of the freeing of desires and the triumph over restraint through power. The elephant is, then, as much a wish-projection as an adversary. This accounts, at least in part, for the two types of elephant riddles.

To point out that the elephant joke mirrors the Oedipal strivings inherent in the Western family system does not explain why, just at this time, such a topic and figure should be of interest to so large a segment of the population. Theoretically, these Oedipal pressures are continually present. Yet rarely are they expressed in such a broadly popular form, a form that has evoked considerable comment and interest. Perhaps there was something unique in the early 1960s that triggered a mass anxiety about authority figures of especially awesome sexual capacities.

Society and the creative individuals within it are too complex to assign any single definitive cause or set of causes for a release mechanism like that represented by the elephant jokes. Nevertheless, certain forces may have been instrumental in triggering such a vital and widespread response. The intensity of the response indicates that the psychic importance of the initiating force must be correspondingly great. The rise of the elephant joke occurred at the same time as the rise of the blacks in the Civil Rights movement. These two disparate cultural phenomena appear to be intimately related; in fact, the elephant may be seen as a reflection of the American black as the white sees him, and that blacks' political and social assertion has caused certain primal fears to be reactivated.

At first glance, this may seem to be a radical hypothesis, but there are a number of parallels between the figures of the elephant and the white stereotype of the black. There is, first of all, the obvious association in the minds of many Americans of both the elephant and the black with the African jungle. Some see the black as a recent descendant of a tree-dwelling wild animal, and this animal sensuality is the source of both attraction and fear. The elephant in the tree, as we have seen, is the same kind of attractive, yet repulsive, superpotent animal. Beyond this, however, the elephant in the cycle has many of the attributes of the black man in his most fascinating and feared form, according to the popular imagination. Both the male black and the elephant are pictured as having unusually large genitals and commensurate sexual capacity. Furthermore, part of their public image has to do with great size, strength, and endurance.

This conception of black masculinity is a fiction at best,[16] but it nevertheless persists. Until the recent black revolution, however, the fear could be dissipated, not only by actual social subjugation but also through folk humor — for example, the "Rastus and Liza" joke cycle, in which the black, depicted as a lazy domestic animal, is unable to work or think. These means of reducing the fear are no longer as available, and in uniting for their cause the blacks produced a contrary image: powerful, enigmatic, and occasionally vindictive (as in the Black Muslim movement). This supplanting image crystallized the previously concealed but long-present sexual fascination and castration fear. The black is now felt as a threatening phallic force to be reckoned with. The defense against this threat is regressive and projective in that the feared object is controlled by recourse to essentially juvenile joking techniques and the casting of the black into the shape of the elephant.

Further evidence for the connection between the black and the elephant is provided by the manifest color content of many of the elephant jokes. Some of the earliest examples had to do with the elephant's color.

> Do you know why elephants are gray?
> So you can tell them from bluebirds (redbirds, black-
>   berries).

But then the elephant began to paint himself or his clothes various colors in order to disguise himself, to avoid being seen or noticed.

> Why do elephants wear green tennis shoes?
> To hide in the tall grass.

Does the elephant, like the black, hope to fit into the natural environment and not be noticed by a simple act of changing his color, as another facet of the public image of the black would suggest? The preoccupation with the elephant's color might then reflect the public's concern with the black as either "colored man" or "man of color."[17]

This hypothetical association of black and elephant might seem implausible if the elephant joke were an isolated phenomenon—but it is not. It is part of a wider contemporary vogue for joking riddles, one important strand of which has been riddling descriptions consisting of enumerations of colors that refer directly to the black. The earliest of these color riddles ridiculed prominent black individuals.

>What's black and catches flies?
>Willie Mays (Centerfielder of the San Francisco Giants).

Around the same time that the elephant jokes were becoming popular, riddles concerning blacks were depersonalized and blacks were referred to by the degrading and generic term, "nigger."

>What do they call a Negro with a Ph.D. in Mississippi?
>Nigger.

Moreover, at the same time that the elephant began to fly, the black also took to the air, and in the process he usurped the powers of the white comic strip hero Superman.

>What's black and has a red cape?
>Super Nigger.

Fear of the black came closer to the surface, and the thought that he might possibly resort to physical attack was expressed.

>What's dangerous, lives in trees, and is black?
>A crow with a machine gun.

>What do they call a six-foot-four Negro with a machine
>   gun in Mississippi?
>Sir.

It should now be clear that the concern with color and the explicit sexual content of the elephant jokes are not mutually exclusive. Instead, the presence of both factors is explicable in terms of a black/elephant equation. Once again, the association of color and sexuality is also found in other joking riddles with specific reference to the black.

What's black and comes in a white box?
Sammy Davis, Jr.[18]

What is black and white and rolls in the grass?
Integrated sex.

Not only is the white awed by the supposed genital superiority of the black, but he also fears for the retention of his women.[19]

⋆   ⋆   ⋆

It is not easy to make sense of nonsense. However, the elephant joke cycle exists as a cultural phenomenon at a specific point in time and space. The widespread and popular nature of these materials can be explained as an outlet for the reenactment and control of Oedipal problems. But a purely psychological analysis alone would not explain why the cycle arose precisely when it did. The social–historical context must also be taken into account. The development of the black freedom movement, causing anxiety even among those sympathetic to the movement, would seem to be the catalytic agent producing such a regressive response. There is no inconsistency in arguing that the elephant may be both the adult sexual rival of the child and the black sexual rival of the white. Both rivals represent power, in part sexual, which threatens and must therefore be conquered. It is easier to conquer in fantasy than in reality. If killing the elephant eliminates either the father, the black, or both, and if it accomplishes this harmlessly under cover of nonsense so that the killer need feel no guilt, then the function and significance of elephant jokes are clear.[20] These jokes, like all expressions of wit, are serious business.

CHAPTER 5

The Curious Case of the Wide-Mouth Frog: Jokes and Covert Language Attitudes

In the early 1970s, a strange piece of whimsy circulated orally in the United States. The modern joke in question concerned a "wide-mouth" frog who evidently didn't know what to feed its newborn babies:

> There once was a mommy wide-mouth frog and a daddy wide-mouth frog. They had a baby wide-mouth frog. They didn't know what to feed their baby wide-mouth frog so the daddy wide-mouth frog went to the zoo to ask mommies what they fed their babies. When he got there, he asked the mommy giraffe, "Mama Giraffe, whaddaya feed your BABIES?" [spoken with a wide open mouth]. The giraffe answered (in a very dignified voice), "I feed them leaves from the highest trees." "OH, IS THAT SO?" [again spoken with a wide mouth]. Then he asked the mommy rhinoceros, "Mama Rhinoceros, whaddaya feed your BABIES?" The rhinoceros said (in a deep voice), "I feed them mud from the swamp bottoms." Again the wide-mouth frog said, "OH, IS THAT SO?" Then he asked the mama hippopotamus, "Mama Hippopotamus, whaddaya feed your BABIES?" "I feed them little wide-mouth frogs." "Oh, is that so?" [with a small tight mouth, in a soft voice].[1]

In the course of attempting to question other animals about their normal regimes of infant diet, the wide-mouth frog is eventually put in the position of having to radically alter its customary speech pattern. This piece of folklore thus contains an explicitly metalinguistic aspect.

It should be obvious that most of the power of the joke lies in the performance, specifically the shifts of "dialect" from wide-mouth speech, to normal speech, and finally to "narrow-mouth" speech. A full appreciation of the story requires more than simply *reading* the text of the joke—it must be *heard* and *seen* in performance. The critical paralinguistic and kinesic features essential to the joke's performance don't really translate successfully into the printed-page format. Nevertheless, here is a second version:

> A wide-mouth frog goes to the zoo and he hops into the lion's cage. And he says, "Hello Mrs. Lion! I'm a wide-mouth frog. What do you feed your babies?" [spoken with mouth widely extended]. Mrs. Lion says, "Go on, get out of here. I don't have time for you." And so he hops out into the tiger's cage and says, "Hello, Mrs. Tiger. I'm a wide-mouth frog. What do you feed your babies?" And Mrs. Tiger says, "Go on, Go 'way." So he hops into the alligator cage and says, "Hello, Mrs. Alligator! I'm a wide-mouth frog. What do you feed your babies?" "Wide-mouth frogs." "Oh, really?" [spoken with lips pursed and brow furrowed in sudden sincerity].

The person who brought this joke to my attention[2] also came across alternative punchlines: **"Is that so?"** or **"You don't say."** Still other informants reported such alternatives as an abrupt implosive, almost hiccoughed, "OH!" or an equally fascinating final sequence in which the wide-mouth frog (narrator) forms a large "OH" with the mouth shaped as if making a huge yawn; but just in the nick of time, before uttering a sound, the frog purses or puckers its lips as tightly as possible in order to produce the /iu/ diphthong[3] or diphthongal vowel[4] instead.

Informants who told or were told this story could say relatively little about what it might mean. This is not unusual. A joke, like beauty, tends to be its own excuse for being and can often be enjoyed without a fully articulated exegesis. However, a joke does not exist *in vacuo* but in a society, where it embodies or reflects concerns of that society. The question is: What concerns, if any, of American society are to be found in the short saga of the wide-mouth frog? How could a sudden change in speech pattern, under threat of death, be relevant to America in the 1970s? To suggest an answer to these questions, let us examine some of the details of the story.

One theme of the joke appears to be the contrast between an open and a closed society. The frog is free, in contrast to the various animals in the zoo who reside in cages. There may even be symbolic or iconic phonological isomorphism, in that the frog in the open society speaks in a wide-mouth or open fashion. At the end of the joke, the frog, in order to survive, must curb its natural way of speaking. It must speak, literally and figuratively, in a close-mouthed way in order to stay alive; it must keep its mouth shut to remain free. One possible moral is that free speech is dangerous in a closed society (the zoo). However, in some versions, the animals questioned by the wide-mouth frog are not in a zoo. Another possible interpretation, which is not at all incompatible with the above interpretation, turns on the notion that big-mouth individuals of whatever political or ideological persuasion inevitably come to grips with the pressures that arise from continually talking "big." The harsh realities of life often demand that habitually outspoken people learn to take advice and perhaps to change their customary style of presenting themselves.

The adaptiveness of the frog who abruptly and drastically changes his mode of speaking is understandable and perhaps even admirable, but there is something both pathetic and absurd in a frog's being forced to deny his wide-mouth nature. (Note that in the second version, the frog bothers to proclaim to each animal visited that he is a wide-mouth frog, suggesting that he is proud of his identity.) The irony is that the danger of being eaten comes from a creature who possesses a truly wide mouth—typically, a hippopotamus or an alligator. But since these creatures speak normally (at least as judged by the dominant society), their wide mouths are not socially significant. It is only the frog who is singled out on the basis of a single physical characteristic: its wide mouth and its wide-mouth manner of speaking.

Another, somewhat unusual, version of the joke provides an important clue about the possible meaning:

> There is a wide-mouth frog standing in her kitchen. She hears a commotion outside and looking out of her window, she notices a crowd standing around a tree. She goes outside and asks, "WHAT'S HAPPENING?" [speaking with a big mouth]. A person answers, "They're hanging a wide-mouth frog!" [talking "regular," as the informant put it]. "Oh, I didn't know!!!" [spoken with a very small, tight mouth].[5]

The reference to a lynching as well as the use of the phrase "What's happening?" strongly suggests that the joke is really about a facet of race relations in the United States. "What's happening?" is a standard greeting formula in Afro-American speech. This hints that the wide-mouth frog might be in some sense a black—even if only a white stereotype of one. The lynching, of course, refers to a long, disgraceful period in American history when white vigilante groups hanged blacks without so much as even a pretense of a formal trial.

If the joke is really about white attitudes towards black speaking patterns, we can more readily understand the joke's popularity in the 1970s. With increased integration through court-ordered school bussing, for example, more and more whites became familiar with black speech patterns. Many whites were both fascinated and repelled by black speech. On the one hand, they delighted in imitating it (mostly in private), which might explain part of the pleasure—both for the joketeller who speaks in a wide-mouth dialect, and for the audience listening to it. On the other hand, most educators, classroom teachers, and the white community generally publicly attack black dialect, demanding that black students learn to talk (and write) "white." In the joke, the wide-mouth frog is forced to do just that in order to continue living (not be eaten, not be hanged). The implication is clearly that if the wide-mouth frog wants to be successful in the larger animal community, he must stop talking like a wide-mouth frog. Black announcers on white radio stations (as opposed to black stations) or black newscasters on major network television stations certainly talk "white"—often eliciting exclamations of praise from white listeners who mistakenly marvel at the sight of a black individual speaking without a trace of black dialect. A wide-mouth frog can "pass," so to speak, by denying his normal speech pattern, even though this means denying any relation to the poor wide-mouth frog being hanged. If a wide-mouth frog wants to remain secure in the kitchen of her home—and the kitchen, like the concern with feeding babies, emphasizes the fundamental nature of an orality theme—she must conform to the dominant majority's speech pattern and renounce any connection with wide-mouth brothers and sisters who cannot or will not change. Also, a wide-mouth frog who doesn't speak like a wide-mouth frog is still a wide-mouth frog. Perhaps this suggests a white view that even if a black makes a concerted effort to *talk* "white," he cannot ultimately *be* "white." He remains black.[6]

Some additional support for this interpretation can be seen in the visual evidence from the phonetic articulation of the joke and from a longstanding detail of the white stereotype of the Afro-American. In fifteenth-century European stereotypes of Africans, there are references to the thick or protruding lips of the Negro.[7] This stereotypic detail carried over to the New World. American folk speech contains a slighting reference to someone's rolling or lighting a cigarette with too much lip motion: an admonishment such as "Don't nigger-lip it." Raven McDavid even noted a 1949 newspaper account claiming that the Negro cannot pronounce postvocalic /-r/ in *beard, bird, bard* because his lips are too thick.[8] The dialogue in the wide-mouth frog joke makes extensive use of words with initial labial consonants or other consonants that entail pronounced lip movement. "What do you feed *your* babies?" involves an initial /w/ in "What," followed typically by an extended or exaggerated /y/ in "your." Often the performance includes an accentuation of the two bilabial /b/s in "babies." Even more convincing is the iconic nature of the initial consonants in each of the three words of the key phrase, "wide-mouth frog." In the version in which the frog proudly proclaims his identity, "I'm a wide-mouth frog," this phonological patterning is especially striking. /w/ is a labial, followed by a diphthong that can easily be extended with lips wide. /m/ is a labial, which is also followed by a diphthong that can easily be extended with lips wide. /f/ is a labial, followed by an American /r/, which tends to involve the lips, to share something of the traits of a /w/.[9] Even though most versions have the alligator rather than the frog utter the key phrase, "wide-mouth frog," there is still a phonological contrast between the lip patterning of the next-to-the-last line and the final punchline. The dynamic lip movement in these words contrasts with the relatively static lip features in the articulation of the punchline. Also, the common use of the diphthong /iu/ in the punchline draws special attention to the position of the lips. They protrude, but in an extremely tightly controlled manner. The particular diphthong itself may be relevant. McDavid states that although it occurs in such words as *puke, beautiful, music, tube, due, new, suit, sumach, grew,* and *blew* in New England as well as along the Chesapeake Bay and the Carolina and Georgia coast, it has an old-fashioned connotation.[10] He further observes that although this diphthong may have social prestige in England, it strikes most Americans as unnatural and affected. Reed discusses it under the rubric of "fancied elegance."[11] The /iu/ diphthong thus smacks of phonetic hypercorrection. This might imply that in trying to conceal its identity, the wide-mouth frog overcorrects its speech.

Yet another piece of evidence supports the present interpretation of the wide-mouth frog. In American minstrelsy of the nineteenth century, part of the stereotype of the Afro-American was his large mouth. Whites took pleasure in acting out their stereotypes of blacks. A recent thorough study of minstrelsy states that "Emphasis on the black man's supposedly large lips and mouth was not new. From the beginning of minstrelsy, white minstrels had made themselves up to appear to have huge mouths, an important part of the physical stereotype that set blacks off from whites."[12] If a huge mouth was part of the minstrel stereotype of the Afro-American, the wide-mouth frog may be seen as a continuation of that tradition. As whites enjoyed talking like blacks (or watching white minstrels in blackface talking like blacks), so the wide-mouth frog joke provides a modern socially sanctioned outlet for whites to talk black. The paradox is that what the whites who talk black say is that blacks ought to be forced to talk white!

One might legitimately ask, Why need there be a facade of fantasy to express stereotypic traits? Why not delineate the stereotype in undisguised fashion? Part of the answer might be that it is always easier to treat unpleasant material in fantasy than in reality. Fantasy—literary as well as folk—has always served as a screen for the projection of racism. But another part of the answer might be that the civil rights movement of the 1960s made it more socially unacceptable to express blatant racism directly. An interesting example from children's literature is Roald Dahl's popular *Charlie and the Chocolate Factory*, first published in 1964 and later made into a film. In this moralistic fable (in which children who are greedy, who chew too much gum, or who watch too much television are appropriately punished), all the work at Willy Wonka's chocolate factory is carried out by "Oompa-Loompas," whose "skin is almost black," who were "imported direct from Africa" by being "smuggled over in large packing cases with holes in them." We are also told "They are wonderful workers. . . . They love dancing and music. They are always making up songs."[13] Perhaps Dahl was not fully conscious of the racist implications of his portrait of the Oompa-Loompas, but racism need not be conscious to be destructive. Animals are commonly used in such racist fictional fantasies. For example, there is probably a racist rationale underlying the appeal of King Kong, a huge gorilla (gorillas come from Africa!) who, in the classic 1933 film, carries off a screaming white woman (to whom he is greatly attracted) to the top of a tall building. The fact that the film was remade in 1976 suggests that the racial tensions involved remain a vital factor in

American society. In any event, there can be no doubt that fantasy, sometimes using animal characters, can be used to express and communicate racist projections. If I am correct, then the curious case of the wide-mouth frog is at least clear, although unfortunately not solved.[14] The idea that a minority group must change its speech pattern under pain of death may overstate the parameters of the problem (although the attempted imposition of Afrikaans upon South African blacks led to riots and death in 1976), but the problem is a very real one in the interrelationship of language and society. Perhaps social judgments based upon distinguishable linguistic differences will last as long as ethnocentrism and prejudice. Then again, perhaps calling attention to the double standard and hypocrisy of a "wide-mouth" alligator preying on a frog because of its "wide mouth" may ultimately lead to greater tolerance for linguistic diversity.

CHAPTER 6

The Jewish American Princess and the Jewish American Mother in American Jokelore

Jewish folklore is endlessly rich, and jokes make up one large component of that folklore. It has been argued that the Jewish sense of humor, especially as revealed in jokes, has helped Jews survive centuries of anti-Semitic prejudice and discrimination, which, in their extreme forms, culminated in pogroms and the Holocaust. Considering the probable—and unfortunate—proportional relationship between repression and jokes (the greater the repression, the more jokes protesting that repression), it's easy to understand why Jews have so long depended on the defense mechanism of jokes.

Many Jewish jokes concern the Jews' relationships with the outside world—the gentile, or goyish, world. However, insiders' jokes have always existed, as well—jokes that treat the Jewish world itself. Themes include the schnorrer, the marriage arranger, the moile, the rabbi, and the rabbi's wife, among others.[1]

This chapter examines the stereotype of the Jewish American Princess (J.A.P.) as displayed in a joke cycle that was popular in the United States in the late 1970s and early 1980s. Since the J.A.P. cannot be understood in isolation from the Jewish American Mother (J.A.M.), that stereotype will be considered as well.

One theme of Jewish jokes in the United States is the Jewish mother. Such jokes are said to be of relatively modern origin. One source, for example, suggests that, "Jokes about the Jewish mother—the biggest cliché in contemporary Jewish humor—are a relatively recent phenomenon. Traditional Jewish humor had no such jokes."[2] And another source claims, "By now, the Jewish Mother is part of all American comedy. Overbearing, overprotective, long-suffering, loudly self-sacrificing, and unintentionally funny, she survives the joke not only as a person of warmth, but as one who cares."[3] There is some question as to just when the stereotype began to come into national prominence, and to what extent the stereotype derives from Eastern Europe.

It was during the 1960s, according to several authorities, that the Jewish Mother became "an integral part of the American scene," especially as a negative stereotype.[4] Sara Reguer, in "The Jewish Mother and the 'Jewish American Princess': Fact or Fiction," sees the Jewish Mother as "a purely American phenomenon,"[5] although she notes the possible connection to the "Yiddishe mama" of Eastern Europe. Zena Smith Blau, writing "In Defense of the Jewish Mother," maintains that "there can be little question that the constellation of maternal traits commonly referred to as the 'Yiddishe Mameh' was the modal maternal pattern among Jewish immigrants from Eastern Europe. . . ."[6] Mark Zborowski and Elizabeth Herzog, in their book *Life Is with People*, agree that the stereotype "has firm roots in the shtetl."[7] Whatever the degree of indebtedness to Eastern Europe for the stereotype or jokes about that stereotype, there can be no doubt that the Jewish American Mother — or J.A.M. — is a distinctive folk character in American jokelore.

The characteristics of the J.A.M. in jokes includes such features as: she is overly solicitous of her children's welfare, especially her son's health; and she is anxious for her daughters to marry well (preferably doctors or lawyers), and for her sons to become professionals (preferably doctors or lawyers). The stereotype includes the J.A.M.'s penchant for forcing food down her children's throats (for reasons of health) and her excessive unending demand for attention, love, and visits from her children, even after they are successfully married.

The J.A.M. enjoys the role of martyr. She is never happier than when she has something to complain about, and the complaint is intended to produce feelings of guilt in her children. It is impossible to totally please the J.A.M., as the following classic joke illustrates:

> A mother gave her son two neckties as a present for his birthday, a red one and a green one. The son, to show his appreciation for the gift, puts on the red one and is wearing it when he picks her up to take her out for dinner. Says the mother, "What's the matter? You didn't like the green one?"[8]

On the other hand, J.A.M.s worship their sons.

How do we know Jesus was Jewish? Because he lived at home with his mother until he was thirty; he went into his father's business; and he had a mother who thought he was God.[9]

Overprotection is a principal element in the J.A.M. stereotype. One theory is that it compensates for Jews generally being underprotected in society.[10] The following text shows the excessively nurturing J.A.M. with her (consequently) spoiled child:

A Jewish mother and her son arrive in a taxi in front of a large plush hotel in Miami Beach. The mother, dressed in a mink and much bejeweled, goes in to register, and she asks several bellboys to bring in the two trunks and twelve suitcases. After they do so, they ask if there's anything else they can do for her. She replies, "Would you please lift my fourteen-year-old son out of the car and carry him up to my room?"
"Oh," says one of the bellboys, "I'm sorry, I didn't realize he couldn't walk."
"He can walk all right," says the mother, "but thank God he doesn't have to."[11]

Perhaps the most common sign of the J.A.M.'s nurturant proclivities is her constant concern with feeding her progeny.

Did you know that there are two signs on El Al airlines planes? "Fasten Your Seat Belts" and "Eat." In another version, the sign reads "Eat, eat, take a little nosh,"[12] while in yet another, the third sign after "Fasten Seat Belts" and "No Smoking" on El Al is "Take a Piece of Fruit."[13]

Did you know they have two stewardesses on El Al airlines? One serves the food, and the other follows, saying, "Eat, eat."

Did you hear about the new ship in the Israeli Navy? the SS Mein Kind [eat, eat my child].[14]

Did you hear about the bum who walked up to the Jewish mother on the street and said, "Lady, I haven't eaten in three days"?
"Force yourself," she replied.[15]

There was often an apparent altruistic reason why the J.A.M. urged her children to eat. As Blau notes, children were exhorted to eat *"for others*, for mama, for poppa, for other members of the family, and inevitably the appeal was made to eat for the 'poor starving children in Europe.'"[16] (Later we shall see that the J.A.P.—who is egocentric rather than altruistic—eats for no one, not even herself!)

One of the best of the food-forcing J.A.M. jokes was reported in 1958. A Jewish gangster has been in a gun fight with the police. As he staggers into his mother's East Side apartment, nearly *in extremis*, his hands covering a big, bloody wound, he gasps, "Ma, ma, I—I've been hit . . ." Mama says, "Eat, eat. Later we'll talk."[17]

The J.A.M. will do anything to make her children eat. What's the difference between an Italian mother and a Jewish mother? The Italian mother says, "If you don't eat all the food on this plate, I'll kill you." The Jewish mother says, "If you don't eat all the food on this plate, I'll kill myself."[18] The J.A.M.'s ploy inevitably involves the martyr threat.

Of course, the J.A.M. makes a difficult mother-in-law, as one might imagine. The antagonism between the J.A.M. and her (prospective) daughter-in-law is sharply delineated in a tale that is also popular in Eastern Europe. A Jewish young man asks his mother for her heart, which his fiancée has demanded as a prerequisite for marriage. The mother gladly accedes to this unusual request so that her son will be happy. Having torn his mother's heart out, the boy rushes back to show it to his bride-to-be. One the way, he stumbles and both he and the heart fall to the ground, whereupon the heart asks, "Did you hurt yourself, my son?"[19] This tale marvelously encapsulates the J.A.M.'s uncanny ability to use solicitude as a devastating weapon to create feelings of guilt. No matter how great the pain for the self-sacrificing martyr-mater, her only concern is for her son's welfare—even if he treats her shamefully!

Not surprisingly, the J.A.M. has a double standard about what she wants for her children versus for their spouses.

> Two women meet on the Grand Concourse in the Bronx. The first one says, "How are your children?"
>
> "Well," says the second, "Oy veh, how awful! My son is married to such a woman. She has to have breakfast in bed, nu, she has to have a mink stole. . . ."
>
> The first woman says, "And what about your daughter? How is she?"
>
> "She's married to a dear man. He serves her breakfast in bed; he bought her a mink stole."

One of the J.A.M.'s most typical complaints is that her married children fail to visit her or to call her often enough. From my own Jewish mother—by telephone, of course, when I called her—I collected the following text:

> A Jewish woman discovers a magic lamp. She rubs it, and a genie appears and says she can have a wish, anything she wants. What does she ask for? Nothing. She didn't want to wish. She had everything she wanted: a daughter who married a doctor and a son who called her once a week.

Another text refers more to the J.A.M.'s daughter.

> An old Jewish woman goes to her lawyer to have her will made out. She arrives at his office and he says, "Hello, what can I do for you?"
> She says, "I want to make my will."
> "Okay, what do you want it to say?"
> "Well, when I die, I want to be cremated and I want my ashes scattered on the first, the second, and the third floors of Nieman Marcus."
> "Okay, but why would you want to do that?"
> "Well, at least that way, I know my daughter will come visit me once a week."[20]

The J.A.M. is such a stock character that she is virtually interchangeable within her cohort. *Any* Jewish Mother can serve, in a crisis. This is beautifully illustrated in the following "big city" joke:

> The telephone rings and the daughter answers.
> "Hello?"
> "How are you?" says the mother.
> "Oh terrible, terrible."
> "What's the matter?"
> "The baby's sick, and the maid called in today, Ma, and she's not coming, and the place is a mess. There's nothing in the refrigerator and we're having company tonight for dinner. I'm supposed to go to the Hadassah meeting. I don't know what to do!"
> "Don't worry. What's a mother for. I got plenty time. I've made gefilte fish; I've got a couple of chickens; I can bring them. I'll be right over. I'll clean your apartment; I'll wait for the doctor to come over. You can go to your Hadassah meeting, and I'll get the dinner ready."

"Oh, ma, that would be wonderful."

"Listen, what's a mother for? Before you hang up, how's Stephen?"

"Stephen, who's Stephen?"

"What do you mean who's Stephen? He's your husband!"

"My husband's name is Marvin."

(Long pause.)

"Is this 841-5656?"

"No, it's 841-6565."

(Pause.)

"Does this mean you're not coming?"[21]

Various explanations of the Jewish Mother stereotype have been proposed. According to some sources, the Jewish mother had to be strong because the Jewish father was weak. In Europe, the husband was concerned with religious devotion to God and the wife ran the household,[22] while in America, Jewish men had to assimilate more to gain employment, leaving the women trapped in the home to serve as bastions of Jewish culture and values.[23] According to this view, the Jewish mother, often married to a weak, unsuccessful Jewish man, had good reason to lavish her attention, love, and hopes for the future on her children instead.[24] So involved is the Jewish American Mother with the lives of her children that she has difficulty letting them leave home. She fears the "empty nest syndrome" more than most.[25]

If this is at all accurate, then it is reasonable to suspect J.A.M.'s apparent selflessness. She has her own personal reasons for serving as relentless nurturer. One finds sometimes an insidious motive attached to the food-providing image. In return for the nurturance, the J.A.M. demands eternal loyalty and love. As one critic has felicitously phrased it, "Too well we know the Jewish mother our male writers have given us, the all-engulfing nurturer who devours the very soul with every spoonful of hot chicken soup she gives."[26] Even the "Eat, eat" jokes have been perceived as "hostile vulgarizations" of the Jewish Mother's role as all-powerful mistress of the home.[27] There is even a hint that what underlies the J.A.M.'s indulgence is hostility towards her demanding, whining children, as the following joke reveals.

Four Jewish women meet.

"Oy!" says the first.

"Oy veh!" says the second.

"Oy veh iz mir!" says the third.

"I thought we weren't going to talk about the kids," says the fourth.

In another text, two Jewish mothers meet. One says to the other, "Do you have any children?"
"No."
"So what do you do for aggravation?"

It is interesting that in the second joke, two Jewish *mothers* meet — even though it turns out that one of the women has no children. This suggests that the J.A.M.'s oversolicitous regard for her children might be an instance of reaction formation caused by guilt for harboring such feelings of hostility and resentment. Reaction formation is a psychological defense mechanism whereby a person has feelings that make him or her feel guilty. As a result, the very opposite of those feelings is expressed. So we might have a mother who resents her children, then feels guilt for having such sentiments, and finally, as a reaction formation, makes a special point of expressing great love for her children.

Perhaps the resentment of the children's seemingly endless demands for nurturance is a relatively late development of the 1980s. A Catholic, a Protestant, and a Jew are debating the question of when exactly does life begin. The Catholic insists that life begins at the moment of conception; the Protestant disagrees, claiming that life begins at birth; the Jew says, "You're both wrong. Life begins when the children leave home and the dog dies."[28]

The image or stereotype of the Jewish American Princess (J.A.P.), on the other hand, varies considerably from the J.A.M.'s. (Interestingly, the fact that a virtually identical stereotype is found in South Africa, where a J.A.P. is called a "kugel," demonstrates that the humor is by no means peculiar to the United States.[29]) The stereotypical traits are consistent ones: The J.A.P. is spoiled rotten. She is excessively concerned with appearance. She diets. She may have had a nose job. Did you hear about the Jewish girl who cut off her nose to spite her race and was a thing of beauty and a goy forever?[30] She worries about her fingernails. She is interested in money, shopping, and status. She shares features such as wealth and status with the J.A.M.; but her characteristics differ dramatically — for example, she refuses to cook (and eat). The J.A.P. is indifferent to sex, and is particularly disinclined to perform fellatio.

One could argue that the J.A.M. is ultimately responsible for creating the J.A.P. Mothers who overprotect their daughters produce women who expect to be catered to and looked after. Julie Baumgold maintains that "A princess is made by only one thing and that is her mother. Her mother telling her that she is beautiful. Unremittingly, over the years, that she is beautiful; that she is precious, the thing that the man has to earn and deserve."[31] While the J.A.M. is bound by "the role of wife and mother, the all-giving selfless nurturer,"[32] the J.A.P. rejects these values. Perhaps the J.A.P.'s obsession with high-style clothing is a reaction to what she perceives as the J.A.M.'s plain, even dowdy hausfrau apparel. The J.A.P.'s refusal to eat (in order to stay slim) may be a direct response to the J.A.M.'s insistence upon eating. The J.A.M. lavishes food to show love; the J.A.P. declines to cook, eat, or indulge in lovemaking.

Perhaps the most common J.A.P. jokes address the refusal to prepare meals.

> What does a J.A.P. make for dinner?
> Reservations.[33]

> How does a J.A.P. call her family to dinner?
> "Get in the car, kids."[34]

> How does a J.A.P. get exercise?
> "Waitress!" (waving one's arm frantically)

An equally popular characteristic of the stereotype is the desire for high-status items, such as trips to fashionable resorts, or standard prestigious material objects.

> What is a J.A.P.'s favorite wine?
> "I wanna go to Hawaii" (Miami)!

> What is a J.A.P.'s second favorite wine?
> "And I wanna go right NOW!"

Other favorite whines include: "You never take me anywhere." "I wanna mink coat!" (diamond ring).[35] The "whining and dining" facet of the J.A.P. starts as early as in the "J.A.P.I.T. joke." A J.A.P.I.T. is a J.A.P. In Training. Her cry is "I want a Diet Pepsi, but I want my *own*."

> What do you call 12 J.A.P.s locked in the basement?
> A whine cellar.

With respect to whining, Zena Smith remarks, "In America Yiddishe Mamehs appeared far more permissive, indulgent and self-sacrificing than the typical Anglo-Saxon mother, at least in the years prior to the nineteen-forties. For example, they were a good deal more tolerant of whining and crying, and dependency behavior generally."[36] This would help explain the J.A.M.'s role in producing J.A.P.s.

But the good life includes more than wine. It includes shopping for quality items.

> How do you tickle a J.A.P.?
> Gucci, Gucci goo.[37]
>
> Why do J.A.P.s like circumcised men?
> They like anything with 20% off.

What three little words does a J.A.P. never hear? "Attention, K-Mart shoppers."[38] K-Mart is a bargain store whose merchandise does not carry the requisite high-status labels, and where there are frequent loudspeaker announcements calling attention to a particularly cheap item on sale. A contrasting ethnic joke is: What are the first three words a Mexican baby will hear? "Attention K-Mart shoppers."

> How does a J.A.P. commit suicide?
> Piles her clothes on top of the bed and jumps off.
>
> What is a J.A.P. with a colostomy's greatest concern?
> Finding shoes to match the bag.[39]

Another reference to undue anxiety about personal appearance is contained in the following text:

> What's a J.A.P.'s idea of natural childbirth?
> Going into the delivery room without any make-up on.[40]

Of course, shopping for expensive name-brands requires adequate financial support.

> Why do J.A.P.'s wear gold diaphragms?
> Because they like their men to come into money.[41]

Despite this last text, it is the antipathy to sex that constitutes the hallmark of the J.A.P.

> How do you keep a Jewish girl from fucking?
> Marry her.[42]
>
> Have you heard the joke about the Jewish nymphomaniac?
> Once a month.[43]
>
> What's the definition of a J.A.P. nymphomaniac?
> One who only has sex on days she gets her hair done.[44]

What is Jewish foreplay?
Twenty minutes of begging.[45]

The previous joke occurs within a larger ethnic-slur tradition crit-
icizing insensitive males oblivious of female sexual needs: What is Irish
foreplay? "Brace yourself, Bridget." What is Italian foreplay? "Hey, you
awake?" (Or, in another version, Slamming the front door and announc-
ing "Hey Honey, I'm home!")

How does a Jewish couple perform doggie style sex?
He sits up and begs and she lies down and plays dead.[46]

What's a Jewish 10?
A 9 without a headache (Or, a 5 with money).[47]

What do you call a J.A.P.'s nipple?
The tip of the iceberg.[48]

How do you know when a J.A.P. has an orgasm?
She drops her emery board (nail file).[49]

What's a J.A.P.'s idea of perfect sex?
Simultaneous headaches.[50]

Why do Jewish girls kiss with their eyes closed?
'Cause they can't stand seeing anyone enjoying themselves.[51]

Many of the J.A.P. jokes combine traits of the stereotype, for example, lack of interest in cooking with lack of interest in sex, the use
of credit cards and sex, and so on.

Why does a J.A.P. close her eyes during sex?
So she can pretend she's shopping.[52]

How does a J.A.P. fake an orgasm?
She thinks of going shopping.[53]

What is a J.A.P.'s ideal house?
6000 square feet with no kitchen and no bedroom.[54]

What's a J.A.P.'s favorite position?
Facing Neiman-Marcus (Bloomingdales),[55] or Bending
over credit cards.[56]

Why do J.A.P.'s use tampons instead of sanitary napkins?
Because nothing goes in without a string attached.[57]

What do you get when you cross a French whore with a
    J.A.P.?
A girl who sucks credit cards. Or, in another version,
    A woman that will suck the numbers off your credit
    card.[58]

In this last text, it is the French whore who accounts for the act
of fellatio, not the J.A.P. The J.A.P. in the joke cycle absolutely refuses
to indulge in such activities.

What's the difference between J.A.P.s and poverty?
Poverty sucks.[59]

What's the difference between a J.A.P. and a job?
Most jobs suck after 20 years.

What's the difference between a J.A.P. and the Bermuda
    Triangle?
The Bermuda Triangle swallows seamen![60]

What do you get when you cross a J.A.P. and an Apple
    (IBM)?
A computer that'll never go down.

Why do J.A.P.s have crow's feet? From squinting and saying, "Suck
what?"[61] In a variant, the question is: Why do J.A.P.s have slanted eyes?
This is of interest in view of the apparent similarity to Japanese facial
features.

What does a J.A.P. think that sucking and fucking are.
Two cities in China.

Why won't a J.A.P. eat soybeans?
Because it's a meat substitute.[62]

How does a J.A.P. eat a banana? Under duress.[63] In a variant, the
answer involves miming a banana held in the left hand, with the right
hand pretending to peel three strips about halfway down the feigned banana. Then the right hand is placed behind the neck whereupon it roughly
forces the head down to eat the peeled banana.[64]
The same theme is found in longer jokes.

Several months after the death of her husband, Mrs.
Goldfarb speaks to the urn containing the ashes. "You
know, Morris, that mink coat I always wanted and you
promised me? Well, now thanks to you, I got it. And you
know, Morris, that trip to Hawaii I always wanted and you
promised me? Well, now thanks to you, I just stopped off

> there on my tour around the world." Mrs. Goldfarb then empties the contents of the urn on the dining room table. "And you know, Morris, that blow job you always wanted and I promised you? Well, here it is!" (blowing the ashes off the table). [65]

Just as the J.A.P. refuses to engage in fellatio, she is equally uninterested in cunnilingus.

> What's the difference between a J.A.P. and jello?
> One moves (shakes) when you eat it. [66]

> What's the difference between a J.A.P. and spaghetti?
> One wiggles when you eat it.

The image or stereotype of the J.A.P. is fairly consistent in these diverse jokes.

There is a male equivalent of the J.A.P., namely, the Jewish American Prince.[67] But he seems derived largely from the Jewish American Princess. In any case, there are not nearly so many jokes about male princes as about female princesses. One joke goes: **What word beginning with A means prince in Jewish? A doctor.**[68]

The J.A.M. and the J.A.P. have entered the mainstream of American culture not just through folklore and jokelore, but also from popular culture. Dan Greenburg's best-selling *How To Be A Jewish Mother*, first published in 1964, reveals "The Basic Techniques of Jewish Motherhood," including such lessons as "Making Guilt Work," "Seven Basic Sacrifices To Make For Your Child," and an entire section devoted to "The Jewish Mother's Guide to Food Distribution." Examples of popular culture devoted to the J.A.P., include a 1971 record, "The Jewish-American Princess," and a paper doll cut-out book, complete with all accessories, including a variety of punch-out credit cards.[69] A 1975 article in the *Journal of Popular Film* names the J.A.P. as one image of the Jew found in American movies.[70] In addition, there are whole books describing the J.A.P., such as Leslie Tonner's *Nothing But the Best: The Luck of the Jewish Princess*.[71] This was followed in 1982 by not one but two entire *J.A.P. Handbooks*,[72] which give detailed descriptions of all the presumed personality characteristics of J.A.P.s and their behavioral propensities. These handbooks, no doubt, are partly a "Jewish" response to the 1980 *Preppy Handbook*,[73] which parodied/celebrated old-line aristocratic WASP culture. The J.A.P. jokes in the bestselling *Gross Jokes* and *Truly Tasteless Jokes* further popularized the cycle. Of course, both J.A.M. and the J.A.P. have been featured in various novels and short stories, such as Philip Roth's *Portnoy's Complaint* and Herman Wouk's *Marjorie Morningstar*.[74]

The contrast between the J.A.M. and the J.A.P. is clear in the light-bulb joke cycle. Significantly, there are texts for both the J.A.M. and the J.A.P., which suggests that the folk consider them two separate stereotypes.

How many J.A.P.s does it take to change a light bulb? One who refuses, saying, "What? and ruin my nail polish?" Or, in a variant, Two—one to pour the Diet Pepsi and one to call "Daddy!"[75] This joke illustrates the familiar themes of nail polish, dieting, and dependence upon Daddy.

The Jewish Mother text differs markedly.

How many Jewish mothers does it take to change a light bulb? None, so I'll sit here in the dark.[76] Here we have the inevitable complaining mother figure who exults in creating guilt feelings in her progeny for their alleged failure to take proper care of her.

Generally, the light-bulb joke cycle delineated the stereotypes represented in that cycle fairly specifically and accurately. How many Harvard students does it take to change a light bulb? One—he holds it, and the whole world revolves around him. Certainly, the pictures of the J.A.P. and the J.A.M. ring true in the light of the other texts reported above.

There is one other minimal pair of jokes that helps illustrate how the folk differentiate the J.A.M. from the J.A.P.

> What is the difference between a Jewish Mother and a vulture?
> A vulture waits until you are dead to eat your heart out.
>
> What is the difference between a J.A.P. and a vulture?
> Nail polish.

One question that invariably arises in any discussion of stereotypes is the extent, if any, to which the stereotypes are "true." Are the J.A.M. and J.A.P. strictly fictional caricatures? Or do these stereotypes correspond to actual personality traits? Predictably, there is a difference of opinion. Some argue that "according to the measurements of social scientists, there does seem to be at least some validity to the Jewish Mother stereotype."[77] On the other hand, a 1984 clinical psychology Ph.D. dissertation, "Personality Traits of the 'Jewish Mother': Realities Behind the Myth," studied 200 women from Houston (50 Jewish women under fifty years of age, 50 Protestants under fifty years of age, 50 Jewish women over fifty, 50 Protestants over fifty).[78] The results did not support the traditional stereotype of the Jewish Mother as domineering, nurturing, and controlling through guilt. The study did, however, indicate the existence of the J.A.P. configuration, which described the younger Jewish mothers as demanding, materialistic, and self-indulging. It is also possible that the time frame is a factor. In 1984, it might be easier to find J.A.P.s than J.A.M.s in Houston. Had the study been carried out forty years earlier, the J.A.P.s might have been outnumbered by the J.A.M.s. In any event, there are those who contend that the J.A.P. stereotype reflects reality.[79]

One of the critical differences between the J.A.M. and the J.A.P. has to do with their respective attitudes toward children. This was perhaps first noted in Martha Wolfenstein's brilliant essay, "Two Types of Jewish Mothers." Wolfenstein contrasted a fifty-one-year-old Russian-Jewish mother with a thirty-four-year-old second-generation American whose parents were of Eastern European origin. The attitudes of the older woman included the idea that her infant was helpless and that a mother's duty was to feed and care for him and to keep him from harm. Even when her child grew up, the clinical data revealed that she continued to think of her adolescent son "as a helpless infant who cannot be trusted to do anything for himself and who, if left to his own devices, will injure himself, probably irreparably."[80] She further observes that, "To this mother, her big athletic boy is still as fragile as an infant, just as vulnerable to the hazards of the environment, and just as dependent on the mother's vigilant care in order to survive."[81] In contrast, the second woman, a college graduate, has adopted American mainstream values towards children, especially with regard to the need for individualism and independence. Her complaint was "When will Karen [her daughter] grow up? Why is she still so babyish?"[82] Wolfenstein ends her fascinating comparison of Eastern European Jewish and American Jewish mother-child relations with the question of "how the transition from the Eastern European Jewish to the American Jewish family is achieved."

Wolfenstein's essay was surely inspired by earlier research by Ruth Benedict, who compared child-rearing techniques in selected European countries. Benedict specifically concentrated upon attitudes towards swaddling in Russia and Poland. In Russia, swaddling was deemed necessary to keep an infant from hurting itself; in Poland, the infant was not considered violent but rather fragile, and so it was swaddled in order to "harden." In contrast, Jewish swaddling in both countries, had a different rationale. There was no suggestion that the baby was inherently violent or that it needed "hardening," Benedict argued. Rather, swaddling provided the baby's first experience of the warmth of life in his own home. It was, in Benedict's terms, an example of a Jewish complementary system she called "nurturance-deference." "The Jewish binder conceives herself as performing a necessary act of nurturance out of which she expects the child to experience primarily warmth and comfort."[83]

What Benedict's and Wolfenstein's speculations suggest is that the Eastern European Jewish tradition of nurturance did not fit in with American ideals of childcare, especially with respect to creating "rugged individualism." Second- or third-generation American Jews felt the need to reject what they considered to be excessive nurturance; hence the J.A.M. stereotype. In the same way, the J.A.P. represents a curious combination of Jewish and American cultural patterns.[84] Jewish culture overprotects its children, and American culture demands and expects upward mobility for all groups. The ideology (though hardly the practice) is expressed in the idealistic egalitarian phrase that "anyone can be president" (except for women, blacks, Jews, etc.). Thus the Jew who had to struggle just to make ends meet in Eastern and Western Europe found that struggling in the United States could yield much greater material reward.

In this light, we can perhaps legitimately argue that J.A.M.s have helped produce J.A.P.s. However, the question, "Can a J.A.P. become a J.A.M.?" is more difficult to answer. My feeling is that the answer is no. To the extent that the difference between J.A.M.s and J.A.P.s is generational, there is no way that a J.A.P., once created, can ever become a true J.A.M. It is not easy to imagine how the spoiled could become spoiler, how the indulged could become the indulger, how someone who refuses to cook could force her children to eat.

Since the J.A.P. joke cycle presents such a decidedly negative stereotype of Jewish young women, and since the jokes are told by Jews (both men and women), we may well have an instance of what is called in the literature "self-hate"[85] or self-depreciation.[86] Martin Grotjahn spoke of the Jewish joke in general as expressing "aggression turned inward." It is, he contended, "a combination of a sadistic attack with masochistic indulgence."[87] Folklorist Dan Ben-Amos has critiqued what he calls the illusion of self-mockery in Jewish humor; an examination of Jewish joke-telling events reveals that the raconteur does not identify himself with the butt of the joke[88] (although it is not clear just how Ben-Amos knows this). "The narrator is not the butt of his story and self-degradation could not possibly be a classical form of Jewish humor." There is, Ben-Amos suggests, a generational factor. It is Jews who speak *without* "Jewish" accents who especially enjoy telling Jewish jokes using accents. "The narrators do not laugh at themselves altogether, but rather ridicule a social group within the Jewish community from which they would like to differentiate themselves."[89] This view echoes the view of Naomi and Eli Katz, who conclude from their study of American Jewish humor that the second-generation American Jew "wished to separate himself sharply from the unassimilated immigrant."[90]

Stanley Brandes' analysis, "Jewish-American Dialect Jokes and Jewish-American Identity," takes issue with this position, arguing that dialect jokes "could be said as much to unite as to divide distinct generations of American Jewry."[91] It seems reasonable to assume that partly or wholly assimilated Jews tell dialect jokes for precisely the opposite reason offered by Ben-Amos—namely, to prove their connection with the authentic, "real" Jews (their parents and grandparents, who did have pronounced accents). Probably both views are correct. The jokes express genuine ambivalence. On the one hand, American Jews are "better" (more assimilated) because they can speak English without an accent, whereas their parents or grandparents could not; on the other hand, American Jews maintain their Jewish identity by telling and listening to Jewish jokes, preferably by using Yiddish in the punchlines. In this way, American Jews succeed in both distancing themselves from *and* associating themselves with the vestiges of their ethnicity through such jokes. So "self-hate" is combined with what might be called "self-love."

But how does all this bear on the J.A.P. joke cycle? Is it merely that, as Katz and Katz suggest, "the contemporary Jewish joke represents . . . a stage of adaptation on the part of young American Jews who reject what they regard as the excessively vulgar, ostentatious and materially oriented conformity of their Americanized parents to the values of well-to-do suburbia?"[92] In this context, the J.A.P. jokes told by young Jewish men and women might represent a rebellion against either the actual values of their materialistic upward-mobile parents, the stereotype of those values, or both. On the other hand, I have encountered young Jewish women who boldly claim that they are J.A.P.s and proud of it. So there is ambivalence. It's possible both to identify with some of the values (despite their caricatures) *and* to attempt to get distance from such values.

This explanation, however, does not really illuminate why the J.A.P. is depicted as being so adamantly opposed to engaging in sexual activity. And why did the J.A.P. joke cycle emerge when it did, in the late 1970s and early 1980s? Both *J.A.P. Handbook*s were published in 1982. Surely there have been overly protective Jewish mothers and whining Jewish princesses before the 1980s! It is just possible that the J.A.P. joke cycle serves another function. After all, the cycle is also popular among non-Jews. This raises the question, should J.A.P. jokes be considered Jewish at all?[93] One *Handbook* even argues that "Not all JAPs are Jewish"[94] and goes on to discuss "WASP JAPs."[95] Reguer goes so far as to claim, "You don't have to be Jewish to be a 'Jewish mother' or a 'Jewish American Princess.'"[96]

While an anti–Semitic element may account for the popularity of the joke cycle to the extent that it lampoons traditional Jewish materialistic values, I suspect that the J.A.P. jokes may be a reflection of anti-feminism. The jokes are, in the large sense, anti–woman. (So are some of the J.A.M. jokes.) The J.A.P. displays the ultimate in bitchy, whining female behavior. It may be more than a coincidence that the joke cycle came into favor at a time when women's liberation and feminist ideology were becoming increasingly better known (and may have been regarded as threatening by old-order "male chauvinist pigs"). Nevertheless, the J.A.P. can hardly be construed as a liberated woman. She very much exemplifies the concept that "a woman's place is in the home" or out shopping. She is a woman who thrives on being looked after by men — first by daddy, later by a husband with a prestigious profession. The jokes don't mention equal rights.

Truly egalitarian values in America, even from a historical perspective, denied the legitimacy of royalty as found in Europe. America has celebrities but no bona fide kings, queens, princes, or princesses. The J.A.P. is therefore something of an anomaly, for her actions and her very nickname suggest that she thoroughly enjoys being treated like a princess.

The acronym for Jewish American Princess happens to form an ethnic slur, Jap (for Japanese), which was commonly used in the United States during the days of World War II. It thus carries at least a nuance of battle and wartime, but in this case, the war is not between the United States and Japan, but the continuing and seemingly endless war between the sexes. The semantic linkage between J.A.P. and Japanese is minimal, but the association is there nonetheless. I remember a freshman at Radcliffe in the fall of 1977 telling me that one part of her dormitory was unofficially called "Little Tokyo" because of the many J.A.P.s lodged there.

In this light, the particular details of the J.A.P. joke cycle encapsulate the view of American women in the early 1980s as perceived by men and by women themselves. Thanks in part to the feminist-inspired women's liberation movement, housewives have become discontent with some facets of the longstanding domestic role customarily assigned to women. That the J.A.P. hates to cook dinner for her husband and her children is an expression of wishful thinking among such discontented housewives. The traditional subservience of such women is also signalled by the sexual demands made upon them by their frequently insensitive husbands. Here another expression of revolt against the status quo takes a sexual form. The J.A.P. is totally indifferent to sex. In her reluctance to perform fellatio (another refusal to "eat"), she signifies her disinclination to engage in acts that presumably give primary pleasure to males. Instead of cooking meals and providing sexual accommodation for male chauvinist pigs, the ideal female is free to spend time for and on herself, shopping for fashionable clothes and beautifying herself. For women, the J.A.P. joke cycle pinpoints what's wrong with the traditional roles women were expected to cheerfully accept in America's upwardly mobile middle-class culture.

It is also true that some women in the 1980s are resentful of the feminist dogma, insofar as they do not enjoy feeling guilty for not pursuing separate careers in business or one of the professions. They would like to continue to be housewives. Such women experience a real dilemma: They want to remain housewives, but they bitterly resent the image of themselves as slaves or chattels. The J.A.P. in this sense embodies an ideal solution—she is a housewife, but one who has successfully freed herself from some of the daily onerous chores, such as feeding the children. She does not want to be a "stay-at-home" but to travel to fashionable resorts and to sample the good life (which includes high-style clothing). When male chauvinist pigs stood in their way, the J.A.P. opposed them, refusing to indulge in sex (oral or otherwise), preferring instead to go off on a shopping spree armed with a large supply of credit cards. The occasional hostile anti-male J.A.P. joke reveals this animosity.

> What does a J.A.P. do with her asshole in the morning?
> Dresses him up and sends him to work.[97]

There are other Jewish jokes that suggest that strong Jewish women demean weak Jewish men:

> A first-grade teacher is calling on her pupils to iden-
> tify animal pictures. She holds up a picture of an elephant
> and calls on Billy Davis. "That's an elephant," he replies.
> Georgie Croft is called on to identify a picture of a bear,
> which he does. The teacher then holds up a picture of a
> deer and calls on Solly Kaplan. Solly stares and stares
> at it and finally announces, "I don't know."
>   "Oh, surely you do, Solly," the teacher says. "Think
> about what your mother calls your father."
>   Solly again stares and stares. "Teacher," he yells out,
> "that's a shmuck??"[98]

This joke would seem to corroborate the contention that "in popular
literature the Jewish man is frequently portrayed as an impotent *schmuck*
who has no authority in his own home."[99]

The underlying message of the J.A.P. joke cycle is: "Let men/hus-
bands continue to look after us (just as our Jewish mothers and fathers
["Daddy"] did), but we shall be our own person, albeit somewhat self-
centered and demanding." If this analysis has any validity, then the
J.A.P. cycle is by no means limited to Jewish American Princesses.
Rather, the stereotype delineated in the joke cycle may be a useful metaphor for *all* upwardly-mobile American females who are dissatisfied
with the traditional norms of a lifestyle demarcated by the duties of
mother and wifehood. To hell with being limited by the restrictive
demands of being "the good wife and mother"![100]

The J.A.P. joke cycle may appeal to men for quite a different reason.
From the male point of view, women want to have it both ways. They
want equality, but they also want to be treated as something special.
So the J.A.P. represents the modern woman who wants to be taken
care of—given unlimited credit cards, taken on glamorous trips—but
who doesn't want to cook or participate willingly in sex. She seems
to be all take and no give! As one source aptly notes, the J.A.P.'s "most
offensive characteristic is her refusal to defer easily to male authority."[101] This may be why some of the J.A.P. jokes project what looks
like unadulterated male misogynistic hostility:

> What do you call 48 J.A.P.s floating face down in a river?
> A start.

If there is any accuracy in this interpretation of the J.A.P. joke
cycle, then the issue is much more than a Jewish issue. The J.A.M.
is thus not just the Jewish American mother, but any American mother

ignorant of the possible ill effects of overindulging her children. Any children who are indulged, who are given more freedom than their parents enjoyed, may grow up to be J.A.P.s—women (and men) who are no longer willing to accept the behavioral and role norms of their parents' generation. J.A.P. jokes may seem to be all parody and caricature, but their basic message stands out for all to see. Just as workers who strike for higher pay and increased benefits withhold the services they normally perform, so the J.A.P.s who refuse to cook dinner or provide sexual gratification for the male "head" of the household do the same thing. The joke cycle may be fantasy, but wishful thinking can nonetheless affect individuals and society at large, especially when it is couched in a joking format.

CHAPTER 7

97 Reasons Why Cucumbers Are Better Than Men

It's a common belief that men, rather than women, tell and enjoy jokes. At parties, it's likely to be men who gather in a corner to exchange jokes (often off-color ones). Still, women also engage in joketelling.

Nevertheless, American joke content does seem to show a marked anti-female bias on the whole. There are jokes about "feminine logic," not "masculine logic"; about "women drivers," not "men drivers"; and about "mothers-in-law," not "fathers-in-law."[1] Jokes about henpecked husbands are not-so-masked attacks on dominant or domineering women, while the numerous "wanton daughter" puns comment on promiscuous younger women. **She was only the stableman's daughter, but all the horsemen knew her** (horse manure).[2] There are also numerous traditional insults involving a girl who is "so dumb," "so fat," "so homely," "so old," and "so thin."[3] Such insults are rarely applied to males.

In *Rationale of the Dirty Joke*, probably the classic compendium of dirty jokes, Gershon Legman gives the male chauvinist position on the origin of sexual humor: "It is, furthermore, unquestionable that most modern jokes on sexual themes are the creation of men and not of women."[4] In a section entitled "Hostility Against the Penis," Legman states, "The real hostility that women often feel, as regards the penis, will not be found in jokes, since jokes are primarily invented by men."[5]

Given how few anti-male or anti-penis jokes, allegedly, were invented by women, it is interesting to report a curious specimen of Xerox folklore that circulated widely in the early 1980s. Xerox folklore, unlike oral folklore, is transmitted via the office photocopy machine.[6]

Yet despite the fact that such machines replicate copies of the original, Xerox folklore manifests multiple existence and variation—the *sine qua non* criterion of all authentic folklore. No two versions of "97 Reasons Why Cucumbers Are Better Than Men" are the same. Even the title may vary—for example, "Cucumbers," "The Cucumber Book," and "124 Reasons Why Cucumbers Are Better Than Men." Variation occurs even in two published versions of this joke cycle: *Cucumbers Are Better Than Men Because . . .,*[7] containing approximately 94 items, and *Why Cucumbers Are Better Than Men,*[8] including some 158 items. The number or order of individual cucumber comments may vary. The type of print may vary, too.

The content of this remarkable instance of cucumber folklore may well reflect the influence of feminist ideology. It is certainly anti-male, in contrast to the anti-female bias in so much of conventional American jokelore. We cannot prove beyond the shadow of a doubt that the author (or authors) of this modern piece of folklore is (or are) female. No names are attached to these Xeroxed sheets of paper. Theoretically, a male could have invented it; but there can be no doubt that these jokes represent a female perspective. Therefore, it is logical to assume that they are the product of female creativity. This goes against the stereotype that feminists have little or no sense of humor. Remember the lightbulb text? **How many feminists does it take to change a lightbulb? That's not funny.**

The cucumber jokes are somewhat daring insofar as they allude to masturbation (although there is a fair amount of masturbation humor among males).[9] The cucumber is a substitute for a phallus; indeed, discussions about dildo forms have reported that the cucumber is in actual use. Sexologist Havelock Ellis mentions both bananas and cucumbers as masturbation aids,[10] while Betty Dodson's 1974 article, "Masturbation as Meditation,"[11] advises, "If a woman desires penetration she can use her fingers or a peeled cucumber."

According to the cucumber folklore, women ought to be able to get along perfectly well in a world without males. Thanks to a convenient cucumber with which to masturbate, women can not only get along without males, they are better off without them. A cucumber is superior to a male. For one thing, it is totally consistent whereas males are not. Women like consistency. So they like cucumbers.

In any event, some of women's most common complaints about men are found in this purported paen to the cucumber. Anyone seriously interested in a detailed critique of male shortcomings with respect to dating strategy or sexual performance will find plenty of information in the cucumber list.

If part of women's liberation means producing the type of humor that has long been produced by men, then "97 Reasons Why Cucumbers Are Better Than Men" should be hailed by women. Let men squirm for a change from the series of barbs. Let there be partial vengeance for the centuries of anti-female jokes told by men.

CUCUMBERS ARE BETTER THAN MEN BECAUSE . . .

1. The average cucumber is at least six inches long.

2. Cucumbers stay hard for a week.

3. A cucumber won't tell you size doesn't count.

4. Cucumbers don't get too excited.

5. Cucumbers are easy to pick up.

6. You can fondle cucumbers in the supermarket . . . and you know how firm it is before you take one home.

7. Cucumbers can get away any weekend.

8. With a cucumber, you can get a single room . . . and you won't have to check in as "Mrs. Cucumber."

9. A cucumber will always respect you in the morning.

10. You can go to a movie with a cucumber and see the movie.

11. At a drive-in, you can stay in the front seat. . . . A cucumber can always wait until you get home.

12. A cucumber won't drag you to a John Wayne film festival.

13. A cucumber won't ask: "Am I the first?"

14. A cucumber doesn't care if you're a virgin.

15. A cucumber won't tell other cucumbers you're not a virgin anymore.

16. With cucumbers, you don't have to be a virgin more than once.

17. Cucumbers won't write your name and phone number on the men's room wall.

18. Cucumbers don't have sex hang-ups.

19. Cucumbers won't make you wear kinky clothes or go to bed with your boots on.

20. Cucumbers aren't into rope and leather, talking dirty or swinging with fruits and nuts.

21. You can have as many cucumbers as you can handle.

22. You only eat cucumbers when you feel like it.

23. Cucumbers never need a round of applause.

24. Cucumbers never ask:
    "Am I the best?"
    "How was it?"
    "Did you come? How many times?"

25. Cucumbers aren't jealous of your gynecologist, ski instructor or hair dresser.

26. Cucumbers won't want to join your support group.

27. Cucumbers aren't into meaningful discussions.

28. Cucumbers won't ask about your last lover . . . or speculate about your next one.

29. Cucumbers will never make a scene because there are other cucumbers in the refrigerator.

30. A cucumber won't mind hiding in the refrigerator when your mother comes over.

31. No matter how old you are, you can always get a fresh cucumber.

32. Cucumbers can handle rejection.

33. A cucumber won't care what time of the month it is.

34. A cucumber won't pout if you have a headache.

35. A cucumber never wants to get it on when your nails are wet.

36. A cucumber won't give it up for Lent.

37. With a cucumber, you never have to say you're sorry.

38. Cucumbers don't leave whisker burns, fall asleep on your chest or drool on your pillow.

39. A cucumber will never give you a hickey.

40. Afterwards, a cucumber won't:
    —want to shake hands and be friends,
    —say, "I'll call you a cab,"
    —tell you he's not the marrying kind,
    —tell you he is the marrying kind,
    —call his mother, ex-wife or therapist,
    —take you to confession.

41. Cucumbers can stay up ALL night . . . and you won't have to sleep on the wet spot.

42. Cucumbers don't leave you wondering for a month.

43. A cucumber won't make you go to the drug store.

44. Cucumbers won't tell you a vasectomy will ruin it for him.

45. A cucumber a day keeps the OB-GYN away.

46. A cucumber won't work your crossword puzzle with ink.

47. A cucumber isn't allergic to your cat.

48. With a cucumber, you don't have to play Florence Nightingale during the flu season.

49. Cucumbers never use your phone or borrow your car.

50. A cucumber doesn't use your toothbrush, roll-on or hairspray.

51. A cucumber won't eat all your food or drink all your liquor.

52. A cucumber doesn't turn your bathroom into a library.

53. Cucumbers won't go through your medicine chest.

54. Cucumbers don't leave hair in the sink or a ring in the tub.

55. A cucumber doesn't flush the toilet while you're taking a shower.

56. Cucumbers don't leave dirty shorts on the floor.

57. A cucumber never forgets to flush the toilet.

58. With a cucumber, the toilet seat is always the way you left it.

59. Cucumbers don't compare you to a centerfold.

60. Cucumbers can't count to ten.

61. Cucumbers don't tell you they liked you better with long hair.

62. A cucumber will never leave you for:
    —another woman,
    —another man,
    —another cucumber.

63. A cucumber will never call and say, "I have to work late, honey" and then come home smelling like another woman.

64. A cucumber never snaps your bra, pinches your butt or gives you a snuggie.

65. You always know where your cucumber has been.

66. A cucumber never has to call "the wife."

67. Cucumbers don't have mid-life crises.

68. A cucumber won't leave you for a cheerleader or an ex-nun.

69. Cucumbers don't play the guitar and try to find themselves.

70. You won't find out later that your cucumber:
    —is married,
    —is on "penicillin,"
    —likes you, but loves your brother.

71. A cucumber doesn't have softball practice on the day you move.

72. Cucumbers never tell you what they did on R&R.

73. A cucumber won't ask for a transfer just when you're up for a promotion.

74. Cucumbers don't care if you make more money than they do.

75. A cucumber won't wear a leisure suit to your office Christmas party.

76. You don't have to wait until half-time to talk to your cucumber.

77. A cucumber won't leave town on New Year's Eve.

78. A cucumber won't take you to a disco and dump you for a flashy outfit.

79. Cucumbers never want to take you home to Mom.

80. A cucumber doesn't care if you always spend the holidays with your family.

81. A cucumber won't ask to be put through medical school.

82. A cucumber won't tell you he's outgrown you intellectually.

83. Cucumbers never expect you to have little cucumbers.

84. Cucumbers don't say, "Let's keep trying until we have a boy."

85. Cucumbers never ask to make love with all the lights on.

86. A cucumber won't insist the little cukes be raised Catholic, Jewish or Orthodox Vegetarian.

87. It's easy to drop a cucumber.

88. A cucumber will never contest a divorce, demand a property settlement or seek custody of anything.

89. Cucumbers never call you "Gail" if your name is "Ann," or vice versa.

90. A cucumber never rolls over and goes to sleep after he's had his, but before you've had yours.

91. A cucumber will never borrow your car to go see your best friend and come home at 7:00 a.m., just in time to take you to work, with a big grin on his face.

92. A cucumber won't brag to his friends that he thinks he got you pregnant.

93. Cucumbers don't mind if you want to be the one on top.

94. Cucumbers can go as fast or as slow as you like, for as long as you like.

95. A cucumber won't be upset if he sees you out with a banana from your office.

96. Happiness is a warm cucumber.

97. No matter how you cut it, you can have your cuke and eat it too.

Perhaps it was only a question of time before males, feeling the sting of the cuke rebuke, would be moved to respond. I do not know if "The Reasons Sheep Are Better Than Women," which follows, is anywhere near as widespread or as popular as the cucumber cycle, but it is definitely influenced by the nature and content of that cycle. It was collected in 1984 from a female doctoral student in chemical engineering who had received it from a male friend in geology at the University of Wyoming.

Just as cucumbers are reportedly used for masturbation by females, so sheep reportedly have been used for acts of bestiality by lonely shepherds for centuries. So it is no surprise that a sheep is used in this joke cycle. Gershon Legman discusses jokes about zoophily: "The animal of choice is traditionally the sheep."[12] Alfred Kinsey's chapter on "Animal Contacts" in *Sexual Behavior in the Human Male* notes, "Because of their convenient size, animals like calves or, in the West, burros and sheep are most often involved."[13] Just as women claim to be able to live without men, so men claim to be able to live without women. The battle of the sexes goes on and will no doubt continue to do so in the forseeable future.

THE REASONS SHEEP ARE BETTER THAN WOMEN:

The Woolgrowers Association isn't nearly as nasty as the National Organization of Women.

There is a livestock auction once a week.

Sheep don't have a gag reflex, or upper teeth.

You can get a better grip on a sheep's ears.

With sheep, you aren't likely to mistake a wrinkle for the real thing.

Sheep don't shy away from boots and leather.

If you fondle a sheep, you won't get chapped hands. Or thighs.

Cotton mouth is easier to get rid of than a social disease.

Nuttin' beats mutton.

A sheep never objects if you are wool gathering.

A sheep won't compare your technique to former boy-friends or her first husband.

Sheep won't argue about whose turn it is to go get a towel.

Sheep won't argue.

Sheep won't drink your liquor, smoke your weed, snort your coke, and then tell you they have to be home early.

Sheep never ask if you're ready to settle down.

Sheep never ask about your former lovers and then get pissed off when you tell them.

No matter how old or ugly you are, you can always find a willing ewe.

Sheep are famous for flocking.

Sheep are never concerned about their reputation.

Sheep won't tell all their friends about the time you couldn't get it up.

Sheep won't ask if you're gay the first time you can't get it up the second time.

Sheep never insist on eating out.

A sheep will never serve you a TV dinner that's still frozen in the middle.

You'll never catch your sheep masturbating to a picture of Robert Redford.

You never have to send a fat sheep to a health spa.

Sheep don't get suspicious if you have to work late.

Sheep don't smell like tuna fish.

Sheep don't get moody once a month.

You can eat a lamb chop without getting wool stuck in your teeth.

A sheep doesn't expect you to support her for the rest of her life after one roll in the hay.

A sheep never wears curlers and a mud pack to bed.

A sheep doesn't stop screwing after the honeymoon.

A sheep won't lead you on and then tell her parents she was raped.

A sheep won't get drunk and throw up in your car.

A sheep won't think that a weekend stay-over entitles her to rearrange your furniture and put up new curtains.

A sheep won't expect you to go to work for her father.

A sheep won't expect you to pay for the babysitter.

A sheep won't expect you to pay her way through school.

A sheep won't expect you to pay $100 an hour to send her to a shrink.

A sheep won't expect you to pay . . . and pay . . . and pay . . . and pay.

A sheep will never try to talk to your friends about elk hunting or gun control.

A sheep will never complain about the spittoon in your pickup.

A sheep will never throw out your old copies of *Playboy*.

A sheep won't care if you keep your fish bait in the refrigerator.

A sheep won't get even with you by spending your paycheck on new clothes, none of which are see-through or meant to be worn in the bedroom.

A sheep won't expect you to trade your pickup for a station wagon with an automatic transmission.

A sheep will never sue you for palimony.

A sheep will never break all your beer mugs in a fit of pique.

A sheep won't care if you screw her sister.

A sheep won't care if your secretary is better looking than she is.

A sheep won't expect you to do your share of the dishes, the laundry, and the cooking, but refuse to learn how to mow the lawn, change a tire, or unclog the toilet.

A sheep won't leave you for: a weightlifter, a psychologist, a gynecologist, the milkman, or another sheep.

A sheep will never tell you the ceiling needs to be painted while you're screwing.

A sheep will never shut you off and then say, "But let's still be friends."

A sheep won't use your razor to shave its legs, or your pocketknife to open a paint can.

Sheep *never* have a headache.

You don't have to explain to a sheep why you are two hours late getting home from work.

A sheep won't suggest that you change your hairstyle, your friends, or your socks.

A sheep won't give your favorite hunting shirt to Goodwill.

With sheep, post-partum depression doesn't last until the kid is old enough to vote.

A sheep won't leave wet nylons hanging all over the bathroom.

Sheep don't ask stupid questions during football games.

Sheep won't ask you to teach them to play poker.

A sheep will never ask you to stop on the way home from work and pick up a box of Tampax.

A sheep won't expect you to spend every weekend at her mother's house.

A sheep will never serve all your imported beer to her bridge club.

Sheep aren't social climbers.

Sheep reach sexual maturity at 18 months, and by the time you're bored with them, you can sell them at profit.

Sheep won't talk about the Myth of Vaginal Orgasm at your office Christmas Party.

A sheep will never leave a vibrator on the living room couch when you're having friends over to watch football.

Sheep grow their own fur coats.

Diamonds aren't a sheep's best friend.

A sheep won't call you at work to tell you she's wrecked the car.

Sheep won't cheat on you with your best friend.

You don't have to take a sheep to a fancy motel, or buy them drinks and dinner first.

A sheep will never ask if you'll still respect her in the morning.

A sheep doesn't mind being just one of the flock.

A sheep won't discuss your sex habits with the neighbors.

A sheep will never make you sell your coon hounds just because they ate her cat.

Sheep aren't into talking before or after.

A sheep never yells at you for leaving the lid up.

A sheep won't nag you into going to a marriage counselor.

A sheep won't send you out after batteries for her vibrator.

A sheep won't leave her underwear soaking in the bathroom sink.

A sheep won't go on a crying jag if you forget to buy her a present for her birthday, your anniversary, Valentine's day, Ash Wednesday, or Halloween.

A sheep doesn't think it's kinky or demeaning to do it doggy style.

A sheep won't mind if you put up mirrors in the bedroom.

Sheep are "ram tough."

A sheep won't tell you that you aren't as romantic as you were when you were dating.

A sheep won't think you're cheap and tacky if you: send daisies instead of long-stemmed roses, tip less than 20%, wear levis with a hole in the seat, open beer bottles with your teeth.

A sheep won't complain if it rains on your camping trip.

Sheep don't mind if you leave the lights on.

Sheep don't mind doing it in the morning.

Sheep don't mind doing it in a pickup truck.

A sheep will never use the excuse that: she just did her
    nails, it's too hot, it's too cold, you'll wake the kids,
    you'll wake the neighbors, she's too drunk to enjoy it,
    she's not drunk enough to enjoy it.

And last but not least:

A SHEEP WILL NEVER LEAVE YOU FOR A CUCUMBER.

The link between the sheep and cucumber cycles cannot be denied.
The Wyoming sheep text cited above was, in fact, attached to a version of the cucumber series.

One is tempted to generalize about the nature and timing of joke
cycles. If the elephant joke cycle was inspired in part by white fears
arising from the black civil rights movement of the early 1960s; if the
dead baby jokes were in any way a response in the 1960s and 1970s
to public debate about abortion; and if the J.A.P. jokes of the early 1980s
were a reaction to a widespread feeling of discontent among housewives
who resented the seemingly endless daily demands imposed by adher-
ence to the good mother and wife roles, then we may safely assert that
joke cycles do not emerge or exist in a cultural vacuum. If this is so—
and it appears to be eminently reasonable—folklorists and others concerned with jokes and joke cycles must study these materials in context. Merely publishing texts of the latest joke cycle is no substitute
for analysis, even if that analysis is admittedly speculative.

In that connection, we may suggest that the cucumber jokes, transmitted almost exclusively by means of the ubiquitous Xerox machine,
constitute a continuation of the impulse that produced the J.A.P. jokes.
Formerly passive and subservient females are becoming increasingly
active and articulate in protesting male behavior they find objectionable.
The cucumber jokes comprise a remarkable enumeration of common
complaints shared by many women about the males with whom they
live. The fact that the cucumber joke cycle appeared in the early 1980s
is a reflection of the attitudes of that point in time—even though the
complaints surely date back much earlier. The "sheepish" reply to the
cucumber attack is presumably a male attempt to fight back against
the cucumber onslaught. It may or may not be symbolic that it is women
who employ vegetables—a reflection of their "lowly" status in the

world? — while men use animals — a reflection of their barely concealed animality?

To conclude, let's remember the extraordinary role of fantasy in joke cycles. Who could have predicted that joke cycles about the behavior of absurd elephants, or wide-mouth frogs, or assorted individuals seeking to change light bulbs would ever have come into public notice or favor? Who could have imagined that female masturbation with cucumbers or male bestiality with sheep might generate a set of jokes that define mutual gender expectations in American society? Yet this is what has happened. We must not underestimate the continuing importance of fantasy and joking. As dreams provide essential outlets for the anxieties of the individual, so joke cycles serve a similar role for the society at large. This is why we should stand ready to observe, record, and analyze the next series of joke cycles that, if history bears witness, are bound to appear in the decades to come.

CHAPTER 8

Slurs International: Folk Comparisons of Ethnicity and National Character

Folklore provides the principal means of transmitting and disseminating national character stereotypes. The study of traditional slurs involves such topics as stereotypes, national character, ethnocentrism, prejudice, imagery, and humor.[1] These topics fall within a number of academic disciplines, and each has its own vast scholarship.[2] Yet it is surprising and disappointing how little attention professional students of "ethnopsychology" or "national stereotypes" have paid to the materials of folklore. A proverb or a joke told by members of one national group about another may be more responsible for the first group's attitudes about the second than any other single factor. Some Americans, for example, have very definite notions about the alleged character traits of the English, the French, and the Germans — even if they, as individuals, have never actually met a member of the national group in question. In the same way, a young WASP child has almost certainly learned the stereotypes of Afro-Americans or Jews years before he encounters a representative of that group. How has he learned them? Most often, by hearing — and perhaps telling — ethnic jokes.

Despite the importance of ethnic and national slurs, folklorists themselves have been slow to study them. One of the earliest studies was Wilhelm Wackernagel's brief essay, *"Die Spottnamen der Völker,"* which appeared in 1848;[3] but the first major work was Baron Von Reinsberg-Düringsfeld's 1863 two-volume compilation, *Internationale Titulaturen.*[4] The first volume treats *"Was die Völker über einander sprechen"*

[What the peoples say about one another]; the second volume concerns *"Was die Völker über sich selbst sprechen"* [What the peoples say about themselves]. The distinction between what a people says about other groups and what a people says about itself is a critical one. Self-image, obviously, is no less free from the influence of stereotyping than are the traditional images of other groups.

The question of self-image dominated the second landmark in international slur scholarship, *Blason Populaire de la France*, by Henri Gaidoz and Paul Sébillot, published in Paris in 1884. Most of their examples are devoted to the French or to the various provincial stereotypes in France. Slurs can be directed against a small village, a large city, a region, or an entire country. A mere one sixth of the work is concerned with foreign (non-French) materials.[5]

It is probably no accident that the serious study of international slurs began in the latter part of the nineteenth century, in view of the rapid rise of nationalism throughout Europe at that time. The discipline of folkloristics itself owes a good deal of its energy to the very same impetus. There is a possible connection between currents of nationalism and the interest in international slurs — one way of building oneself up is obviously at the expense of someone else. This connection is further suggested by the dedication in the next (and, regrettably, last) significant book-length contribution to the scholarship, A. A. Roback's 1944 *A Dictionary of International Slurs*.[6] The collection is dedicated to "General Charles de Gaulle, the Conscience of the Allied Command." Roback tried in vain to coin an acceptable term, "ethnophaulisms" for international and ethnic slurs, but the term has not enjoyed much acceptance among scholars. Archer Taylor's *The Proverbs*, which gives an all-too-short consideration of *blason populaire*, remarks on the lack of an appropriate English term. "The brief characterizations of a neighboring village or people which the French call 'blason populaire' and the German 'Ortsneckereien,' and for which there is no convenient English term, are truly popular."[7]

Even without a proper term, it is clear that slurs refer equally to ethnic or other folk groups within a country as to national groups outside a country. Moreover, within a folk group, there may well be slur traditions breaking down that group into smaller groups. For example, there are Jewish jokes that distinguish among Orthodox, Conservative, and Reform Jewish groups, just as there are Catholic jokes distinguishing among Benedictines, Franciscans, and Jesuits. By the same token, in Germany as in many other countries, northerners direct slurs against southerners and southerners use slurs against northerners. The Prussian-Bavarian instance in Germany is only one variation on a large number of north-south antagonisms in which the efficient, industrious northerners are contrasted with the lazy, backward southerners. (In the southern hemisphere, e.g., Brazil, the stereotypes appear to be reversed: It is the southern Brazilian who is busy and industrious, while the northern Brazilian is depicted as lazy and foolish.)

One reason why it is so difficult to define the subject matter of slurs is because of the difficulty in defining the term "folk." If a folk is defined as any group of people whatsoever who share at least one common factor, then a group as large as a nation or as small as an individual family could qualify as a folk. And the point is that there are traditional slurs against all different kinds of folk groups, including nations and families. Conceivably, one good test of whether a given group is or is not a folk would be the existence of slurs about the group in question. There are abundant slurs against occupational and religious groups. Interestingly enough, the same basic structural technique may be used in any slur, no matter what the group.

A typical technique depicts two or more individuals (representing their respective folk groups) performing the same act, a splendid exemplification of the comparative method. The act is held constant while presumably the only variable is the characteristic, stereotyped behavior of each folk group represented. According to an illustration from American campus folklore, a chemist, a physicist, and an economist are marooned on a desert island without food. Suddenly a cache of canned goods is discovered, but there is no opener. The chemist begins looking about for chemicals in their natural state so he can make up a solution that will dissolve the tops of the cans. The physicist picks up a rock and begins calculating what angle, what force, what velocity he will need to use to strike the can with the rock in order to force it open. The economist merely picks up a can and says, "Let us assume this can is open." (Or, in another version, "Let us assume we have a can opener.")

The desert island turns out to be a fairly conventional setting for international slurs. A 1962 text from El Paso, Texas goes as follows:

> Two Englishmen, two Germans, and two Americans were on a ship that sank. They were the only survivors, and they swam to an island where they were stranded for ten years. After ten years, a ship finally appeared. After thus being rescued and after returning to their homelands, the two Germans started an Army, one American started a

factory, and the other American started a labor union. The two Englishmen didn't know each other yet.

Another American text includes the French.

The ship sinks and the survivors are left on a desert island. The Americans go into business immediately. The French begin building night clubs. The Germans build armament plants. Then one turns to the other and asks, "Who's that group standing there?" The reply: "That's the English, they're still waiting to be introduced."[8]

The American texts show fairly consistent stereotypic traits, such as the militarism of the Germans and the stand–offishness of Englishmen. It is interesting that essentially the same traits are reported in versions from other countries. For example, the following desert island text, collected from a Greek informant, has a slightly different initial situation and represents more nationalities.

Two men and a woman are shipwrecked on a desert island. If they are Spanish, the men will fight a duel and the survivor gets the girl. If French, one man becomes the husband, and the other the lover. If English, nothing will happen because no one is there to introduce them so they won't speak. If Italian, they will play cards to decide who will have the girl. If Greek, they will start fighting over politics and forget the girl. If Turks, one will have the front way and the other the back passage.

Finally, we have a German version of the last initial situation:

A ship goes down in the Pacific. Nobody survives except two men and one woman. They save themselves on a small island. What happens if the two men are Italian? The one murders the other in order to possess the woman for himself. If they are Frenchmen, they live peacefully *a trois*. If they are English or Germans, then the men move to another island and leave the woman alone. If they are Russians, they set a bottle afloat for Moscow for further instructions.[9]

Women share the same national stereotypic traits as men. Here, in still another form of the desert island setting, is an Egyptian (Cairo, 1974) version of a standard joke:

Girls of different nationalities were asked: "What would you do if you found yourself on a deserted island alone

with a bunch of men on the island trying to attack you?"
The German girl said, "I'll fight."
The English girl said, "Rather ungentlemanly, rather
bad taste."
The American girl said, "I'll close my eyes and say no."
The Indian girl said, "The best way is passive re-
sistance."
The French girl said, "I understand the situation, but
I don't see the problem."

Although the basic structure of a joke may remain constant, the specific content may reveal definite character traits. These culture-specific traits are what form the essence of international slurs. It is important to distinguish culture-specific traits from generalized insults. There are literally dozens of standard numskull tales and classic negative comments that can easily be incorporated into A's stories about B (with A and B standing for any two cultures with some awareness of one another). For example, the well-known tale of the dream bread[10] involves three travelers who agree that the one who has the most wonderful dream shall eat the last loaf next morning. After the first two tell their dreams, the third relates that he dreamed the others were dead and therefore that they wouldn't need the bread, so he got up during the night and ate it. Clearly, any three groups could be represented. To be sure, it *is* always of interest to see which particular groups the taleteller chooses to fill the three slots, especially which two are selected as dupes to be foiled by the trickster. But unless some particulars are added to the delineation of the three actors, there is relatively little in the way of culture-specific national character traits.

Other examples of slot-filler jokes of this kind include the following Flemish text, collected in 1970:

Why do the Americans have the Negroes and the Belgians
have the Flemish?
Because the Americans had first choice.

In American versions, groups included "Italians and Negroes," "Polacks and Negroes," and so on. Proverbs provide a more elaborate form of rank ordering national or ethnic groups. A Polish proverb is typical. The Pole is deceived by the German, the German by the Italian, the Italian by the Spaniard, the Spaniard by the Jew, and the Jew by the devil.[11] In this folk hierarchy, the Pole places himself at one end, with the devil at the other. A Russian version of the same proverb offers a different list: A Russian can be cheated only by a Gypsy; a Gypsy by a Jew; a Jew by a Greek, and a Greek by the devil.[12] A Levantine text has still another ordering: It takes three Jews to cheat a Greek, three Greeks to cheat a Syrian, and three Syrians to cheat an Armenian.[13] While it is fascinating to have a folk listing of other peoples in ascending order of trickiness, this provides not a true comparison of traits but merely a single trait and merely a comparison of degree.

Even less information is provided by a number of popular jokes that, on the surface, appear to concern diverse national groups. For example, there is a widespread joke in which three or more individuals are in a boat or airplane that because of some difficulty, can carry only one of them. In the majority of American versions, the Englishman cries, "God save the Queen" and jumps out. The Frenchman cries, "Vive la France" and jumps out; and a Texan cries, "Remember the Alamo" and pushes out a Mexican. While the joke does indicate the existence of aggressive impulses toward Mexicans and Mexican–Americans, it tells us almost nothing about the national character stereotypes. The joke structure tends to raise Texas to the status of nationhood by juxtaposing it with England and France, but we learn little about the stereotype of Mexicans. Equally unproductive is the standard joke in which three protagonists are forced to seek shelter in a cave with a goat or pig. Each of the first two is forced to flee because of the great stench of the animal, but after the third enters the cave, the animal evacuates his abode. This joke turned out to be one of the most popular jokes told in Denmark, where it is localized to refer to the three principal subdivisions of the country: Jutland, Funen, and Zealand.[14] Again, apart from demonstrating lines of rivalry, the joke contains no reference to specific character traits.

One cannot rule out *a priori* any joke as a source of folk national character attributes. Sometimes a given joke will contain culture–specific traits in some versions. For example, in the standard joke in which three or more individuals at a bar each find a fly in their drink, there may be such traits delineated. In a version reported by A.A. Roback, we find little more than a sequence from politeness to crudeness:[15] Should a fly fall into his cup, the Englishman will take it out and not drink; the German will take it out and drink; the Russian will drink, fly and all. In a version I remember from my own childhood, There is an Englishman, Irishman, and a Scotsman. The Englishman calls for a spoon and scoops out the fly before drinking. The Irishman uses his fingers to remove the fly before drinking. The Scotsman carefully picks out the fly and wrings

it out before drinking. The presence of the Scottish stereotype of economy bordering upon miserliness reminds us that there are international
slurs that contain very specific and very consistent character traits.

One difficulty in studying ethnic or international slurs, although
not an insuperable one, stems from the lack of genre distinction. A
slur may be a single word or phrase; it may be a proverb, a riddle,
or a joke. The idea of slur is therefore a functional one, entailing a
rhetorical intention: namely, of making fun of the characteristics of
self and others. Yet are all slurs pejorative? Sometimes the negative
import is determined by who utters the item to whom in the presence
of whom else! A joking self-deprecation told in the intimacy of the in-
group becomes a serious insult if articulated by an outsider or stranger.
But even apart from all important context, is there a slur involved in
such phrases as *Irish stew, Hungarian goulash, Welsh rabbit, English muffins,
French toast,* or *Danish pastry?* (In Denmark, by the way, the latter is
attributed to Austria, as indicated by the term *"Wienerbrød."*) All references to national identity are not necessarily slurs. What about *German measles, Scotch tape,* and *Spanish fly?* Metaphorically, I suppose, one
is *attacked* by German measles. Scotch tape might have an economic
reference — mending an old item rather than buying a new one. Spanish
fly, an aphrodisiac much celebrated in adolescent jokes, may refer to
the Spanish subtype of the Latin lover stereotype. Unquestionably
many slurs *are* negative. Examples include *to be in Dutch* (in trouble),
to Jew someone down in price, and to *Welsh on a deal.* But if all slurs, or
what we are calling slurs, are not pejorative, then the term may not
be very apt. The possibility of positive traits or neutral traits would
certainly seem to make the term "slur" inappropriate.

Another critical issue has to do with whether or not international
slurs are true — that is, do they accurately reflect empirical reality? The
original definition of stereotype by Walter Lippmann in 1922 definitely
implied that stereotypes were false.[16] Yet they are like any other gen-
eralizations: They may be false, they may be true, they may be a combination of partly false and partly true. Social psychologists holding
the "kernel of truth" theory of stereotypes suggest (as the name itself
implies) that there may be an element of validity in the traditional por-
traiture.[17] Of course, since some scholars deny that national character
exists at all, it is difficult to prove conclusively that international slurs
correspond in any meaningful way with the actual personality traits
of specific nations. Even cross-cultural comparative research may be
inconclusive. For example, if a dozen or more countries have slurs

against the Germans, portraying them as militaristic and authoritarian, that does not necessarily mean that Germans *are* militaristic and authoritarian, merely that some individuals in these countries perceive the Germans as possessing these traits. Moreover, even if there were an observable correspondence between a group's self-image and how other groups perceived that same group, it would not necessarily follow that the group in question actually possessed those traits. Even if Germans saw themselves as militaristic and authoritarian (as some slurs suggest they do) that fact still would not prove that Germans are militaristic and authoritarian. Stereotypes in slurs deal with traditional images of reality rather than reality itself. In some cases, a group has come to accept the stereotype of itself as defined by outgroups — for example, the acceptance by some Afro-Americans of the white racist stereotype that black is considered an evil color (and that lighter skin color is valued). Within recent years, Afro-Americans have made a conscious attempt to throw off the yoke of color stereotypes: **Black is beautiful! The blacker the berry, the sweeter the juice.** But the stereotype remains, as a version of the above proverb shows: **The blacker the berry, the sweeter the juice, but if you too damn black it ain't no use.**

Since most traditional slurs are insulting and derogatory, the idea that there might be a kernel of truth in slur traditions is not likely to please any group that is the subject of slurs. On the other hand, scholarship is not a popularity contest. If slurs contain a kernel of truth, then scholars have a moral obligation to seek and document it. My own view is that there may well be some truth in slurs, just as in caricature. The exaggeration may be false, but it may be esthetically necessary to make the point. Often the exaggeration makes the issue one of degree. Thrift is normally deemed a good quality, but stinginess is not. At what point does thrift become stinginess? And who decides? Unkind jokes about stinginess (found in countless slurs about Scots and Jews) may well reflect a genuine concern with thriftiness, which is not at all a negative trait.

It seems wisest to judge each slur tradition individually. Some slurs may have a kernel of truth, others may not. In order to determine which ones do, and precisely what the kernel or element of truth might be, the personality and national character studies of the group under investigation must be examined rigorously.

Multi-group international slurs are the focus of this chapter. The stereotypes contained in multi-group slurs are often found in slurs about single groups, but it's the comparative aspect that particularly interests me. A typical single group slur would be **Whenever there are four Irishmen, there is bound to be a fifth,** referring to the alleged penchant of the Irish for drinking. Multi-group international slurs, usually have only a single trait for each nation. This means that the folk are forced to select the one trait they feel is most characteristic—in effect, a folk rank-ordering of national stereotype traits for each nation. It is not difficult to ascertain which traits occur most frequently.

Then there are slurs that mention at least *two* groups. Roback's *Dictionary of International Slurs* reports only nine pages of "National Comparisons," as opposed to over two hundred pages of mainly individual slurs (organized generally by country or group).

One type of multi-group international slur is in riddle or pseudo-riddle form. For example, there is the cross-breed riddle.[18] **What do you get when you cross an Italian with a Mexican? A gangster on welfare.** The cross-breed riddle is limited—it can handle only two ethnic or national groups at a time. **What would the son of a Jewish mother and a Polish father be? A janitor in a medical school.**[19] Such occupational stereotypes are quite consistent. **What do you get when you cross a Negro with a Polack? A retarded janitor.** This text may be followed by another **What do you get when you cross a Negro with a Jew? You still get a janitor, but he owns the building.** This suggests that in a series of linked texts the cross-breed riddle can accommodate more than two groups. However, such series are relatively rare. More common are texts like **Did you hear about the man who had dinner at a German-Chinese restaurant? Two hours later he was power hungry.** This plays on the stereotypes of the militaristic, politically ambitious German and the notion that Chinese food is not filling.

Occasionally, a comparison of just two national groups yields more than one single personality-trait attribution. For example, a German text contrasts French and Germans:[20]

Ein Franzose ist ein Vagabund.	One Frenchman is a vagabond.
Zwei Franzosen ist Liebe.	Two Frenchmen is love.
Drei Franzosen ist eine Ehe.	Three Frenchmen is a marriage.
Ein Deutscher ist ein Philosoph.	One German is a philosopher.
Zwei Deutsche ist eine Organisation.	Two Germans is an organization.
Drei Deutsche is der Krieg.	Three Germans is war.

A Polish version speaks only of Germans: One German—a beer; two Germans—an organization; three Germans—a war.[21]

The cross-breed riddle is not the only riddling form to serve as a vehicle for multi-group international slurs. A number of questions, as well, provide conventional points of departure. These questions include: What's the shortest book in the world? What's the most dangerous thing in the world? What is Hell?

What are the three shortest books in the world? *Italian War Heroes, Jewish Business Ethics,* and *Who's Who in Puerto Rico.* Other titles reported in variants include: *The Polish Mind, 200 Years of English Humor, Democracy in Germany, Negroes I Have Met Yachting,* and *La Dolce Vita in Scotland.*

> Who are the three most dangerous men in the world?
> A drunken Irishman with a broken whiskey bottle in his hand, an Italian with an education, and a Greek in sneakers.

> What are the four most dangerous things in the world?
> A Negro with an education, a Chinaman with a driver's license, a Jew with authority, and a Greek with tennis shoes.

> Who are the three most dangerous men in the world?
> An Italian with a gun, a Mexican with a driver's license, and a Frenchman with a chipped tooth.

From these variants we can see that some traits are transferrable—an Italian or a black with an education, a Chinaman or a Mexican with a driver's license—but some traits are not. The most devastating of the nontransferrable stereotypes are sexual ones. The first refers to the alleged proclivity of the Greeks for anal intercourse—presumably a Greek with tennis shoes could sneak up quietly behind one, while the second refers to the supposed inclination of the French for cunnilingus, a special variation of the French lover stereotype which, in turn, is related to the larger Latin lover image. It should be noted that these pseudo-riddles assume that *the stereotype is already known to the audience!* A member of the audience unfamiliar with the supposed pederastic penchant of Greeks or the oral-genital taste of the French would almost certainly fail to understand the reference to Greeks wearing sneakers or Frenchmen with chipped teeth. In this sense, folklore reinforces rather than initiates stereotypes. On the other hand, it is also quite likely that many individuals are first introduced to stereotypes through folklore of this kind, which they ask knowledgeable friends to explain to them.

> **What is hell? Hell is a place where the cooks are English, the mechanics are French, and the lovers are all American.**

This joke, incidentally, is told by Americans.[22] A longer version reported from a San Franciscan of Japanese ancestry features additional groups:

> **Hell is a place where the French are the engineers, the British are the cooks, the Germans are the policemen, the Russians are the historians, and the Americans are the lovers.[23]**

Not only do slurs show "wrong" occupations associated with various nations, but they also claim to reveal "right" (stereotypical) vocations. For example, a German text from 1784 relates:

> **Among three Italians will be found two clergymen; among three Spaniards, two braggarts; among three Germans, two soldiers; among three Frenchmen, two chefs; and among three Englishmen, two whoremongers.[24]**

More common than riddling forms are proverbs reflecting international slurs. Consider the German proverb: **The German originates it, the Frenchman imitates it, and the English exploits it.**[25] We find variation in a Polish version: **The Englishman conceives it; the Frenchman realizes it; the German improves it; and the Pole seizes upon it and buys it.**[26] It is not always clear whether it is better to have invented something or to have had the perfected use of it. Another version makes the Pole's self-image clearer: **What an Englishman cares to invent, a Frenchman to design, or a German to patch together, the stupid Pole will buy and the Russian will deprive him of it.**[27] As we shall see shortly, the technique of ending not with oneself but with one's rival or hated enemy is common in Eastern Europe.

Several other proverbs may illustrate the nature of slur traditions. **The Spaniard lives in arms; the Italian in temples; the Briton in the navy; the German in fortresses. The Spaniard sleeps; the Italian plays; the German smokes; the Frenchman promises; the Englishman eats, and the American boasts.**[28] A Czech proverb reveals the common French stereotype: **The German woman excels in the shed; the Czech woman will have people fed; and the French woman is best in bed.**[29]

Some proverbs comment upon comparative writing styles. An Italian proverb declares, **The English write profoundly; the French gracefully; the Italians divinely, and the Germans muchly.** Another version: **The Spaniard writes little; the German writes much; the Italian writes much and well; the Englishman writes excellently, and the Frenchman still better.**[30] However, except for the emphasis upon the voluminous writing of Germans, this may be simply a rank-ordering of nationalities.

One interesting type of proverb containing international slurs uses a careful juxtaposition of contrasting positive and negative statements. In a version reported from 1614:

> An Italian traveller used to say that the Portuguese seems
>   a fool and is so;
> The Spaniard seems wise and is a fool;
> The Frenchman seems a fool and is wise;
> The Englishman is wise but cannot show it;
> The Italian is wise and seems so,
> and the Dutchman would be wise but for the pot [of ale].[31]

Reinsberg-Düringsfeld attributed a shorter version to Charles the Fifth:

> The Italian is wise and appears so;
> The Spaniard appears wise and is not;
> The Frenchman is wise without appearing so.[32]

Roback also has a version:

> The Spaniard seems to be wise, but is not;
> The Frenchman seems to be a fool, but is not;
> The Italian seems to be wise and is so,
> while the Portuguese seems to be foolish and is so.[33]

From 1614 to 1863 to 1944, there is remarkable consistency—all three texts proclaim nearly the same traits for the Frenchman, Italian, and Spaniard. Although the traits are fairly general, the consistency suggests that national character stereotypes may remain fairly constant through time; however, there is always the possibility that they will be affected by the impact of changing historical events, which cause enemies to become allies or allies to become enemies.

One of the finest examples of the proverbial form of the international slur is a German text that compares the English, Germans, French, and Russians in a strikingly compact paradigm.

> *In England ist alles erlaubt, was nicht verboten ist.*
> *In Deutschland ist alles verboten, was nicht erlaubt ist.*

In Frankreich ist alles erlaubt, und auch wenn es ver-
boten ist.
In Russland ist alles verboten, auch wenn's erlaubt ist.

In England everything is permitted that's not forbidden.
In Germany everything is forbidden that's not permitted.
In France everything is permitted, even if it's forbidden.
In Russia everything is forbidden, even if it's permitted.[34]

Despite the various riddling forms and the popularity of the proverb, the joke is almost certainly what constitutes the major folkloristic
carrier of international slur traditions. We have already discussed a
number of standard texts, such as the various nationalities marooned
on a desert island. Here are two additional jokes that demonstrate once
again the relative uniformity of the content of the slurs.

One extremely popular multi-group international slur compares
what the women of various nations say after sexual relations. A 1966
Swedish text offers this comparison:

English: "Oh, good thing we're married."
German: "I would like to take a shower."
French: "Do you feel better now, darling?"
Italian: "More."
American: "Do you think the ceiling would be nice if it was
painted blue instead of yellow?"
Swede: "I'm hungry."

A 1970 American version is entitled, "What They Say the Morning
After":

American Girl: "Jeazus Christ! I must have been drunk.
What did you say your name was?"
French Girl: "For this I get a new dress, oui?"
Russian Girl: "My body belongs to you. My soul will always
be free."
Jewish Girl: "Goniff! Next time I'll have the mink coat first."
Chinese Girl: "I hope I've given you some new slants."
English Girl: "It was rather pleasant. We'll have to meet
again sometime."[35]

A Jewish-American version of 1965 manifests the same stereotypes
in somewhat sharper focus. The title of this version is, "What the
Women of Various Nations say after conjugal relations":

American wife: "Gee, honey, that was great."
French wife: "Mon cherie, what a beautiful lover you are."

> Jewish wife: "I should have held out for a fur coat."
> German wife: "Ach, mein herr, what authority. How masterful."
> English wife: "There dear, do you feel better now?"

It is noteworthy that the Jew is evidently considered by the folk to be a functional equivalent of a national group (much like the Texan in the airplane joke). A possible reason for this might be the long-standing popularity of the Jewish stereotype in all European countries.

One of the very finest illustrations of the multi-group international slur traditions is set in an academic context—supposedly, an international congress devoted to the study of the elephant, attended by scholars from various countries. It is probably true that there are national or cultural biases in the selection of problems for research (just as there are surely individual personality biases within a given culture that affect the choice of a topic for study as well as the approach taken to that topic). The titles of the elephant-congress communications papers reveal national character stereotypes par excellence. Here's an American version of the joke.

> The Englishman gives his paper on "Elephant Hunting in India."
> The Russian presents, "The Elephant and the Five-Year Plan."
> The Italian offers, "The Elephant and the Renaissance."
> The Frenchman delivers, *"Les Amours des Elephants."* ("The Love Life of the Elephant" [or, in some versions, *"L'Elephant dans la Cuisine,"* "The Elephant in the Kitchen or "The Elephant in Cooking"—that is, the French cuisine]).
> The German gives "The Elephant and the Renazification of Germany" (or, in other versions, "The Military Use of the Elephant," or *"Ein kurze Einführung in das Leben des vierbeinigen Elephanten"* [A Short Introduction to the Life of Four-footed Elephants] in 24 volumes, but dies after preparing the seventeenth for press).
> Finally, the American rises to give his paper on "How to Build a Bigger and Better Elephant."[36] (In other American versions, the final participant is a Jew whose paper is entitled, "The Elephant and the Jewish Question" or a black whose communication is "The Negro and the Elephant.")

Even just a few selected versions from other countries demonstrate convincingly that this joke is an international one. Here's a Czech version:

> The Swiss announced a competition for the best book on elephants.
> The British submitted a volume called, "The Elephant and the British Empire."
> The French submitted a book called, *"L'Elephant et l'Amour."*
> The Germans sent in 57 volumes entitled, *"Eine Elementare Einführung in die Grundlagen der Elefantenohrlehre"* ("An Elementary Introduction into the Foundations of the Science of the Elephant's Ear").
> The Russians sent a volume, "The Superiority of the Soviet Elephant."
> The Czech entry was, "The Soviet Elephant is Our Idol!"[37]

A Rumanian version I collected in Bucharest in 1969 is similar to the Czech text:

> The German writes a three-volume "Introduction to the Study of Elephants."
> The French scholar publishes a small, perfumed, leather-bound volume (with a ribbon attached) entitled, *"Les Amours des Elephants."*
> The Russian writes a two-volume work published by the Foreign Language Press, "Marx, Engels, Lenin, and Stalin on Elephants."
> The Rumanian writes, "The Soviet Elephant, the Most Advanced Elephant in the World."[38]

Clearly, the fact that in both the Czech and Rumanian texts the scholars from these countries chose Soviet–related topics is a biting commentary. Among international scholars, those residing in countries behind the Iron Curtain are obliged to deny their own national interests and identities in favor of rendering obsequious, but no doubt politically expedient, homage to the Soviet Union. It seems to be a fairly common device in East European slurs to have the Russian be the final participant (rather than a member of the culture of the joketeller). In any international slur, it is surely relevant to consider whether the teller's group is represented—and, if so, does it come last, and is the featured attribute negative (as is, presumably, the case of the other groups mentioned) or positive? These Eastern European texts pretend to praise the Soviet Union, but the context of the joke structure itself makes it abundantly clear that the praise is meant as not very veiled criticism. The Russian is the final participant in the following Czech gesture joke, collected in Prague in the summer of 1971. The premise involves the use of fingers. The Poles need all five — they're so awkward (narrator makes gesture using whole hand to wipe nose). The Germans need four (for their Sieg Heil salute). The Americans need three (for money, with rubbing gesture of thumb over the third and second fingers of the same hand). The Czechs need two: one for "Shh" (pointer finger held over the lips) and the second (the thumb pointing back over the shoulder) for indicating someone is back there watching. The Russians need only one (a wagging finger) meaning, "Don't!" Despite the purely political cast of the Czech and Russian portions, the boorishness of the Pole, the German glorification of militarism, and the American interest in economics appear to further illustrate the traditional stereotypes already discussed.

Finally, a Norwegian version of the elephant conference is distinguished by its own special punchline.

> The German: "150 Ways to Use the Elephant for War."
> The Frenchman: "The Sex Life of the Elephant."
> The American: "How to Grow a Bigger and Better Elephant" (or, in another Norwegian text, "The Biggest Elephant I Ever Saw").
> The Swede: "The Political and Social Organization of the Elephant."
> The Dane: "150 Ways to Cook an Elephant."
> The Norwegian: "Norway and the Norwegians" (or, in another version, "Norway and We Norwegians").

Here, the nationalistic bias is admitted openly: Whatever the assigned topic, the real concern is the nation and the citizens of that nation. The punchline may be a gentle gibe at excessive patriotism, but it underlies an essential function of these international slurs. Each country wants to assert its own unique identity, and one way of doing this is vis-à-vis other recognized nations. Indeed, a small country may gain status, in its own eyes, simply by listing itself in a slur along with major world powers. In this way, an international multi-group slur is an ideal form for expressing national consciousness.

The punchline is, in effect, a play on the internal structure of the joke. The expectation — which is denied — is that the Norwegian, like all the others, will find some stereotypic approach to the common theme, the elephant. There are, of course, jokes whose whole point is to play on the nature of a joke cycle. For example, a man walks into a bar and asks the bartender if he's heard the latest Polack joke. The bartender coldly replies, "No," and that he happens to be Polish. The first man says, "That's all right, I'll talk slow." So it is a Polack joke after all, just as the Norwegian paper is an appropriate part of the elephant congress joke.

Extrapolating from this brief but largely representative sample, it should be fairly easy to identify some of the principal stereotypic characterological attributes of a number of nations: The Scotsman is stingy; the Jew is mercenary; the Irishman is crude and inclined toward drink; the Pole is stupid; the French is concerned with cooking and love-making; the English is unduly concerned with propriety and cold in interpersonal relations; the German is a longwinded scientific pedant, as well as being excessively militaristic; the American is prone to exaggerate and to boast; and so on. The folkloristic evidence from proverbs, jokes, and other forms of international slurs is fairly consistent. Yet these traditional trait associations are not necessarily those reported in other studies of national stereotypes. Mariana Birnbaum's 1971 survey, which was limited to folk speech and proverbs (and which did not include jokes), failed to turn up the standard German stereotype, other than a reference to drinking.[39] Birnbaum even comments, "It is of interest that although they were enemies of this country in two world wars, except to actual military slang, there exist far fewer anti-German expressions than the historical relationship would suggest."[40] However, the texts presented here indicate that there is hardly a dearth of anti-German expressions!

More important by far is the comparison of the data gleaned from folkloristic sources, such as those presented here, and the results obtained in the extensive social science literature devoted to national stereotypes. Judging from the folklore, one can see large lacunae in the attitudinal tests that supposedly are designed to elicit stereotypes. For one thing, such tests typically impose upon the individuals questioned either a particular list of countries (or groups) or a specific list of adjectives (traits). For example, the list of adjectives used in an elaborate UNESCO survery were: hardworking, intelligent, practical, conceited, generous, cruel, backward, brave, self-controlled, domineering, progressive, peace-loving, and impossible to characterize.[41] Clearly, there is some discrepancy between the list of *a priori* adjectives selected (and precisely how *were* they selected?) and the adjectives that actually appear in traditional international slurs. In terms of reliability and validity, it should be obvious which set of adjectives is more likely to reflect existing stereotypes. Moreover, examining the inventory of slurs from each country shows which other countries normally are compared (rather than insisting on a comparison between the country of the individuals questioned and one or more other countries selected somewhat arbitrarily by the test administrator). Also, the number of culture-specific traits found in slurs appear to make it difficult to find adjectives that would apply equally well to a large number of countries. The propensity for excessive militarism, for instance, is not attributed to the French or the Italians. In the case of the Italians, it is quite the contrary — their principal military association appears to be cowardice in the face of war. Consider, **What's the first thing an Italian soldier is taught? How to hold his hands above his head.** Or the newspaper ad: **Italian Army rifle for sale—just like new, never fired, just dropped once.**

In fairness, the results of the present sampling of folk humor does support one of the findings of the UNESCO study, namely, that "stereotyped views of certain peoples are common property of Western culture rather than the effect of bilateral national outlooks that differ from one country to another."[42] We have seen that the association of love-making with the French is a national character stereotype widely held in Europe and the United States. In many cases, the stereotype is held even by the country being stereotyped. The Germans, for example, in the 1784 text cited, say that two *soldiers* are found among any three Germans. Further, there is the *German* paradigm of one, two, and three Germans, which ends with three Germans equalling a war. This kind of self-stereotyping does *not* conform to the UNESCO finding "that stereotypes of one's own countrymen are invariably in flattering terms."[43] Here again, the data from folklore seem eminently more trustworthy than the data from questionnaires filled in as part of an international survey. For it is in folklore, after all, that we find the most authentic indicators of attitudes held. The UNESCO questionnaire, like so many social science questionnaires, reflects the prejudices of the test-makers rather than the test-takers!

One must not overlook the role of humor in international slurs. It is humor that masks the aggression toward others — and, in some cases, toward self. The Henri Bergson notion of the "mechanical superimposed upon the living" seems beautifully exemplified in the slurs: The Germans routinely insist upon making war, just as the French routinely insist upon making love. It is humor that provides the ever so crucial leavening agent that enables people to picture their own negative characteristics, real or imagined.

If comedy and tragedy are merely opposite sides of the same coin, then we must look long and hard at the humor of international slurs. Stereotypes are a factor in the formation of prejudice, and prejudice often prevents people from accepting one another as individuals. In this respect, the study of international slurs is not trivial. The same motivating factors that led to the 1949 UNESCO-sponsored opinion polls are just as important now, and will be for decades to come. The resolution that urged "inquiries into the conceptions which the people of one nation entertain of their own and of other nations" was part of a larger study of "Tensions Affecting International Understanding."[44] As the world continues to shrink dramatically, thanks to more efficient means of travel and communication, and as more and more nations begin to interact with one another, the interference of stereotypes with cross-national human understanding becomes more and more of a threat to world peace. One way of identifying both the stereotypes and one of their prime sources lies in the study of international slurs.

Some may argue that a scholarly discussion of ethnic and national stereotypes accomplishes nothing more than helping to popularize and further circulate them. That is a risk, but it is one worth taking. After all, the slurs exist whether or not a folklorist chooses to collect and study them. The folklorist doesn't invent the slurs; he merely reports them. It is difficult to meaningfully attack prejudice in general; it is more effective to attack specific traits. The traits must be identified in order for someone to attack them.

I believe that any individual traveling to another country should be aware of what that country thinks of his nationality. Just as important is what members of his country think of the inhabitants of the country being visited. One may be equally well victimized by one's own prejudices as by the prejudices held by others!

So there is an applied aspect of this consideration of multi-group international slurs. We cannot expect international slurs to disappear — evidently, there is a deep human need to think in stereotypes. What folklorists *can* do is examine the slurs to see what the stereotypes are, and to label them as stereotypes. We should not let the humor of the slurs fool us into underestimating the potential danger of national character stereotypes. What a tragedy it would be if the world were to die laughing.

CHAPTER 9

The Jew and the Polack*
in the United States:
A Study of Ethnic Slurs

One of the most interesting aspects of the study of man concerns the alleged or actual character traits of different cultures and subcultures. Anthropology and psychology have a vast literature devoted to "national character," ethnic psychology, or *Volkscharakter.*[1] While some scholars have despaired of ever arriving at a rigorous description of the "modal personality," or fundamental character, of different groups, there is little doubt that different peoples manifest different personality traits.

The literature on man's apparently universal propensity to stereotype is equally large. Ever since journalist Walter Lippmann coined the term in 1922 in his book, *Public Opinion,* social psychologists have actively sought to refine the concept and to document its existence and influence,[2] attending to stereotypes both of self and of others. There have also been special studies on the relationship between stereotypes and prejudice,[3] revealing that stereotypes contribute materially to the formation and perpetuation of deep-seated prejudices.

---

*"Polack" is, in and of itself, an ethnic slur, offensive to Polish-Americans. It belongs to the same set of demeaning terms as nigger, canuck, kike, dago, and wop. I decided to use it primarily because it is the term of choice in the joke cycle about the alleged characteristics of Polish-Americans. For a discussion of such terms, see Irving Lewis Allen, *The Language of Ethnic Conflict: Social Organization and Lexical Culture* (New York: Columbia University Press, 1983).

Yet the extensive national character and stereotype scholarship has surprisingly little reference to the materials of folklore. Stereotypes are described almost solely on the basis of questionnaires or interviews, in which informants assign an a priori set of adjectives, such as "honest" or "stingy," to national or ethnic groups. One wonders what method the researchers use to select the initial list of adjectives, and whether their personal biases reflected in the list don't partially invalidate the results. What psychologists and others fail to realize is that folklore represents an important and virtually untapped source of information for students of national character, stereotypes, prejudice. The folk have been making national (folk) character studies for centuries.[4] People A have numerous traditions (expressed in proverbs, songs, jokes, and so on) about the character of People B, as do People B about People A. And it is precisely these traditions that transmit stereotypes from one generation to another. The stereotypes are thus "already recorded" and are presumably free from the inevitable investigator–bias present in the unduly leading questionnaires. Furthermore, the folkloristic evidence may clarify a number of bothersome ambiguities. Most of the traits contained on the conventional questionnaire lists of adjectives have both positive and negative associations. Thus, as W. Edgar Vinacke points out, "thrifty" is positive, while "stingy" is negative.[5] The basic trait is the same, but the degree differs. The folkloristic context of a joke ordinarily makes it clear whether a Scotsman is being thrifty or stingy.

In the United States, as elsewhere, individuals acquire stereotypes from folklore. Most of our conceptions of the French or of the Jew come not from extended personal acquaintance or contact with representatives of these groups but rather from the proverbs, songs, jokes, and other forms of folklore we have heard all our lives.[6] The stereotypes may or may not be accurate character analyses — they may or may not be in accord with actual, empirically verifiable personality traits. The point is that folk stereotypes exist, and that countless people make judgments on the basis of them. There is probably no other area of folklore where the element of belief is more critical and potentially more dangerous, not only to self but to others.

Comparison is a method of research that may conceivably help prove or disprove the degree of validity of folkloristic stereotypes. Does the French folk self-concept of French coincide with the delineation of French national character made by French psychologists, sociologists, or social historians? And what of the American conception of French character? Is it the same or different from the German conception of the French? Or the Spanish? The question includes whether folk stereotypes are cross-cultural. Some seem to be—for example, the Jew as mercenary and mercantile-minded. E. Terry Prothro and Levon Melikian, among others, suggest that cross-cultural agreement or "types" might tend to support the idea that such stereotypes contain at least a "kernel of truth."[7] On the other hand, considering the mass media's encouragement of international propaganda efforts, one must proceed with great caution. The fact that a fiction is shared cross-culturally does not necessarily make that fiction true. Still, cross-cultural agreement that Germans are militaristic constitutes much more impressive evidence than merely a single American folk stereotype of the Germans as militaristic.

Comparative studies of folk stereotypes may also be undertaken with just two groups. As Wm. Hugh Jansen attempted to show, two groups may produce a variety of interrelated stereotypes.[8] Let's assume two groups, A and B. These can stand for any of a number of pairs of groups: northerners/southerners, Greeks/Turks, Jews/Gentiles, and so on. This pair produces the following potential stereotypes:

A's conception of A vis-à-vis B. (Example: a white's conception of a white in contrast to a black.)

B's conception of A vis-à-vis B. (Example: a black's conception of a white in contrast to a black.)

A's conception of B vis-à-vis A. (Example: a white's conception of a black in contrast to a white.)

B's conception of B vis-à-vis A. (Example: a black's conception of a black in contrast to a white.)

A's conception of B's conception of A vis-à-vis B. (Example: a white's conception of a black's conception of a white in contrast to a black. This may or may not be the same as a black's conception of a white in contrast to a black.)

B's conception of A's conception of B vis-à-vis A. (Example: a black's conception of a white's conception of a black in contrast to a white. The question here is whether the black stereotype of the white stereotype of the black was or was not identical to the white stereotype of the black.)

A's conception of B's conception of B vis-à-vis A. (Example: a white's conception of a black's conception of a black in contrast to a white.)

B's conception of A's conception of A vis-à-vis B. (Example: a black's conception of a white's conception of a white in contrast to a black.)

The possibility of "stereotypes of stereotypes," in addition to the conventional stereotypes, is no mere theoretical premise. Jokes contain not only stereotypes but also plays upon the stereotypes—for example, where a black will make fun of the white stereotype (or what he believes to be the white stereotype) of the black. Part of the white stereotype of blacks, for instance, is that black males are sexually superior. In a joke told by blacks, reported by Langston Hughes in 1951, a white man comes home one cold winter night to find his blond wife on the couch in the arms of a great big black. Petrified with astonishment, the white man forgets to close the front door and the icy winds rush in. Thinking his wife was being raped, the man cried, "Darling, what shall I do to this Negro?" The wife sighed from the couch, "Just shut the door so he won't catch cold."

Sometimes the stereotype and the "stereotype of a stereotype" are mutually reinforcing. One American concept of the Frenchman is that he is a great lover (which may, in fact, be part of the larger Latin Lover stereotype that includes Italians and Spaniards). Another American stereotype is that the French consider Americans to be poor lovers. (Thus there is some congruence between A's conception of B on the one hand, and A's conception of B's conception of A on the other.) The latter stereotype is illustrated in the following text:

> A French girl was very despondent over a sad love affair, so she went to the banks of the Seine and jumped in. A man passing saw her jump in so he dove in after her and pulled her out. But she was already dead. Oh, she'd taken off all her clothes—she was nude. So he ran to get a gendarme. In the meantime, another Frenchman came along and he saw this girl lying nude on the banks of the Seine so he ran up and started making advances. And since she didn't seem to resist him, he started to make love to her. In the meantime, the other Frenchman came back with the policeman and he said, "Monsieur, monsieur, stop, stop, she's dead." And the man jumps and says, "Oh, *sacrebleu,* I thought she was American."

Jokes like this, together with other folkloristic treatments of stereotypes, may be loosely classified under the rubric of ethnic slur. One difficulty, however, is that ethnic slur, like the French term *blason populaire,* normally has a pejorative connotation.[9] Yet clearly many elements of folk stereotypes have positive value. Jews tell and enjoy apparently anti-Semitic jokes, just as Catholic priests relish anticlerical tales. The term "ethnophaulism" proposed by A.A. Roback refers to "foreign disparaging allusions."[10] Whether an ethnic slur is truly disparaging depends in part upon who is using it and about whom.

Another difficulty with a concept like "ethnic slur" is that it crosses genre lines. An ethnic slur may consist of a single word—for example, frog, referring to a Frenchman. Or it may be an extended epigram or proverb: With a Hungarian for a friend you don't need an enemy. Count your fingers after you shake the hand of a Hungarian. How do you make a Hungarian omelet? First you steal a dozen eggs. . . . Both a Hungarian and Rumanian will sell you their grandmother, but only a Rumanian will deliver her. There is some ambiguity in the last example. On the one hand, anyone so callous as to make money by selling his own grandmother is obviously not to be trusted. On the other hand, the Hungarian is contrasted with the Rumanian insofar as the Hungarian fails to live up to his bargain to deliver his grandmother. This failure is negative in that it is yet another instance of the untrustworthiness of Hungarians; they do not fulfill contracts. At the same time, it is positive in that the Hungarian is a trickster who, in the final analysis, would not actually sell a member of his own family into bondage, while the Rumanian would. The Rumanian, by contrast, is more honest but not so clever as the Hungarian whose ruthless behavior he attempts to imitate.[11] Still another problem with the notion of ethnic slur is that there are many slurs that are not strictly ethnic, but have to do with a geographical region or city. For example, Did you hear about the big new prize contest? The first prize is one week in Philadelphia; the second prize is two weeks in Philadelphia. A similar anti-Philadelphia slur is, The best thing about Philadelphia is the Express [train] to New York. There are many other anti-Philadelphia slurs, although its reputation as a "dead" town with little to do or its lack of late-night life is no doubt also applied to other cities. For example, I spent a week in Philadelphia one day, or I was in Philadelphia once, but it was closed.[12] There are obviously also slurs involving religion. In fact, part of the stereotype of the Jew would have to be considered a religious rather than a pure ethnic slur.

The inadequacy of the term "ethnic slur" concerns essentially the definition of "folk" itself. Some folk groups are ethnic groups, in which case the label "ethnic slur" seems very appropriate; however, many folk groups are not ethnic, in which case the term seems inappropriate. This is clear if one accepts the modern, flexible definition of "folk" as not a peasant society but any group whatsoever that shares at least one common factor.[13] The linking factor might be ethnicity, but it might just as well be political or religious affiliation, geographical location, or occupation. Any group is potentially both producer and victim of slurs. Some slurs are very much in-group traditions; some are strictly out-group traditions; some are used as often by the in-group as by the out-group.[14] One reasonably empirical and eminently practical way to determine whether a given group has a "folk" identity separate from the general culture surrounding it is: Does that group have, or is it the subject of, slurs? In medicine, general practitioners have jokes about proctologists (**rear admirals**). In academic life, university professors have jokes about deans: **Old deans never die, they just lose their faculties.** Within Catholicism, there are jokes about Jesuits, often commenting upon their intellectual rather than mystical approach to life and religion. For example: **There was a meeting of three clergymen, and the three were in a room. There was a Dominican, a Franciscan, and a Jesuit. In the middle of the meeting, the lights go out. Undeterred by the darkness, the Dominican stands up and says, "Let us consider the nature of light and of darkness, and their meaning." The Franciscan begins to sing a hymn in honor of our Little Sister Darkness. The Jesuit goes out and replaces the fuse.** It is sometimes difficult to collect such in-group traditions; the subgroups may close ranks when confronted by what they take to be a threatening outsider who is only posing as a harmless folklorist-collector.

The term "ethnic" or "national slur," then, is a functional rather than generic category, and there are slurs that have nothing to do with ethnicity. The ethnic slur depends on an alleged national or ethnic trait. More often than not, the traits are mocked and demeaned. What is of primary interest here is determining precisely the trait or set of traits that the folk has singled out for emphasis.

Not only have the folk undertaken informal national character studies in the form of ethnic slur or national stereotype traditions, but they have even attempted modest comparative studies. Although admittedly of limited scope, such comparative listings of slurs indicate the general human tendency to compare one's own group with other groups. Almost all the multigroup ethnic slurs, in which a host of cultures are lampooned, reveal a similar compositional technique. Members of different cultures are placed in an identical situation or are each made to perform the same act. It is the responses to the fixed situation or the different ways of carrying out the set task that provide the outlet for supposedly stereotypic behavior. Consider, for example, the

remarks made by women from different countries after sexual intercourse in a 1969 Spanish text:

> The Russian woman: "Romanov, this night we have cre-
> ated a perfect being for the party."
> The German woman: "Hans, this night we have created
> a perfect being."
> The French woman: "Rene, you know a lot about love, but
> you still have more to learn."
> The English woman: "What did you say your name was?"
> The Spanish woman: "Come on, Pepe, get out of bed. We
> have to go to the two o'clock (a.m.) mass."

In this one example we find typical ethnic slurs expressed with the
usual praiseworthy economy of the folk. There is the French glorification of lovemaking, the Russian concern for political dogma, the German love of power, which harks back to the notion of a "Master Race,"
and the English aloofness in personal relations, combined with the notion that sexuality is a wifely duty devoid of pleasure. Of course, these
traits often occur in single slurs. For example, there was the Englishman
who was making love to his wife. And he said, "Oh! Pardon me, darling.
Did I hurt you?" And she said, "No, why?" And he said, "Oh, you moved."

Now let's turn to national and subcultural slurs. In the United
States, with its unmelted "melting pot" of immigrant groups, it is
sometimes difficult to distinguish between international and subcultural
ethnic slurs. An anti-Italian slur probably refers to Italian-Americans
rather than Italians, but it may refer to both. Sometimes, the point
is simply to force the utterance of the folk reference term, as in What
does a pizza sound like when you throw it into a wall? Wop! (One folk
etymology for the word "wop," a common term of disparagement for
Americans of Italian descent, is that in the early 1920s many Italians
tried to enter the United States illegally. These would-be immigrants
were rounded up by U.S. officials and sent back to Italy with docu-
ments labelled "W.O.P.," which supposedly stood for "Without Papers,"
referring to the papers needed for legal immigration.)[15] Probably the
most common anti-Italian ethnic slur concerns cowardice. Here, the
reference is clearly to Italians rather than Italian-Americans, although
the latter are presumably tarred with the same brush. An example is
the following joking question: What's this? (narrator raises both hands
well above his head as if to surrender). Answer: An Italian getting ready
for World War III (or, An Italian out on war maneuvers). The same gesture
is also the answer to the question, What's the Italian soldier's salute?

Cowardice is also the subject of the following slurs: How many speeds does an Italian tank have? Five—four in reverse and one forward, in case they're attacked from the rear. What happened two hours after the Arab-Israeli war broke out? The Italians surrendered. There are other anti-Italian slurs, but these are representative.[16]

In analyzing the content of ethnic slurs, one critical question is whether a specific character trait is limited in distribution to one particular ethnic group. For example, one anti-Italian joke reported by Simmons is, How many Italians does it take to change a lightbulb? Three—one to hold the bulb and two to turn the ladder. However, this joke is also told about Polacks and many other groups. If this joke is simply a floating tradition of the "moron-noodle-numskull" variety, then it raises the question, how feasible is it to undertake a meaningful content analysis of ethnic slurs? And just how specific and consistent are the ethnic slur traditions attached to any one particular group? There is no doubt that stereotypes may change in time, subject to the vagaries of historical events. For example, in 1941, Americans perceived the Japanese as sly, treacherous, and sneaky; twenty-five years later, however, these traits are largely absent. Generally speaking, traits of a stereotype manifested at any one point in time demonstrate considerable consistency, and many ethnic slur traditions have proved remarkably stable over long periods of time. Part of the consistency and stability may be explained in terms of pattern strength. In a "multiple-trait stereotype," it is precisely the combination of traits that makes a particular stereotype unique, and it is the combination of traits that contributes to the stereotype's remarkable, if maleficent, staying power. To illustrate the consistency of the patterning of multiple-trait folk stereotypes, let's briefly consider the Jew and the Polack as they appear in current American oral tradition.

I will discuss the generic Jew who appears in American ethnic slurs in contrast to the gentile.[17] One profitable way to deal with Jewish subcultures is by means of ethnic slurs—for example, the Russian Jews versus the German Jews, or Orthodox versus Conservative versus Reform Judaism. But for the present purposes, it's enough to delineate some of the more typical traits of the Jew in general, as he is depicted in ethnic slurs. What are these traits?

1. One of the dominant traits is the concern with making money, which the following texts should illustrate.

When Billy Graham sang "All I Want is Jesus," five thousand people joined the Protestant church. When Pope

Pius sang "Ave Maria," ten thousand people joined the Catholic church. When Pat Boone sang "There's a Gold Mine in the Sky," one hundred thousand Jews joined the Air Force.

Jesus Saves: Moses Invests.

Have you heard the Jewish football yell that goes: "Get that quarter back!"?

How do they take a census in Israel? They roll a nickel down the street.

2. A related trait is the alleged penchant for mercantile trade; for example, the Jew is depicted as always looking for a bargain, or looking to make a sale:

God comes down to a Babylonian one day. He says, "Say, I have a commandment; I'd like to give it to you." And the Babylonian says, "Well, what is it?" "Thou shalt not steal." And the Babylonian says, "Well, no thanks." So God went over to an Egyptian and offered him the same deal. And when the Egyptian heard it, he said, "No thanks." And then God met Moses and God said, "I have a commandment for you." And Moses said, "Well, how much is it going to cost me?" "Nothing." And Moses says, "I'll take ten."

It is surely noteworthy that the Jewish Moses doesn't even bother to ask what the commandments are—more important is what they cost. The critical factor is the bargain, insofar as there is no charge for the commandments. Moses says he'll take ten, and he has not even asked what it is he is getting. But usually, in the stereotype, it is the Jew who offers the cut rate:

This is station KVY, Tel Aviv, 1400 on your dial, but for *you,* 1395!

Perhaps one of the bitterest examples of the exalted importance of commerce is the joke in which two clothing manufacturers are waiting anxiously for a telegram of confirmation or cancellation of a big business order. Finally a telegram arrives. Neither wants to open it. Confirmation? Cancellation? Finally, one opens the telegram. "Good news, Morris," he says to his partner, "your brother died." A final example of this part of the stereotype pasquinades the black as well:

> A Protestant, a black, and a Jew die and go to heaven. When they get there, St. Peter says to the Protestant, "What do you want?" The Protestant answers, "Nice food, a nice pasture, and some nice sheep." St. Peter then asks the black what he wants. He says, "A big flashy Cadillac, a million dollars, and a big white house." St. Peter then asks the Jew what he wants and the Jew replies, "All you got to give me is a suitcase full of trinkets and the address of that black."

The point here, of course, is that the Jew elects to gain wealth by taking it away from someone else through a sharp and unfair business trade. In terms of the joke's premise, he presumably could have been given the wealth by St. Peter, just as the black had been. However, as the stereotype suggests, the Jew is consistently portrayed as being business oriented before all else.

3. A prominent trait is the desire for status, often achieved by males by becoming professional men and by females by marrying professional men.

> What did Mr. Mink give Mrs. Mink for Christmas?
> A full-length Jew.

Normally the path to such financial success is presumed to lie in careers in medicine or law.

> Two Jewish women meet on the street, one with children. The other says, "Such beautiful children how old are they?"
> "The doctor is seven and the lawyer is five."

In the same vein:

> There is a little Jewish lady running along the seashore yelling, "Help, help, my son, the doctor, is drowning."

Still another expression of this facet of the stereotype is found in the following joking question:

> What is the definition of a C.P.A. (Certified Public Accountant)?
> It's a Jewish boy who can't stand the sight of blood and who stutters.

I suspect that this particular ethnic slur might not be understood by all members of the outgroup. The point here is that a Jewish boy who can't stand the sight of blood cannot become a doctor, and similarly a Jewish boy who stutters cannot become a lawyer. Hence the only course left is to become a C.P.A.

The Jewish female's means of attaining status has traditionally been through a good marriage, preferably to a doctor. This stereotype is illustrated by the following texts:

> In a crowded theater, a Jewish lady trips and falls downstairs. In mortal pain and half dying, she screams, "Is there a doctor in the house?" Finally, a man comes over and says, "Yes, Madam, I'm a doctor."
> "Doctor, I have a young daughter who is of marriageable age."

> Two Jewish women are walking along, and one says, "Ach, my son—he gives me both sorrow and pleasure." So her friend asks her, "How does he give you sorrow?" And she says, "He's a homosexual." So her friend asks, "How does he give you pleasure?" And she says, "He's going with a doctor."

Did you hear about the Jewish girl who accidentally married the Good Humor man? (Good Humor men are ice cream vendors in the streets. They normally wear white uniforms, somewhat similar to the white hospital coats worn by doctors.)

4. Another feature of the folk stereotype, but a physical rather than a motivational one, has to do with the so-called large Jewish nose. Sometimes, this feature is combined with another stereotypic trait:

> Why do Jews have big noses?
> Air is free.

Usually, however, the nose appears alone, as in the following sick joking question:

> Do you know what happened to the pregnant Jewish woman who took Thalidomide?
> She had [gave birth to] a ten-pound nose.

One of the most elaborate expressions of this element of the stereotype is a folktale parody:

> Once upon a time there was a little Jewish girl, and her name was Little Red Rosenthal. Little Red Rosenthal lived at the edge of the woods with her mother. One day Little Red Rosenthal's boubie [grandmother] was sick. So Little Red Rosenthal's mother gave Little Red Rosenthal

a basket with *pchaw, kishka, sup mit kreplach,* and *shtrudel* for Little Red Rosenthal to take to her boubie. Her mother told her to be very careful of the wolf and not to talk with him and to go straight to her grandmother's house. On the way Little Red Rosenthal met the wolf and he said, "Darling, ver are you goin'?" "I'm going to take this basket of food to my boubie," she replied, and went on her way. The wolf went ahead, straight to the boubie's house and ate up the boubie. When Little Red Rosenthal got to her boubie's house she knocked on the door, "Kom in," said the wolf.

"Boubie! What big ears you have!"
"The better to hear your beautiful voice mit, my dear."
"Boubie! What big eyes you have!"
"The better to look on you mit, my dear!"
"Boubie! What a big nose you have!"
"*You* should talk!"

5. The stereotype traits having to do with money, business, professionalism, and nasal physiognomy are perhaps the most obvious and recurrent. Nevertheless, this by no means exhausts the stereotype. Among the other traits that occur in ethnic slur tradition is the alleged propensity of some Jews for pro-Semitism (as opposed to anti-Semitism). According to this trait, Jews tend to interpret or evaluate anything that happens in the world in terms of its importance to Jews. This next text illustrates such stereotypic ethnocentrism:

One day during the time when Babe Ruth was the hero of every boy in America, little Bennie came running in to his grandfather and excitedly yelled, "Grandfather, grandfather, Babe Ruth just hit his sixtieth home run." His grandfather gave him a long, somber look and acidly replied, "So, how's this going to help the Jews?"

But if pro-Semitism is part of the stereotype, so is anti-Semitism. A most important facet of the stereotype is the Jew who tries to disown or conceal his heritage. The gist is that Jews should not, or rather cannot, stop being Jewish. Often this is revealed in the punchline of a joke in which a traditional phrase of Yiddish folk speech proves the continued Jewishness of the character. Here is a representative text:

A young Jewish couple from New York decides they want to go to Florida for a vacation, but the hotel they want to stay at is restricted. ("Restricted" means that Jews are not welcome and that the clientele is supposedly restricted to white Christians.) The man tells his wife he thinks it will work out and they will be able to stay at the hotel just as long as she doesn't open her mouth, because nobody will know they are Jewish. So they make the trip, and everything goes just fine. They check into the hotel, and the wife never opens her mouth. They go up to their room and pretty soon the wife decides she would like to take a swim. The husband tells her to go ahead but reminds her not to say anything. So she goes down to the pool for her swim. She sticks her toe into the water and it is just terribly cold, and she yells out, "Oi vey!" Then, looking around horrified, she adds, "Wat ever dat means."

Perhaps the best examples of the Jew's unsuccessful attempts to renounce his heritage are found in the large number of Jewish–Christian jokes. The idea is essentially that a Jew cannot convert to Christianity, however much he may try.

Do you know the one about the little old devout Orthodox Jew who decides in the latter part of his life to turn to Catholicism? Well, the Catholic church is so delighted, because this is wonderful propaganda for the universal appeal of the church, and they invite him to speak at the next congregation. So the little Jew gets up and says, "Fellow goyim. . . ."

"Goyim" is a humorous, disparaging Jewish term for non-Jews or gentiles. Many Jewish jokes end with the utterance of this term. The point in the above joke is that the Jew, even when supposedly converted, cannot do other than consider the Catholics as goyim—as members of the out-group, as opposed to the Jewish in-group. Here's another example of a "goyim" joke that serves as a pro-Jewish story, thereby reinforcing group solidarity.

The Israelis decide to make a huge bell by melting down all the guns used on the Gaza strip, and they're going to send this bell to be rung on the day of the Pope's coronation in St. Peter's Square. So on the day of the coronation, the Pope gets up and says what a glorious tribute this is to brotherhood, and so on, and there is great anticipation; and he turns to the monk who is waiting to ring the bell. The monk pulls the cord and the bell rings out "Goyimmmm."

The following tale offers one of the finest comments on the practical reasons for converting from Judaism to Christianity, coupled with an editorial judgment as to the ultimate sham of such an attempt.

There was this Jewish man who moved to an all-Catholic neighborhood. And he couldn't make a friend because of his religion. What's more, everybody hated him because on Friday night, when everyone would cook fish, this man would cook chicken and the neighborhood would reek with the smell of chicken. So finally this Jew decides to give in to the social pressures exerted on him, and he decides to become a Catholic. So he goes to the church, and he tells the priest that he wants to convert. So the priest says, "Fine. All you do is cross yourself every time you see someone and say, 'Once a Jew, now a Catholic,' and be sure to follow all the laws, and come to church and eventually you'll become a Catholic." So the man goes around crossing himself saying, "Once a Jew, now a Catholic" and he goes to church. And soon he has a lot of friends. But he still cooks chicken on Friday nights, and no one can figure out why. So the neighbors report the fellow to the priest. And one day the priest visits the ex-Jew, and he tells him that he has heard that he was still cooking chicken on Friday. And the Jew denies this. No matter how much proof the priest presents, the ex-Jew still will not admit that he cooked chicken on Friday. So the priest says, "Okay, I'll believe you." And the following Friday the priest decides to go over to the new convert's house. And as he approaches the house, he can smell chicken cooking. So he asks himself what's going on and he decides to peek in the kitchen window and see if the man is cooking chicken. And he looks in the window. Here's the ex-Jew standing over a pot, cooking a chicken. And he's crossing the chicken saying, "Once a chicken, now a fish."

The point is, of course, that the Jew has become a good Catholic only to the extent that a chicken can become a fish! Clearly the Jew uses the magic conversion formula strictly as a practical measure. If a Jew converts, argues the stereotype, there must be an eminently practical and pressing reason for it, and in any case, the conversion does not alter the essential Jewishness of the individual. This is also illustrated in the following story:

A devoutly religious Jew is on his deathbed. His family clusters around to hear his last wish. To their surprise, he asks them to send for a priest. They are shocked and ask if he means a rabbi. No, he wants a priest, he insists. Despite their dismay, the family obeys the command and sends for a priest, who converts the old Jew and administers the last rites according to the requirements of Catholicism. After the priest leaves, the family rushes in to demand an explanation. Why, after living his whole life as a religious Jew, did he now suddenly at the very end convert to Catholicism? His answer: "Better one of them should die than one of us!"

The failure of conversion attempts is also featured in jokes about the Christian nuclear family of the New Testament. The Jewish origin of Christianity is stressed, often by noting that Jesus was a Jew. What happened in A.D. 13? Jesus was "bar mitzvahed." The following text also demonstrates the nature of "Jewish origin of Christianity" jokes.

This lady went down to a restricted hotel in Miami. She went up to the manager and said, "Podden me, so I'd like to have a small room."

The manager said, "Sorry, all our rooms are taken." Just as he said that, a man came down and checked out.

"Isn't that vunderful," she said, "now I can have a room."

The manager said, "Look here, I don't want you to think I am prejudiced or anything, but we don't allow Jews in this hotel."

"That's O.K., I don't happen to be Jewish. I'm Catholic."

"No! I can't believe it," the manager said.

"I'm telling you, I'm Catholic."

"Do you know your catechism, then?"

"I'm knowing my catechism."

"Who's the son of God?"

"Who's the son of God? Jesus son of Mary."

"Do you know how he happened to be born in a stable?"

"Soitenly, nu, a son of a bitch like you wouldn't give a Jew a room."

In modern American society, however, Jews fear that they may be losing their identity. This loss of identity may be caused by successful conversions to Christianity or by Jews marrying non-Jews. Thus the following text contains not only the "Jewish origin of Christianity" theme, but also the fear that Christianity may be replacing Judaism:

> A Jewish man is very disturbed when his son comes home from college on vacation and tells him that he is converting to Christianity. The man rushes to tell his neighbor about it and the neighbor says, "Strange you should mention that. My boy also came home from college and he also converted to Christianity." The two men commiserate and try to think of what they should do. They decide to see the rabbi. They tell the rabbi their problem and the rabbi says, "Strange you should mention that. My son also came home from college and converted." Now the men are really upset. They ask the rabbi what to do. He decides there is only one thing to do. They must all go down to the temple and pray to God. They pray to God and tell Him of their troubles. Suddenly they see a flash of lightning and hear a crack of thunder and a booming voice rings out, "Strange you should mention that."

A final trait in the stereotype concerns the antipathy to intermarriage. Jews are endogamous and there is often resistance to the idea of a Jew marrying a non-Jew. Here is a classic example.[18]

> There's this girl from a very Orthodox Jewish background and she goes away to school. One day she phones up her mother and says, "Mom, I'm getting married."
> And so the mother says, "*Mazel Tov*, my dear. Congratulations."
> So the daughter says, "But Mama, he's not Jewish."
> So the mother says, "That's all right, dear, I'm sure he's a nice boy, you picked him out, he's a nice boy."
> So the daughter says, "Another thing about him, Mom. He's black."
> So she says, "Vell, you picked him out. I'm sure he's a fine boy. I'm sure he's got a fine job."
> So the daughter says, "Well, about the job, Mother. He doesn't have one."
> So the mother says, "Vell, he's a good boy, he'll get a good job." Then the mother asks, "Ver are you going to live?"
> So the daughter says, "Well, uh, Mom, that's what I

called about. We were wondering if we could stay with you."

So the mother says, "That's vunderful, daughter, you can stay with us. Your father will sleep on the couch and you and your husband can take the bedroom."

So the daughter says, "But where are you going to sleep, Ma?"

So the mother says, "Don't worry about me, as soon as I hang up I'm going to drop dead." (An alternate punch line is: "Don't worry about me, but would you mind turning off the gas when you come in.")

The double standard of the intermarriage problem is also the subject of stereotyping. The Jewish girl must marry a Jewish boy, but the Jewish boy is more free to marry a gentile girl. This is made clear by the following text.

A Jewish girl brings home a *shagits* (non-Jewish boy) whom she wants to marry. And she introduces him to her father. And the father asks, "Is he Jewish?"

And she says, "No, Dad."

He says, "I will never permit my daughter to marry a *shagits*."

So they have a conference about it and the boy says, "Well, look, Dad, supposin' I converted. I'm perfectly willing to go through the ritual to be converted into Judaism. I'm in love with your daughter and I want to marry her."

The father said, "Well, that's different."

So the boy goes through the whole business. He's circumcised; he goes through the whole ritual. And when they're ready for the wedding, the daughter falls out of love with him. She says she doesn't want to marry him. So the boy comes rushing to the girl's father and he says, "You know, Dad, I did everything I could possibly do. I agreed to become a Jew and I did. I've been circumcised and now your daughter doesn't love me any more and she won't marry me. What shall I do?"

The father says, "Marry a *schicksah* [non-Jewish girl] like the other Jewish boys."

The father's inconsistency is obvious. He insists that his daughter marry a Jewish boy, but he recognizes the tendency for Jewish boys to marry gentile girls. The girl is clearly intrigued by the prospect

of marrying a non-Jew, for when the latter becomes a Jew she is no
longer interested. Loss of identity through Christianization or intermarriage is a genuine concern of the Jewish community in the United
States; thus, it comes as no surprise to see such anxieties expressed
in folklore. These latter jokes are probably told more by Jews than
non-Jews, but almost all of the above texts are in fact told both by
Jews and non-Jews. Whether one takes offense at an ethnic slur depends
on the identity of the teller and of the audience. Some Jews take offense
at ethnic slurs regardless of whether the raconteur is Jewish or not.
Others enjoy the slurs *en famille*, but would resent them if related by
a person they considered to be an anti-Semitic gentile.

There is an endless amount of Jewish humor. The present sampling
is merely to delineate various features of the stereotype of the Jew in
American folklore. The principal traits are obvious enough: the concern with money, trade, status, professionalism; the large nose; the
undesirability and, in fact, impossibility, of renouncing one's ethnic
identity as a Jew; a prideful consciousness of the Judaic elements of
Christianity; and a fear for the loss of ethnic identity through conversion to Christianity or through marriage with gentiles. Much of the
stereotype has existed for some time in the United States, not to mention other parts of the world.[19] The point here is that there is a fairly
consistent, composite stereotypic picture of the Jew. Most of the traits
in question are not attributed to other national or ethnic groups, although sometimes one trait may be, as in the stinginess slur: **What's
the difference between a Jew (Scotsman) and a canoe? A canoe tips?**
But it is important to note that the particular combination of stereotypic
traits is unique. Thus, while both Jews and Scotsmen are alleged to
be unusually stingy, this may be the only trait the two stereotypes
share. Scotsmen are not said to have large noses and are not depicted
as being particularly anxious to become doctors, for example.

There was even a psychological experiment in which jokes about
Jews and their supposed stinginess were transformed into jokes about
Scots and the same trait. Jewish subjects continued to find the jokes
less humorous than gentile subjects.[20] It is also worth noting that not
all of the stereotypic traits "recorded" in folklore are reported in the
psychologists' studies of stereotypes.

As a final test of the specificity of the multitrait ethnic slur
stereotype, I will contrast the Jewish traits with those of the Polack,
as found in recent popular cycle of ethnic slurs.

Polack jokes have been noted by folklorists and by the mass media.[21] The fact that some of the jokes told about Polacks in the midwestern section of the United States are the same told about Italians or Puerto Ricans in the eastern states suggests that we may have nothing more than a "lower-class" stereotype that can be applied equally well to any immigrant group registering low on the social scale at any given moment.[22] Nevertheless, the fact that the American cycle of Polack slurs has similar traits to those found in European (especially German) stereotypes of Polish people (stereotypes reported some years ago)[23] suggests that there may be some continuity in Polack ethnic slurs in particular. Here, at any rate, are some of the dominant traits.

1. The Polacks are poor.

> Why is the Polish suicide rate so low?
> Did you ever try jumping out of a basement window?
>
> What's a Polish barbeque?
> A fire in a garbage can.
>
> What is a description of a Polish funeral?
> Ten garbage trucks with their lights on.
>
> How do you describe Polish matched luggage?
> Two shopping bags from Sears.
>
> What is a Polish vacation?
> Sitting on someone else's steps.

2. The Polacks are dirty.

> Why aren't Polacks allowed to swim in Lake Michigan?
> Because they leave a ring.
>
> Why did the Polish couple get married in the bathtub?
> They wanted a double-ring ceremony.
>
> How do you get 86 Polacks in a Volkswagen?
> Throw in a nickel.
>
> How do you get Polacks out of a Volkswagen?
> Throw in a bar of soap.

The first of these joking questions could conceivably fit the stereotype of the Jew, but the second, related, part would not.

> Where do Polacks hide their money?
> Under the soap.

Do you know how to get a Polack out of a bathtub?
Turn on the water.

3. Polacks are stupid.

The teller of this joke puts his left hand behind his head. He puts his right hand perpendicular to his face and above his eyes, as if looking for something. Then he asks, What's this? A Polack looking for his left hand. In another charadelike slur, the narrator covers his eyes with his left hand and stomps the ground wildy with his right foot and asks, What's this? A Polack looking for land mines. In others, the body movement is found in the answer rather than the question. How does a Polack tie his shoe? He puts one foot up on a chair and ties the shoe on the foot on the floor (instead of the one in the chair). Why do Polacks have hunched shoulders and sloping foreheads? Because every time you ask them a question, they go . . . (gesture of shrugging their shoulders, indicating they don't know the answer) and every time you tell them the answer, they go . . . (gesture striking the forehead with the palm of the hand indicating "Of course, how stupid I am"). Reminiscent of gesture is the statement that Polish mothers are strong and square-shouldered from raising dumbbells.

Why does a Polack wear a hat while taking a crap?
So he'll know which end to wipe.

Did you hear about the Polack who was asked if he would like to become a Jehovah's Witness? He said he couldn't because he didn't see the accident.

Definition of a cad: A Polack who doesn't tell his wife he's sterile until after she's pregnant.

Did you hear about the lazy Polack?
He married a pregnant woman.

What is the definition of gross ignorance?
One hundred and forty-four Polacks. (A gross is, or course, twelve dozen.)

Did you hear about the Polish space scientists who're planning to land a man on the sun? When asked if the sun's heat would burn him up, they replied they had thought of that and they were going to land him at night.

Why did the Polack lose his job as an elevator operator?
He couldn't learn the route.

Did you hear about the Polack racing driver who entered the Indianapolis 500? He came in last and he made 14 pit stops, four for repair and maintenance and ten to ask directions.

What's this? (A piece of paper, on the left side of which is written the word "in" with an arrow pointing from left to right. On the right side is written the word "out" and there is also an arrow pointing from left to right.)
Answer: A Polish maze.

How do you keep a Polack busy?
Give him this. (A square of paper on both sides of which is written, "Please turn over.")

Do you know why they don't give Poles a coffee break? It takes too long to retrain them.

What is stamped at the bottom of Coca Cola bottles in Poland?
"Please open other end."

What has an I.Q. of 300?
Poland.

4. Polacks are inept.

How did the Polack get 35 holes in his head?
Trying to learn to eat with a fork.

A woman ran into a police station yelling, "Help, I've been raped by a Polack." The officer said, "How do you know he was a Polack?" She said, "Because I had to help him."

A Polack and an Irishman were out hunting when a beautiful naked girl ran by. The Irishman yelled, "Hey lass, are you game?" She replied, "Yes." So the Polack shot her. (The Irishman meant "game" in the sense of "willing to be daring, that is, in terms of sexuality"; the Polack understood "game" in the sense of the object of hunting.)

Did you hear about the Polish fish? It drowned.

5. Polacks are vulgar, boorish, and tasteless.

What is a Polack's biggest decision before attending a formal dance?
Whether to wear red or green socks.

The Polack was asked in a political discussion, "What would you do with Red China?" He said he would put it on a purple tablecloth.

How do you tell the bride at a Polish wedding?
She's the one with the clean T-shirt (or with the sequins on her tennis shoes, or with braided armpits).

How do you tell the difference between the bride and the groom at a Polish wedding?
The groom is the one with the finger in his nose.

How do you break a Polack's finger?
Punch him in the nose.

What do you find when you turn a Polack's nose inside out?
Fingerprints.

What happens to a Polack who picks his nose?
His head collapses.

Why do Poles go around with their initials written on the backs of their hands?
They want to have monogrammed handkerchiefs.[24]

How do you kill a Polack?
Hit him on the head with the toilet seat while he is taking a drink of water.

There seem to be a large number of jokes associating Polacks with feces, such as, How do you brainwash a Polack? Give him an enema. Why do Polacks carry a piece of shit in their wallets? For identification.[25]

These Polack ethnic slurs should illustrate the nature of the stereotype. There are, of course, many others, although they do not demonstrate any consistent trait: What's the difference between a Polack wedding and a Polack funeral? One less drunk. Who won the Polack beauty contest? Nobody. Why do Poles learn English? So they can read Joseph Conrad in the original. Did you hear about the Polish heart transplant? The heart rejected the body. Did you hear about the breakthrough in Polish medicine? They transplanted an appendix.

It should be obvious that the most common stereotypic features of poverty, dirtiness, stupidity, ineptness, and vulgarity are not to be found in the stereotype of the Jew. By the same token, the principal mercenary and status-seeking elements of the Jewish stereotype are not to be found to any great extent in the Polack stereotype. Interestingly enough, the folk has its own comparison of the Jew and Polack stereotypes. One version of the common, **What are the three shortest books in the world?** has the answer: *Italian War Heroes, Jewish Business Ethics,* and *The Polish Mind.* A similar contrast is afforded by the following cross-breed riddles: **What do you get when you cross a black with a Polack? A retarded janitor.** (Here we find the Polish trait of low mental ability coupled with a menial occupational trait of the black stereotype.) **What do you get when you cross a black with a Jew? You still get a janitor, but he owns the building.**

One possible reason for the popularity of the Polack (or Italian) joke cycle is that it takes the heat off the black. Lower-class whites are not militant and do not constitute a threat to middle-class white America. White jokes involving stereotypes of blacks had to become more and more disguised, as overt "Rastus and Liza" jokes yielded to elephant jokes and "colored" riddles involving (g)rapes.[26] With the Polack cycle, it is the lower class, not blacks, that provides the outlet for aggression and the means of feeling superior. The examples make it quite clear that the folk do differentiate stereotypes. While there will always be floating slurs or numskull tales that may be attached to almost any group, there are also definite constellations or clusters of character traits contained in folk stereotypes.

Despite the clearcut pejorative cast of nearly all the ethnic slurs, most of the slurs are told and enjoyed by members of the group concerned. Jews help perpetuate the stereotype of the Jew and, perhaps to a lesser extent, Polish-Americans tell Polack jokes. This may be partly because ethnic slurs are part of ethnic identity. While many may protest that the slurs are nothing but false caricatures, they may secretly take pleasure in the fact that their group is vital enough to stimulate such traditions. Then again, it is also possible that the stereotypes may have some basis in ethnographic fact. If Jews are at all materialistic, do stress family solidarity, and are ambitious in terms of the careers of their children, then these slurs reinforce the group's value system.

Whether the stereotypes are accurate or not, they exist. And it may be very important to know what a group thinks it is like, just as it is important to know what other groups think a group is like. These traditional self-images and images held by other groups may even be more important than how the group actually is. If a fat boy believes that fat boys are jolly or if he thinks that other people think that fat boys are jolly, then he may force himself to play a jolly role. This is why the study of group images is essential. If so, then to the extent that such images are transmitted and perpetuated by folklore, the task of analysis definitely falls within the province of the professional folklorist.

No doubt some will argue that the study of ethnic slurs may serve no other purpose than to increase the circulation of such slurs and by so doing unwittingly assist the rise of further ethnic and racial prejudice. However, a more realistic view would be that the slurs are used by the folk whether the folklorist studies them or not. Most children in the United States hear these slurs fairly early in their public school careers. Therefore, an open discussion of the slurs and an objective analysis of the stereotypes they contain can do no harm and might possibly do a great deal of good in fighting bigotry and prejudice. Only by knowing and recognizing folk stereotypes can children be taught to guard against them so that they may better judge individuals on an individual basis.

CHAPTER 10

Polish Pope Jokes

On October 16, 1978, Cardinal Karol Wojtyla, archbishop of Krakow, became the first Polish Pope in history and the first non-Italian to hold the office in more than 450 years. Within days or even hours of the announcement of the news, folklore was created in the form of additions to the previously existing Polish joke cycle. This disappointed the many Polish-Americans who had very much hoped that the prestigious election of a Polish Pope would "end the respectability of Polish jokes."[1]

The Polish joke cycle has been reasonably well documented by professional folklorists[2] and has been attacked by Michael Novak in his 1976 *Newsweek* essay, "The Sting of Polish Jokes," for its demeaning of Polish-Americans. Novak suggested that Southern and Eastern Europeans in the United States are "subject to the last respectable bigotry," and he deplored the Polish joke cycle's adverse impact on the self-image of Polish-Americans, who are forced to grow up hearing endless and mindless repetitions of the "dumb Polack" stereotype. He called for an end to "ethnic jokes of the inherently demeaning kind" (as opposed to jokes in which he claims all ethnic groups are equal and that are "truly amusing").[3] Novak's ideals are praiseworthy, but he is quite naive about the nature of *blason populaire* traditions, which as a genre are probably universal. Most such traditions are demeaning and they exist precisely for the reason Novak notes: namely, to make a majority feel superior to a minority. If ethnocentrism is a universal, then it is predictable that any one group will be able to express its uniqueness (and superiority) only at the expense of some other group, which must serve as foil or inferior. In any case, halting Polish jokes wouldn't solve the basic problem. Prejudice and stereotyping exist, with or without folklore. Folklore is a mirror of culture; it doesn't work to blame the mirror for the ugliness of the view. Breaking the mirror might destroy an image temporarily, but it would not change any of the essential features of the object mirrored. Ethnic humor is more of a symptom than a cause of ethnic stereotyping and ethnic prejudice, though it certainly contributes to the formation and perpetuation of deep-seated prejudice. The problem is that it's not possible to halt Polish jokes (or any other kind of jokes)—folklore thrives most in the face of conscious attempts to regulate and censor its content! The futility of the Polish-Americans' hope that the election of a Polish Pope would curtail or contain the Polish joke cycle was probably inevitable. Quite the opposite occurred—the election provided a fresh impetus for a new burst of creativity in the cycle.

The themes of the cycle—stupidity, ineptness, tastelessness, dirtiness, and so forth—remain consistent and appear to derive from an earlier anti-Polish joke cycle popular in Germany.[4] Polish jokes of the late 1970s demonstrate the same general themes as earlier texts. Representative recent texts include:

> Did you hear about the Polish jigsaw puzzle?
> It had one piece.

> Did you hear about the Polish fox in a trap?
> It chewed off three of its legs and was still caught.

> Did you hear about the Polish woman who tried to get an abortion because she didn't think the baby was hers?

> The abortion clinic's so popular in Warsaw that there's a two-year wait.

> Why don't Polish mothers nurse their babies?
> It hurts too much to boil their nipples.

> Did you hear about the Polish terrorist who was assigned to blow up a bus? He burned his lips [from the hot exhaust pipe].

> Did you hear about the Polack who thought his wife was trying to do away with him? He opened the medicine chest and saw a bottle labelled "polish remover."

> Why did five Polacks push a house down the street?
> They were jumpstarting the furnace.

Did you hear about the five Polacks who were sent to the basement of a house on a rat-control mission? Two got purple hearts and three got war brides.

Did you hear about the Polish lesbian?
She does it with men.

One of the earliest Polish Pope jokes concerned his election. Do you know how the college of Cardinals selected the new Pope? They took a poll. In a variant, the cardinals convene and one of them says, "Let's take a poll" whereupon the Polish cardinal yells "I accept." This variant actually is a better illustration of the basic cycle, as it involves a Pole's misunderstanding of a word. Another joke that circulated widely within the first day or two of the announcment of the Pope's election was: Did you hear what the Pope's first big decision was? To wallpaper the Sistine chapel. Incidentally, this joke and others were frequently told by Catholics (though not of Polish descent). In a later joke, they asked the Polish Pope whether he thought priests should marry. His response: "Only if they're in love."

An early joke that exemplified the alleged propensity for blundering ineptitude was: Did you hear about the new Pope's first miracle? He made a lame man blind. Variant answers include: He made a cripple blind, He made a blind man lame, He made a blind man walk and a lame man see, and He turned a blind man deaf. There are other Polish Pope miracle jokes, for example, He turned wine into water, and He cured a ham.

One miracle refers to bowling. Did you hear about the Pope's new miracle? He bowled 305. A perfect game, that is, the maximum score possible in bowling, is 300. The same association is equally evident in: Why doesn't the Pope say Mass on Tuesdays and Thursdays? They're his bowling nights. (The implication here is that bowling is somehow understood to be a sport enjoyed by the "lower class.")

Perhaps the most interesting Polish Pope jokes articulate the folk's perception of the Italians' presumed unhappiness with the election of a non–Italian. Did you hear the new Polish Pope's opening prayer? "Hail Mary full of Grace, the dago came in second place." (In other versions, "Italian" and "wop" are substituted for "dago.") But if the Italians don't like the Polish Pope, the feeling in mutual. The new Pope called his mother and said, "Mama, I have good news and bad news for you. What do you want to hear first?" she says, "Son, first let your mama hear the good news." "I've been named Pope, mama!" he exclaimed. "Wonderful, my son. I'm so proud of you!" Her voice dropped. "But what's the bad news?" "Mama," he said, "I have to live in an Italian neighborhood." The Italian–Polish rivalry is also reflected in Did you hear that the Pope got a new helicopter? You see, the old one went "wop, wop, wop, wop." Do you know what the new one will sound like? "P-lock, P-lock, P-lock, P-lock." This is clearly an update of the older joke, How to tell a Polish car? Its wheels go "po-lack, po-lack, polack."[5] This text makes fun of both Italians and Poles, a combination found in non-Pope jokes as well. A cross-breed riddle, for example, merges two stereotypes: Did you hear about the man who had an Italian father and Polish mother? He made himself an offer he couldn't understand. Another Polish Pope joke that ridicules both groups was collected from an Italian-American male informant. Before the Pope could be elected, he was told that he would have to perform a miracle, so he set out to do it. When he came back and said he had done it, they asked him, "Well, what was the miracle you performed?" and he said, "I built a bridge over the Sinai Desert." They said, "Hell, you're never going to get elected now! You're going to have to go back and tear it down!" And he said, "Tear it down? shit, there's already a thousand Italians fishing off it!" This last text is an interesting one. It has a number of possible implications. First, although the Pope was stupid enough to build a bridge over land, the Italians were even more stupid in trying to fish from it. Perhaps it hints that the blind faith of Italian Catholicism will lead Italians to follow a blind leader such as a Polish pope without questioning his acts. If a pope builds a bridge, then one can fish from it, by definition. (One early Polish Pope joke consisted simply of, There goes the myth of papal infallibility.[6]) Of course, the joke also expresses the hope that the new Pope may be able to build a bridge between Arabs and Jews in the Middle East and thus ensure peace in that troubled area.

There are other Polish Pope joke texts. For example, You know, Pope John Paul the second thinks he's the eleventh. This is based on the notion that a Pole couldn't distinguish between the Roman numeral two (II) and the conventional numeral eleven (11). But the above examples should suffice to illustrate this innovative continuation of the Polish joke cycles. It is interesting that this joke cycle has sometimes become so generalized that it refers to American foreign policy: Do you know how Poland would have handled the Viet Nam war? Same way we did. No doubt the creation of further texts will depend somewhat on the future events of the current papacy and how John Paul II responds to them. Folklorists interested in ethnic humor should take advantage of this unique opportunity to observe the interplay between historical events and folklore — in this instance, an ethnic joke cycle.

CHAPTER 11

Many Hands Make Light Work, or Caught in the Act of Screwing in Light Bulbs

Folklorists never lack data. Not only is there the accumulation of folklore from centuries past, but new folklore is constantly being created in response to each succeeding generation's social and psychological needs. The distressing feature of folkloristics — the scientific study of folklore — is that new folklore is not any better understood than old. Even though modern folklorists can virtually observe an element of folklore at its moment of inception, they seem able to do little more than report its existence. Folklorists somehow cannot bring themselves to depart from the longstanding tradition of merely describing. What is needed, of course, is description *and analysis.* Granted that it is much easier to describe than to interpret, but that is no excuse really for the dearth of analytic commentary on folklore old and new.

Among the dozens and dozens of Polack jokes so popular in the late 1960s and 1970s, one particular text asked: **How many Polacks does it take to screw in a light bulb? Five — one to hold the bulb and four to turn the ceiling (chair, ladder, house).** William M. Clements indicates that the Indiana University Folklore Archieves contained more than twenty versions of this joke.[1] And this joke, in turn, was simply one of many purportedly commenting on the physical ineptitude and stupidity of Polacks.[2]

What is of special interest is that apparently this single joke provided a model or impetus for a whole new cycle of jokes, all based on the initial formulaic question, **How many _____s does it take to screw in a light bulb?** This leads to speculation on the possible genetic interrelationships of joke cycles. Just as the light bulb cycle may have spun off from the Polack joke cycle, so the Polack cycle may, in turn, have derived from some earlier cycle.[3] It's worth wondering what new joke cycle, if any, may be inspired by one or more of the light bulb jokes.

By 1978 and 1979, the light bulb cycle had swept the country. By 1980, a short note on the subject appeared in the *Journal of American Folklore*, and a popular anthology of some forty texts entitled *How Many Zen Buddhists Does It Take to Screw in a Light Bulb?* was published.[4] The anthology contains texts only (accompanied by cartoon illustrations) and ends by inviting readers to "join the newest and fastest-growing joke craze since the Knock, Knock!" by sending in additional examples of the genre. Judith B. Kerman's note, "The Light-Bulb Jokes: Americans Look at Social Action Processes," presents some of the better-known light bulb jokes and concludes by asking why the cycle came into being. Kerman claims the answer is complicated and suggests that complex social movements and decision-making in the 1980's "call for comment" (presumably, the joke cycle is a response to that call). She also argues that the underlying impulse behind the formation of such jokes may "be more a matter of esthetics." However, these vague notions do not explain at all why the particular metaphor of screwing in light bulbs was selected as a paradigm for social commentary. Why wasn't one of the many other available Polack (and other) riddling jokes used as the datum for a new cycle? In short, what is the significance, if any, of the choice of the act of screwing in light bulbs as the basis of a series of jokes?

The original (?) Polack joke reflected a stereotype, namely, that Poles or Polish-Americans are stupid — that is, not too *bright*. Inasmuch as an illuminated light bulb is a standard popular iconographic symbol for "idea" — as found, for example, in comic strips — it makes a certain amount of sense for a Polack to be unable to screw in a light bulb, (to be unable to come up with a bright idea). But the attribute of stupidity is *not* necessarily part of the stereotypic features normally associated with the various groups named in the light bulb jokes. **How many WASPs (White Anglo-Saxon Protestants) does it take to change a light bulb? Two. One to mix martinis and the other to call an electrician.** The WASP is not stupid but rather is above carrying out such menial tasks as changing a light bulb. Instead he pours himself a drink and pays for a high-priced specialist to come to perform a simple household chore that he could easily do himself.

In ethnic slurs based upon a common action, the stereotype is supposedly revealed in the manner in which the action is carried out. So the only variable in the first line of each joke is the name of the group being pasquinaded. The principal variation occurs in the "answer" to the joking question. In this way, we are told that Californians are "laid back," New Yorkers are rude, and so on. Here are a number of groups and their stereotypic activity:

> "How many _____ does it take to change a light bulb?"

> Californians: "Ten. One to screw it in and nine others to share the experience."[5]

> New Yorkers: "Three. One to do it and two to criticize." (Or, "None of your fucking business!")

> Pennsylvanians: "None. You just hold it up and it glows by itself" (referring to the Three Mile Island nuclear facility and its radiation crisis).

> Democrats: "Thirty. One representative from every social/economic group."

> Republicans: "Three. One to change the bulb, and two to see how good the old one was."

> Graduate students: "Only one, but it takes nine years." (Or, "Depends on the size of the grant"; "Two, and a professor to take the credit"; "Could you repeat the question, please.")

> Football players: "One, but eleven get credit for it."

> Law students: "Six. One to change it and five to file an environmental impact report."

> Pre-med students: "Three. One to stand on a stool to screw it in and two to kick the stool out from under him."

> Gay men: "Five. One to screw in the Art Deco light bulb and four to stand back and yell 'Fabulous!'" (or "Marvelous!")

> Feminists: "That's not funny." (Or, "Five. One to do it and four to write about it"; "Five. One to change the bulb,

> two to discuss the violation of the socket, and two to secretly wish that they were that socket.")

Psychiatrists: "Only one, but the light bulb has to really want to change."

Zen Buddhists: "Two, One to screw it in and one to not screw it in." (Or, "Two. One to screw it in and one to unscrew it.")

Jews: "So how many Jews does it take to change a light bulb?"

J.A.P.s [Jewish American Princesses]: "One who refuses, saying, 'What, and ruin my nail polish?'" (Or, "Two. One to call her father and the other to open a can of Diet Pepsi.")

Jewish mothers: "None. So I'll sit here in the dark."

Blacks: "Hey man, whussa lightbulb?"

Mexicans: "Ask me *mañana, señor*, if you still want to know."

These are representative, although the list is not exhaustive. For example, several texts have been aimed at the Iranians to vent anger over the unwarranted seizure of more than fifty American citizens housed in the U.S. Embassy in Iran:

Ayatollahs: "None, they didn't have light bulbs in the thirteenth century."

Beverly Hills real estate agents: "Fourteen. One to screw it in and thirteen to learn Farsi."

Iranians: "One hundred. One to screw it in and ninety-nine to hold the house hostage."

In a joke about the joke cycle, the Iranians are also featured. The *Village Voice* in New York City ran a light bulb joke contest. First prize was $200. The winning joke was sent in by the Iranians: "How many Iranians does it take to screw in a light bulb? You send us the prize money and we'll tell you the answer."

Having sampled the tradition, we remain in the dark about why the act of screwing in light bulbs should have been selected as a base metaphor for a joke cycle. I believe the efficacy of the metaphor turns on the word "screw." To screw is a common slang term for sexual intercourse. And this very usage is found in the light bulb cycle itself. In one version of How many Californians does it take to screw in a lightbulb? the answer is: None. They screw in hot tubs (or Jacuzzis). (In Northern California, this same joke is told about Marin County residents, rather than Californians.) In another light bulb joke, How many Lilliputians does it take to screw in a light bulb? the answer is, Two. You just put them in a light bulb and let them do it. The published anthology offers What's the difference between a pregnant woman and a light bulb? You can unscrew the light bulb! and How many mice does it take to screw in a light bulb? Two (with a drawing of two mice engaged in intercourse—in a human face-to-face position).

The underlying sexual nature of the light bulb joke cycle suggests that the jokes are essentially about impotence. Sexual impotence is a common enough theme of oral (and written) humor. Certainly, some of the light bulb jokes have more to do with delineating alleged stereotypic features of various groups than with anything else, but the basic premise that a person has trouble screwing in a light bulb has a definite sexual connotation. In addition to the nuances of the verb "screw," there is also the phrase, "turn on." To "turn on" means to become emotionally aroused, either through drugs or through sexual attraction. Thus someone who needs help in "turning on" a light by "screwing" a bulb into a light socket is someone who is sexually inept. This double sense of "screwing in light bulbs" is explicitly signalled in the "They screw in hot tubs" text above, as well as in the feminist text treating the violation of the socket.

Most of the stereotypes delineated in the light bulb cycle are not new. The cutthroat competition surrounding admission into medical schools, which causes students to actually sabotage fellow students' experiments in chemistry labs in order to finish higher on the class grade curve is a sad fact of undergraduate academic life. The spoiled daughter of indulgent Jewish parents who is unduly concerned with her appearance (nail polish, slimness) and the aggressive rudeness of New Yorkers predate the light bulb cycle. This cycle simply utilized already existing stereotype traditions in American culture. And inasmuch as the light bulb joke itself already existed in the Polack joke cycle, the "new" cycle consists of "recycled" older forms and content. Still, the Iranian texts are new, sparked by American shame and fury over the Iranian government's holding American citizens hostage for billions of dollars. And the articulation of older stereotypes in the light bulb joke format also represents something new. Folklorists are accustomed to seeing endless combinations of new and old elements in a given item of folklore.

But one question is why the light bulb cycle came to be so popular at the end of the 1970s. The sexual significance of screwing (assuming that this interpretation is valid) does not in itself explain why the cycle arose when it did. As far as fears of sexual impotence are concerned, it could theoretically have arisen at any time. That is hardly a new anxiety peculiar to the late 1970s. My hunch is that the cycle is about power, or the lack thereof. Power in modern times depends upon having sufficient energy resources. Americans began to fear that rising oil prices and/or diminishing oil supplies would severely decrease energy supplies, ranging from gasoline for automobiles to heating oil for homes or electricity for household appliances. The question became, "Will there be enough 'power' to go around?" The burgeoning pressures of increasing population growth around the world suggest that there may well be energy shortages in years to come, just as there are shortages of food and housing now in many parts of the globe. Modern society, with its inevitable bureaucracy, has made it increasingly difficult to carry out even the simplest tasks. A maze of rules and requirements must be fulfilled before a need can be met. As we become more and more specialized in our work, more and more intermediaries intervene in the chain of events between a need and the fulfillment of that need. Whether one calls an electrician to change a light bulb or has to wait until an environmental impact report has been filed before changing a bulb, the upshot is the same. The "deferred reward" philosophy remains in effect—one must wait for the light. The Iranians' seizure of American citizens confirms Americans' sense of a lack of power. And the fact that the Iranian government (as opposed to terrorists) demanded exorbitant sums (such as $24 billion) before releasing the hostages could have been easily construed as an attempt by Iran to "screw" the United States!

Historically, American society has had a positive attitude toward change: change is a good thing in a worldview system that places a high premium on progress. And Americans are impatient with the slowness of other societies with respect to change. Yet as the United States becomes enmeshed in more and more webs of conflicting legislation, it becomes harder and harder to implement change. And so it seems to the average American that it has become increasingly difficult for an individual to effect change—social change, political change, technological change, and so on. Groups, not individuals, appear to have become the agents of change. So we can understand the inflation of numbers with respect to how many people (of a particular group) it takes to change a light bulb. In theory, one person can change a light bulb; in practice, it may take more than one to carry out the task.

If this analysis is at all valid, we may better understand the popularity of the light bulb jokes. On one hand, they reflect the age-old theme of sexual impotence, a metaphor that lends itself easily to minority groups seeking power. On the other hand, they may reflect a widespread malaise that Americans share about energy supplies and the power that comes from energy. Such simple necessities as cheap gasoline and electricity, once taken for granted, are now in some jeopardy. Without electricity, we will all be unable to screw in lightbulbs to any useful purpose. We shall all join the Jewish mother who complainingly sits in the dark. Add to this the American concern about losing political power in the world and about the individual's losing power to control his or her own destiny, and we can see other reasons why the cycle might have mass appeal. We should not be misled by the presence of particular groups named in the cycle; for when we joke about the impotence of others, we are joking about our own potential lack of power.

CHAPTER 12

Misunderstanding Humor: An American Stereotype of the Englishman

The folk evidently believe (or at least want us to believe) that different nationalities may be distinguished by their alleged ability or inability to understand humor. Social psychologists may be even more interested than folklorists in whether there are definable distinctions in national or ethnic "senses of humor."[1] But folklore, if not folklorists, offers ample data for anyone intrigued by the question. A typical American version of a standard joke compares French, English, German, and Jewish senses of humor.

> When a Frenchman hears a story, he always laughs three times: first when he hears it, second when you explain it to him, and third when he understands. That is because a Frenchman likes to laugh.
>
> When you tell a joke to an Englishman, he laughs twice: once when you tell it and a second time when you explain it to him. He will never understand it, he is too stuffy.
>
> When you tell a joke to a German, he only laughs once, when you tell it to him. He won't let you explain it to him because he is too arrogant. Also, Germans have no sense of humor.
>
> When you tell a joke to a Jew—before you finish it, he interrupts you. First, he has heard it before; second, you are not telling it right; and third, he ends up telling you the story the way it should be told.

Certainly there is a legitimate question as to whether this joke about responses to jokes describes national character or national stereotypes. It is not clear whether the comment on the Englishman, "He will never understand it, he is too stuffy," truly epitomizes an actual problem the English have in comprehending jokes, particularly jokes told by American raconteurs. But the very existence of this particular joke, as well as others that appear later in this chapter, strongly suggests that Americans consistently *perceive* the English as unable to understand American humor. Even if the focus is only with a national stereotype and not national character, it still points to an important facet of the American image of the Englishman—a facet that requires explanation. Why do Americans portray Englishmen as having difficulty in understanding American jokes?

Before addressing the issue, let us briefly document the existence of the stereotype. Perhaps the most striking illustrations of the American depiction of the Englishman's inability to understand a joke told him come from what W. Carew Hazlitt's *Studies in Jocular Literature* called the "marred anecdote."[2] In the marred anecdote, A tells a joke to B and later, when B attempts to repeat the joke to C, he gets a critical part of it wrong, thereby completely ruining the joke. What we have is a double structure. First there is the original joke; second there is the botched retelling of the initial text, which constitutes a separate joke. Such a double structure is reminiscent of the unsuccessful repetition pattern so common in folktales in which an evil sister, brother, or dupe attempts in vain to replicate an earlier rewarding activity carried out by the tale's protagonist.[3]

In Hazlitt's examples, the joketellers have no national identifications. Typical is the account in which one scholar laughs at another because the latter's garment is too short. The second scholar responds by remarking that "it would be *long enough* before he got another." The first scholar has occasion to repeat the response to a third party, varying it just slightly, but enough—as Hazlitt says, "so as to give the deathblow to the witticism." "Jack," quoth he, "I've just heard a capital joke." "What is it?" "Why, I told Tom that his coat was too short, and he answered that it would be a *long time* before he got another." "Well, I don't see anything in that." "Ah! well," returned the first, "it seemed a very good joke when he made it."[4] Another illustration given by Hazlitt concerns an Archbishop Herring who fell into a ditch near St. John's College. A passing wag called out, "There, Herring, you are in a fine pickle now!" A Johnian, overhearing this, went back to his college, and was asked by some of his friends what made hims so merry. "Oh," says he, "I never met such a good story before. Herring of Jesus [College] fell into the ditch, and an acquaintance said, as he lay sprawling, 'There, Herring, you are in a fine *condition* now.'" "Well," observed someone, "where is the wit in that?" "Nay," replied the first, "I am sure it was an excellent thing when I heard it."[5]

These illustrations from Hazlitt should serve to demonstrate the basic joke type. They also show that the type exists without the Englishman necessarily being the butt of the joke. Hazlitt's study was published in 1890. Charles C. Bombaugh's 1905 *Facts and Fancies for the Curious from the Harvest-Fields of Literature* has a section entitled "Missing the Point of Jokes," with a dozen examples of the genre. None of them has any mention of an Englishman misunderstanding an American joke.[6] This strongly suggests that the tradition of making the Englishman the butt of the marred anecdote cycle may be a twentieth-century innovation.

Let us now consider some representative texts of the most recent cycle. Evan Esar's 1952 treatise, *The Humor of Humor*, gives one of the classic instances:[7]

> A British visitor was admiring an American canning factory. The superintendent, showing him about, said in jest: "In spite of everything you've heard, we're really economical here in America. This plant proves it. We eat all we can, and all we can't we can." The Englishman looked puzzled. But that evening while dining with an American friend, he suddenly saw the point and burst out laughing. "What is it?" asked his friend. "I'm laughing at the wit of you Americans," said the Englishman. "The superintendent of the canning factory I visited this morning said something rather amusing to me. He said: 'We eat all we're able to, and all we're not we tin."

The joke plays in part upon one of the many differences between English and American usage: "can" versus "tin." Britons talk of a tin of peaches and a tin-opener.[8] It also displays another feature of the stereotype, the Englishman's delayed "understanding" of the joke. In the same vein are such texts as, Why don't you tell an Englishman any jokes on Saturday night? So he won't laugh in church or the variant: How do you make an Englishman laugh on Saturday? Tell him a joke on Wednesday. Of course, in the can–tin joke, the Englishman is portrayed as thinking that he understands the American joke. The joke is that he has totally misunderstood the original wordplay.

A number of other texts invariably show how the Englishman comes to America, hears a joke, and later blunders when he attempts to retell it, usually after his return to England. The following exemplify the pattern:

> A man named Strange dies. According to his wishes, he is buried under a blank tombstone. People walk by, see the blank tombstone, and say, "That's strange." Each visitor to the town would be shown the stone and told the story. An Englishman saw it, heard the story, and recounts the incident to friends upon his return to England: A man named Strange dies. According to his wishes, he is buried under a blank tombstone. People would walk by, see the blank tombstone, and say "How very peculiar!"[9]

> A good-looking young lady was sitting on a park bench one Sunday morning. As she sat there communing with nature, three men passed by. Each one tipped his hat and said good morning as he passed. The men that passed by were a pedestrian, an equestrian, and a motorist. Which one knew her? Of course, the horse manure [horseman knew her]. An Englishman heard the joke and thought it was jolly good, and he decided to tell it to his friends. All went well until he got to the answer. He explained that "the equestrian was the one who was acquainted with the young lady" and started to laugh. When he saw that no one else got the point, he stopped laughing and said, "Don't you get the point? It was the equestrian. You know, the answer is horse shit."[10]

> An Englishman was at a dinner party and his host, while carving a boiled tongue, inadvertently knocked it off the table into his guest's lap. He immediately said, *"Lapsus linguae"* (slip of the tongue) and it raised such a laugh that the Englishman wished to repeat it. He purposely knocked the meat into somebody's lap at his next dinner party, saying "Lapsus linguae." However, nobody laughed. It was leg of lamb.[11]

Sometimes the Englishman misremembers other folklore genres such as toasts, limericks, and riddles. Consider, for example, the following variant of a traditional, Oedipal toast.[12]

An Irishman, upon meeting an Englishman, said, "Here's a little story:
'Here's to the sweetest days of my life
Spent in the arms of another man's wife . . .
   my mother.'"
The Englishman then encountered a Frenchman and said, "Here's a little story:
'Here's to the sweetest days of my life,
Spent in the arms of another man's wife . . .
   but I can't remember who she was.'"

One of the very best known examples of the marred anecdote tradition involving an Englishman includes a limerick.

An Englishman was told a limerick in America. It went like this:
There once was a fellow named Skinner
Who invited his girl friend to dinner,
They started to dine
At a quarter past nine
And by ten thirty-five, it was in 'er.
(Not the dinner, but Skinner).
He was terribly amused and determined to share it with the boys in the pub back home. Arriving there later, he said, "Hey old chaps, I heard a jolly good one in the States. Let's see if I can get it straight. . . .
'There once was a chap named . . . uh . . . Tupper,
(That's right, Tupper) . . .
Who invited his lady to supper,
They sat down and ate
At a quarter past eight,
And by nine forty-two it was up 'er . . .
er . . . not the supper . . . not Tupper . . .
but some bloody bloke named Skinner!'"[13]

If toasts and limericks can be botched by the visiting Englishman, so also can riddles.

There was an international convention being held in one of the large New York City hotels. During one of the breaks, an Englishman was wandering around the lobby and began talking to a bellhop (hotel porter, in English usage). During the conversation the bellhop said, "I have a riddle for you: I am the son of my father and the father of my son. Who am I?" The Englishman thought for a while and then said, "Blimey, you've really got me stumped on that one. I give up. Who are you?" The bellhop replied, "I'm me!" The Englishman broke up: "By George, that's really good, extremely funny." A few months later the same Englishman was back in England and talking with some of his colleagues there, telling of his trip to America. "While I was in America I really heard a funny one. I bet you can't figure this one out: I am the son of my father and the father of my son. Who am I?" His friends thought for a while and they finally said that they couldn't figure it out. So he quickly replied, "Well, strange as it may seem, I am a bell-hop in the lobby of a New York hotel."[14]

These examples should suffice to indicate the general nature of the tradition in the United States. The question is, why did the tradition arise and what possible functions does it serve? I believe we may answer the question by using the concepts of reciprocal stereotypes and projective inversion.

Most scholars are familiar enough with ethnic or national stereotypes, how members of group A perceive members of group B. What is less well studied is what I am calling reciprocal stereotypes—integrally related, mutually reinforcing stereotypes held by each of two groups about the other. For example, the English perceive the Americans as culturally inferior[15] and the Americans perceive the English as culturally superior. Or the English view the Americans as exaggeration-prone, and the Americans view the English as favoring understatement. One can probably find instances of reciprocal stereotypes among any two groups who are in contact. For example, the English see the French as good lovers and good cooks, while the French see the English as poor lovers and poor cooks.[16] Not all stereotypes are necessarily part of a reciprocal pair. In an asymmetrical stereotype, A's view of B is not matched by a converse or inverse view of A held by B.

Stereotypes, whether national or ethnic, do not occur in a vacuum. Rather they are historically and semantically related to other stereotypes. Accordingly, it should come as no surprise to discover that A's stereotype of B may be related in terms of content to B's stereotype of A. In the present context, remember that the United States began its existence as a group of colonies of Great Britain. England was the authority figure, the superordinate power, the supreme arbiter of taste and fashion. America was the dependent variable, the subordinate, the follower rather than the leader. It has taken several centuries for America to try to overcome its longstanding national inferiority complex, especially vis-à-vis Europe in general and England in particular. Mark Twain wrote entertainingly about the American in a European setting—*A Connecticut Yankee at King Arthur's Court* and *Innocents Abroad* (note the title!). Henry James, as well as other men of letters and artists, felt they had to go to Europe to learn their trade. Americans were content enough with their rapidly developing technology and their rising standard of living, but for "civilization" and "culture," they tended to be embarrassed by Americanisms, preferring instead to ape the "superior" intellectuals of Europe. Even in the late twentieth century, many Americans continue to look to Europe for trends in art, wine, and literature. American literature, for example, is rarely a department of its own—like French literature, Italian literature, Spanish literature, and so on—but rather occupies a small niche in the English department, where the works of Chaucer, Shakespeare, and Milton hold sway. In short, it remains a colony in the empire. The position of American literature (and American studies generally) at American institutions of higher learning demonstrates the difficulty in changing the self-deprecatory attitudes of Americans toward their own culture. The same pattern is discernible in American folklore scholarship. Ballad scholars, for example, devoted far more energy to collecting, classifying, and analyzing English and Scottish ballads than to ballads indigenous to the United States.

The English view of Americans is well documented, thanks to numerous travellers' accounts by such writers as Frances Trollope and Charles Dickens.[17] The relevant reciprocal stereotypes appear to be the English view of Americans as naïve innocents, incapable of understanding the intricacies of world events and the subtleties of the English language, and the Americans' view of the English (or at least the upper-class English) as urbane sophisticates who are worldly wise and masters of nuance and stylistic complexities of spoken and written English. Margaret Mead's remarkable comparative essay on American and English national character recounted questions repeatedly raised by Americans: "Why is it the British always insist on their own way in international affairs and we always lose?" and "Why do the British pull the wool over American eyes?"[18] Mead noted that Americans tend to arrange objects on a single scale of value, from best to worst, biggest to smallest, cheapest to most expensive ". . . and that Americans tended to ask about every piece of English behavior 'Is it better or worse than ours?'"[19]

It is true that Americans as a nation want to be number one. Whether it is "winning" the Olympics (in terms of amassing the greatest number of gold medals) or winning the nuclear rearmament race (with the Soviet Union), Americans dread the thought of being second best. Members of winning American football teams hold up one finger for the television camera, signifying "We're number one" "Winning isn't everything; it's the only thing." The American insistence on rank-ordering absolutely everything from best-selling books, popular songs, boxing contenders, football teams, industrial corporations, to academic departments (nearly every self-respecting university department claims to be among the top five or ten in the nation) is a deep-seated facet of American national character.

If Americans want to be number one but feel that they are inferior to Europeans in many areas of creativity, what can they do about it? One possibility is boasting. A common mask for feelings of inferiority is braggadocio, and it is no accident that American culture enjoys the "bigger and better" theme. (And as Americans brag to conceal their feelings of inferiority toward Europe, so Texans and Californians brag to conceal their feelings of inferiority toward the eastern seaboard.) Anyone who thinks he constantly has to prove how superior he is clearly has a serious inferiority complex. Americans have had an inferiority complex from the beginning of their history as English colonies, and this inferiority complex has not yet disappeared.

If the Americans' poor self-image consists in part of feeling like poor imitations of the English, then we can understand why in American folklore it is the English who are depicted as poor imitators of American culture. Projective inversion allows the subject and object in a relationship to be transposed.[20] Thanks to this simple transformational device, it is not the Americans who cannot speak proper King's or Queen's English, but it is the English visitor to the United States who is incapable of understanding American English.[21]

The emergence of the marred anecdote cycle with the Englishman featured as dupe seems to have occurred around or shortly after World War I. (The war also provided an opportunity for increased contact between the Americans and the English.) If so, then it likely accompanied the rise of America as a world power — and the gradual decline of England as a world power. On the other hand, I am not persuaded that the jokes reflect historical accuracy. We are dealing with national stereotypes. The English are not humorless nor are they incapable of understanding American culture. In one sense, it is irrelevant whether the British actually look down on Americans. What is important is that Americans *think* that the English look down at Americans.[22]

Is the marred anecdote cycle likely to continue in American folklore? If my analysis is sound, then, I speculate, it will. It is likely that Americans will continue to prefer the English pronunciation of English (especially upper-class accents) to any of the available prestigious accents in the United States, including the cultivated New England and southern accents. (The pride of American educational television consists of mostly BBC productions on Masterpiece Theatre, introduced by the dulcet tones of suave Alistair Cooke.) I'm not sure the Cadillac has replaced the Rolls Royce, that the American President has more splendor than the King or Queen of England, or that Harvard and Yale outrank Oxford and Cambridge. So long as Americans remain bothered by the nagging underlying feeling (due, in part, from the historical beginnings of America) that American culture (education, language, international diplomatic skills) is second to English culture, the popularity of the marred anecdote cycle featuring the Englishman in the second portion of the jokes will probably continue.

CHAPTER 13

Laughter Behind the Iron Curtain: A Sample of Rumanian Political Jokes

Americans, like other Westerners, have definite if stereotypic ideas about the evils of socialism and communism. Most of these value judgments have been formed on the basis of indirect sources, ranging from films and newspaper reports to outright patriotic propaganda. Relatively few Americans have had direct experience living under a socialist or communist regime, and most rely on second-hand sources. These sources clearly are the products of differing points of view. One author of a given article on modern life in Rumania may be sympathetic to the Rumanian government, while another may give a report independent of the government's position on the subject.

Frequently, allusions to the writings of political idols seem contrived, and it is not at all clear whether lip service is being rendered so that the article may be published or whether the author honestly believes in the infallible wisdom of the political idol(s) in favor at a given point in time. In any event, one wonders if it is possible to bypass individual reporters to get right at the people who live in countries behind the Iron Curtain and to discover what they think of the political system that governs them. Since internal published criticisms of any regime in power are extremely rare, to say the least, it is not easy for Americans to learn just how popular or unpopular socialism/communism is among the peoples of Rumania and the other countries of Eastern Europe.

There *is* one source of information about popular attitudes toward politics in Iron Curtain countries, which may be considered more or less unimpeachable: folklore. Folklore, which is passed on primarily by word of mouth, from person to person offers little opportunity for official censorship to be exercised. The mouth of the folk cannot be closed, as it were, and in the various manifestations of oral literature, the folk invariably have their say.

Of all the important forms of folklore in the modern world, none is more powerful than the joke. It thrives in cities; and as urbanization increases around the world, urban folklore, including jokelore, also increases. The content of jokes is as varied as humanity itself, but one favorite subject (along with sex and religion) is politics. A country's political jokes contain caricature to be sure. But behind the extremes of exaggeration, one often finds a kernel of truth, or at least a genuine expression of sentiment. Political jokes in Iron Curtain countries frequently express what many individuals feel but dare not utter. Jokes are, by definition, impersonal. They provide a socially sanctioned frame that normally absolves individuals from any guilt that might otherwise result from conversational articulation of the same content. Thus, jokes provide a much-needed vent for emotion. Hypothetically, the more repressive the regime, the more jokes there will be about that regime. The following sampling of political humor, collected for the most part in Bucharest in late August 1969, illustrates how well jokes encapsulate popular attitudes.[1] It was not always easy for an American to collect political jokes in Rumania: Some people were reluctant to tell jokes to strangers. Informants usually spoke in low tones, after glancing about nervously to see if there were anyone else listening. Even ordinary conversations with strangers may be politically dangerous; one never knows what use may be made of the content of the conversation. A cardinal rule is therefore to know to whom one is speaking:

> **Two Rumanians are looking at a huge Cadillac parked outside the Athenee Palace (a large luxury hotel in downtown Bucharest). One says, "Look at that Volga (a well-known Russian make of car). Have you ever seen such a car?" The other says. "It's not a Volga; it's a Cadillac." The first continues, "Oh, look at the Volga with its chrome and its leather upholstery." The second says, "I've told you. It's not a Volga; it's a Cadillac." The first goes on, "It certainly is a magnificent Volga. Look at those white wall tires." The second, a bit angrily, says, "Look, stupid, I keep telling you. It's not a Volga; it's a Cadillac. It's obvious**

you don't know very much about cars." The first replies,
"I know plenty about cars but I don't know very much
about you!"

The same theme of knowing the identity of an addressee before
speaking freely is the subject of this Rumanian localization of a common joke found in many countries, including the United States:

> Two Rumanians are on a bus. One is sitting down.
> The other is standing, but he is standing on the first man's
> foot. The man sitting asks, "Are you a member of the
> Communist Party?"
> The man standing answers, "No, I'm not."
> The first man asks, "Are you in the military?"
> "No, I'm not."
> "You mean you don't work for the government in any
> capacity?"
> "No, I don't."
> "Then get the hell off my foot!"

It is particularly dangerous to tell political jokes, or at least so
it would seem from the following texts: There was a competition of
political joke-telling and do you know what the first prize was? 15 years.
(In another version, the answer is: third prize, 5,000 lei, (the basic
monetary unit of Rumanian currency); second prize, 3,000 lei; and first
prize, 5 years.) In the same vein is the report that there was a big canal
to be built. The left bank was to be built by those who told political jokes
and the right side by those who listened. (It is interesting inasmuch as
the Rumanians do use the "left–right" metaphor to express ideological
positions that the more serious crime, telling jokes, is punished by placing the guilty on the "left" side. It is also noteworthy that just listening to political jokes is also considered to be a crime.)

Some of the Rumanian political jokes are in the familiar What's
the difference between . . . form. For example, What's the difference between communism and capitalism? In capitalism, man exploits man. In
communism, it is vice versa. In another text, What is the difference between socialism and capitalism? Capitalism makes social mistakes (referring to the class system and other forms of social inequality) and socialism
makes capital [large] mistakes.

In terms of the contrast between capitalism and socialism, one thing
that immediately strikes an American visitor to Rumania, Yugoslavia,
Czechoslovakia, and other Eastern European countries is the slower

pace of life. In shops (most of which are owned by the state) or in restaurants, the service is poor, by American standards. It may take minutes to hours to get waited on and just as long to get the bill. An American explanation of the consistently indifferent and slow service might be that there is little incentive for salesmen to sell. The salary system is fixed by the state and is not affected by individual efforts. The people are well aware of this fundamental difference, in which individual initiative is rarely if ever rewarded. One revealing slogan in Rumania is: **Our country pretends to pay us and we pretend to work.** But even more impressive is the following text, in which the Rumanians appear to recognize how Rumanian working conditions must look to American eyes:

> **An American worker falls in love with a Rumanian girl and he takes a job in a factory in Bucharest. He comes each morning exactly when he is supposed to, he works very hard until ten, he eats his sandwich in fifteen minutes (this reflects the stereotype of Americans eating quickly) and continues his work. Around him, the other workers work as they always do. When payday comes, the American receives the normal amount (that is, the same as that given to all the workers) and he says, "I didn't participate in the strike so why am I given strike pay?"**

This joke suggests that Americans work hard while Rumanians do not. It is also an indictment of the low wage scale; the American, who mistakenly thinks his fellow workers have been on strike, complains of receiving only a token strike payment. In fact, it is the normal full paycheck.

Of all the current joke cycles in Rumania and elsewhere behind the Iron Curtain, surely one of the most popular concerns the alleged transmissions of an incredibly naive and outspoken radio station supposedly located in Soviet Armenia. One need only mention the phrase "Radio Erevan" to a Rumanian to elicit a suppressed grin or smile. There is, apparently, a real Radio Erevan (Erivan, Yerevan) in Soviet Armenia, but the raft of jokes attributed to it are purely apocryphal. The premise usually involves a listener's sending in a question, which Radio Erevan then attempts to answer. Sometimes the content is sexual. For example, **A listener asks whether drinking a glass of water can serve as a means of contraception. The answer is yes it can. The listener also wants to know whether it should be 'before' or 'after' intercourse. The answer is 'instead of.'** Another typical text, which seems to be especially popular, goes as follows: A listener asks Radio Erevan what should a pair of collectivist farmer newlyweds do on the first night of marriage not to dirty the bed? And our answer is "Wash their feet." (The innuendo is obviously that collectivist peasants are uncouth and dirty.) The combination of sexuality and politics in East European humor is not unusual. There is, for example, a Hungarian joke about little Moricka (Maurice), a clever Jewish schoolboy. In school one day, the teacher gives every child a picture of Marx. "Go home and put it somewhere, and tomorrow tell the class what you did with it," orders the teacher. The next day the teacher asks the children where they put their pictures. First he asks Johnny, and Johnny says that he put it in the kitchen. "Why?" asks the teacher. "So that Marx could see how well the workers eat in a socialist country." Next, the teacher asks Paul, and Paul says he put the picture right over his parent's closet. "Why?" asks the teacher. "So that Marx could see how well the workers dress in a socialist country." Next the teacher asks Moricka, who says he put the picture right over his parents' bed. "Why?" asks the teacher. "So that Marx could see how the workers of the world unite."

The purely political jokes in the Radio Erevan cycle are even more devastating. Here are two representative texts: A listener asks, "Dear Radio Erevan, would it be possible to introduce socialism into Switzerland [or, in some version, the United States]?" And our answer is: "Yes, it would be possible to introduce socialism into Switzerland, but it would be a pity." Another listener asks, "Dear Radio Erevan, would it be possible to introduce socialism into the Sahara?" And our answer is, "Yes, it would be possible to introduce socialism into the Sahara, but after the first five-year plan, the Sahara will have to import sand." Folk recognition of the importance of radio jokes is demonstrated by the following: Why has the radio reception recently been so bad? Because it is now transmitting from Magadan (in Siberia). Apparently, wayward radio stations, like troublesome individuals, can be banned to Siberia!

Some of the Rumanian jokes are not just about socialism in general, but about the Soviet Union in particular. One reason might be that Rumania is fundamentally a Romance culture and there are deep lines of resistance to what is perceived as a gradual but insidious process of "Slavicization" (for example, "yes" in Rumanian is the Russian "da"). One noticeable tendency is to make fun of the self-proclaimed great accomplishments of the Soviet Union. In the Rumanian version of the well-travelled joke about the international conference on the elephant, the books are as follows: The German writes a three-volume *Introduction to the Study of Elephants*. The French scholar publishes a small, perfumed leather-bound (with a ribbon attached) volume entitled *Les Amours des Elephants.* The Russian writes a two-volume work published by the Foreign Language Press, *Marx, Engels, Lenin, and Stalin on Elephants.* The Rumanian writes, *The Soviet Elephant, the Most Advanced Elephant in the World.* (In the American version of this joke, the final punch-line has the American delegate giving his communication on *How to Build a Bigger and Better Elephant.* In another Rumanian joke, there is a dwarf in New York, who lives on the 150th floor of a building, but he can reach only the fiftieth button in the elevator. Someone else must push the top button for him. In the Soviet Union, there is also a dwarf who lives on the 150th floor but he pushes the top button himself. Why? Because he's the greatest dwarf in the world!

Even the genuine accomplishments of the Soviet Union, such as the exploration of space, are put in perspective by the folk. An East German visits a friend in Moscow. A little girl answers the door. The East German asks her, "Where is your father?" "He is not home." "When will he be at home?" "At 8 hours, 40 minutes, and 23 seconds." "Where is he?" "He is going around the world 33½ times." "What about your mother? Is she at home?" "No she isn't." "When is she expected?" "I don't have any idea." "How come you know the hour, minute, and second when your father will return but you have no idea when your mother will return. Where is she?" "She is at the market in the line for meat." This slam at the Soviet space program, contrasting it with acute domestic problems (which include very long lines in shops and critical item scarcities), is strikingly similar to some American criticisms of the U.S. space effort.

It is probably not entirely accidental that an East German was a character in the preceding joke. East Germans seem to be regarded by some Rumanians as excessively adamant with respect to political ideology. (This attitude may ultimately be related to Rumanian memories of their unfortunate alliance with Germany in early World War II.) The following text also has to do with East German and Russian ideology. An East German was asked, "Have you any Stalinists in your country?" He replied, "I shall give you the same answer that a cannibal from Malaysia gave when he was asked, 'Have you cannibals?' 'No,' he answered, 'we ate the last cannibal yesterday.'" (The equation of Stalinism with its purges to cannibalism is interesting and possibly even a fairly accurate metaphor. In any case, the joke suggests that the Rumanians think that the East Germans are specially prone to be Stalinists.)

Other commentaries on the quality of life in the Soviet Union and Eastern Europe include the following: A dog is launched in an early Russian space vehicle and as it orbits the earth, it receives invitations from all of the nations of the world to descend. "Come land in our country," urge the French, and the Italians. "No," replies the dog, "I must return to Moscow." "Why must you return to Moscow?" "Because Moscow is the best place in the world to lead the life of a dog." The "life of a dog" allusion is not at all unusual. There is, for example, a text in the Radio Erevan Joke cycle: A listener asks, "Dear Radio Erevan, is it possible for a dog to have a nervous breakdown?" And our answer is, "Yes it is possible but only if the dog leads the life of a man." In still another Rumanian joke, told to me by a Jewish informant, a Jew is trying to escape across the border of an East European country. Unfortunately, he is caught by some frontier guards. "What are you doing?" one of them asks. "Nothing," the Jew replies. "Come on now, what were you doing?" "Well, I had terrible stomach cramps and I just had to go." "Show me." The poor Jew scratches around in the underbrush and finds a dog feces. "Voila!" he says. "But that's a dog's," objects the guard. The Jew shrugs and says, "With such a life, such a pile!"

A less pathetic jibe at the harshness of life in the Soviet Union is the following multi-national slur: There is a dispute between different nations concerning the origin of Adam and Eve with particular regard to their probable nationality. The Englishman argues that they must have been English because only an Englishman would be so much a gentleman as to give his twelfth rib to make a woman. The Frenchman contends that they were French because only a Frenchman could be so elegant while completely naked. The Jew insists they must have been Jews because the Bible says that the creation took place in the Holy Land. Finally the Rumanian claims that they must have been Russian because only a Russian could eat so poorly (only an apple) and be dressed so badly and still call it Paradise.

These examples might suggest that little overt aggression (or rather, overt physical aggression) is expressed in Rumanian political jokes. But this is not entirely true. In one very popular Rumanian joke, a Czech is standing at the edge of a cliff (or a river) saying over and over, "Thirty-two, thirty-two, thirty-two." A Russian official approaches him, and demands to know what he is doing. The Czech continues, "Thirty-two, thirty-two, thirty-two." "Why are you saying 'thirty-two?'" asks the Russian. The Czech continues, "Thirty-two, thirty-two, thirty-two." "If you don't stop saying 'thirty-two,' I'm going to arrest you." says the Russian. Just as he is about to seize the Czech, the Czech grabs the Russian and throws him off the cliff and says, "Thirty-three, thirty-three, thirty-three. . . . " This type of anti–Russian sentiment is similar to that found in an anecdote I collected in Czechoslovakia in August 1968, right before the Russian occupation. Khrushchev is being driven in a limousine in a rural area of Czechoslovakia. Suddenly, the car strikes and kills a pig that has wandered onto the road. The chauffeur asks Khrushchev if he wants to drive on, and Khrushchev replies, "No, we'd better go up to the nearest farmhouse and pay some damages." And so Khrushchev sends his chauffeur off to the farmhouse on the hill with instructions to offer to the farmer some compensation. A half-hour passes and the chauffeur does not return. Then another half-hour. Khrushchev begins to wonder what has happened. Still another half-hour passes and finally Khrushchev sees the chauffeur returning. To his surprise, the chauffeur is staggering under the weight of all sorts of packages and gifts. "What happened?" asks Khrushchev, "I sent you to pay *them*." "I don't know," replies the chauffeur, "All I said to them was: I have Khrushchev in the car and I killed the pig."

The Rumanians are very sympathetic to the plight of the Czechs, as they too have strong nationalistic tendencies. During the Russian invasion of Czechoslovakia, the Rumanians were extremely uneasy, fearing that they too might be "occupied." This anxiety was reflected in part by the sudden flowering of political jokes at that time. The jokes were clearly a collective defense mechanism and were recognized as such by a rhyming slogan that spoke of them (the Russians) with their tanks; us with our 'bancs' ('banc' is a slang term for joke).

Part of the anti–Russian sentiment takes pleasure in the Russians' difficulty with communist China. This is beautifully illustrated in the following Pied Piperesque anecdote: There is a terrible plague of rats in the Kremlin. There are millions of them. Brezhnev issues an order that all comrades are urged to do what they can to solve the problem. The leading chemists develop a formula, which does kill a million rats but there are more than ten million left. The biologists and physicists also try, but without success. Nothing works. Finally there is just one little man who says he can find a solution. "But what can you do after the great scientists have failed?" asks Brezhnev. "I can do it. Just give me a chance." "All right, go ahead." And so the man makes a mechanical rat, winds it up, and places it on the ground. All the millions of rats follow it into the river, where they drown. Brezhnev is delighted and rewards the man with many rubles. As the man is about to leave, Brezhnev calls him over and whispers, "You did well, but tell me, could you make a small mechanical Chinese?"

A joke that depends largely on gestures shows how the Rumanians would like to use the Russian-Chinese difficulties to the advantage of Rumania. Brezhnev and Ceaucescu are sitting at a table across from each other. Each has his elbows on the table with his chin supported by his two hands. Brezhnev, without moving his hands, wags his right index finger at Ceaucescu (as if to warn him about getting out of line with Soviet policy). Ceaucescu replies without moving his hands by pulling the corners of his eyes towards his ears to as to make them slanting (i.e., like the eyes of the Chinese).

But the Rumanians do not always portray Ceaucescu as a hero in their jokes. They have made a realistic appraisal of him and of the chances for improvement in Rumania. In one revealing joke (which is also told in Yugoslavia about Tito), there are three cars driving in a line. In the first is Brezhnev, the second Nixon, and the third Ceaucescu. The cars come to a fork in the road. Of course, Brezhnev turns to the left. Nixon turns to the right. Ceaucescu turns to the right but signals to the left. The implications of this joke are clearly that despite Ceaucescu's pretenses that he intends to move further towards the left, his actual movements in effect smack of fascist totalitarian control. There is also the hint that although he might like to turn right (following Nixon), he cannot do so without at the same time indicating that he is turning further to the left (following Brezhnev). In this way, he is attempting to keep all contingents partially satisfied. Truly the joke provides a superb metaphor for the political realities of contemporary Rumania.

As for the future of Rumania, one must reflect on the following text: God is walking and he meets Brezhnev, who is weeping. "Why are you weeping?" God asks him. Brezhnev says, "Because Americans have a better standard of living." God says, "Don't feel bad, you are ahead in the space race [this joke was collected before the American lunar landing] and you should be happy." And God leaves him feeling much better. Then God walks further and he meets Nixon weeping. He asks why and Nixon replies, "Because the Russians are ahead in the space race." So God says to comfort him, "But you have a better standard of living so you should be happy." Nixon leaves consoled. Then God walks a little further and sees Ceaucescu sitting on a step weeping. (Pause) And God walks over, sits down beside him, and begins to weep too!

My experience in collecting these jokes suggests that there is reason for sadness in Rumania. Informants related these jokes to me in hushed whispers. They refused to actually utter the name of Ceaucescu, but used such indirect terms of reference as the initial letter of his name. In several instances, prospective informants stated their suspicion that the collector might be a paid agent in the employ of the Rumanian government. Yet despite the fears and the reference to tears, there is, in the final analysis, laughter. And it is my belief that the data presented here probably represent a truer expression of the feelings of the Rumanian people than could be obtained by the more conventional means of eliciting attitudes in questionnaires or controlled interviews. It is not enough to study only political leaders and their views. The people's attitudes toward politics and politicians are also important, and there is probably no better source material for the study of such attitudes than folklore in general and jokelore in particular. I hope therefore that this sampling of Rumanian political jokes not only provides some insight into the Rumanian people's actual attitudes toward the political system under which they live, but also serves as a reminder to all those living or working abroad that if they wish to know what is really on a people's collective mind, there is no more direct and accurate way of finding out than by paying attention to precisely what is making the people laugh.

NOTES

PREFACE

1. Antti Aarne, *Verzeichnis der Märchentypen* (Helsinki: Suomalaisen tiedeakatemian toimituksia, 1910); later revised by Stith Thompson in 1928 and 1961. See Aarne and Thompson, *The Types of the Folktale* (Helsinki: Academia Scientiarum Fennica, 1961).

2. Gershon Legman, *Rationale of the Dirty Joke: An Analysis of Sexual Humor* (New York: Grove Press, 1968); Legman, *No Laughing Matter: Rationale of the Dirty Joke,* 2nd Series (New York: Breaking Point, 1975).

3. For information, see such survey volumes as: Ralph Piddington, *The Psychology of Laughter* (New York: Gamut, 1963); D. H. Monro, *Argument of Laughter* (Notre Dame: University of Notre Dame Press, 1963); William E. Fry, Jr., *Sweet Madness: A Study of Humor* (Palo Alto: Pacific Books, 1968); Paul E. McGhee, *Humor: Its Origin and Development* (San Francisco: W. H. Freeman, 1979); John Morreall, *Taking Laughter Seriously* (Albany: State University of New York Press, 1983).

4. Lutz Röhrich, *Der Witz: Figuren, Formen, Funktionen* (Stuttgart: J. B. Metzler, 1977); Mahadev L. Apte, *Humor and Laughter: An Anthropological Approach* (Ithaca, NY: Cornell University Press, 1985).

CHAPTER 1   *The Dead Baby Joke Cycle*

1. Louise Pound, "American Euphemisms for Dying, Death, and Burial," *American Speech* 11 (1936): 190–202. Reprinted in Louise Pound, *Nebraska Folklore: Selected Writings of Louise Pound* (Lincoln: University of Nebraska Press, 1959), 139–47.

2. Harry Graham, *Ruthless Rhymes for Heartless Homes and More Ruthless Rhymes for Heartless Homes* (New York: Dover, 1961), 10.

3. Lewis Copeland, *The World's Best Jokes* (New York: Blue Ribbon Books, 1936), 290. Copeland includes twenty-four Little Willies (290–94).

4. Ibid., 290–91.

5. Evan Esar, *The Humor of Humor* (New York: Bramhall House, 1952), 282. Esar's suggestion sounds plausible, but "the willies" allegedly dates from circa 1895, which precedes even Harry Graham's 1899 poem. See Harold Wentworth and Stuart Berg Flexner, *Dictionary of American Slang* (New York: Thomas Y. Crowell, 1967), 580.

6. Graham, *Ruthless Rhymes*, 19.

7. Ibid., 51.

8. Copeland, *World's Best Jokes*, 290. In the version reported by Esar, the last line is "Willie, dear don't mar the paint." See Esar, *Humor of Humor*, 282.

9. Copeland, *World's Best Jokes*, 292.

10. Louis Untermeyer, ed., *A Treasury of Laughter* (New York: Simon & Schuster, 1946), 303.

11. Copeland, *World's Best Jokes,* 292.

12. Cornelia Chambers, "The Adventures of Little Audrey," in *Straight Texas,* J. Frank Dobie and Mody C. Boatright, eds. (Austin: Texas Folklore Society 13, 1937), 106–10. Reprinted in B. A. Botkin, *A Treasury of American Folklore* (New York: Crown, 1944), 372–75.

13. Brian Sutton-Smith, "'Shut Up and Keep Digging': The Cruel Joke Series," *Midwest Folklore* 10 (1960): 11–22; Roger D. Abrahams, "Ghastly Commands: The Cruel Joke Revisited," *Midwest Folklore* 11 (1961–1962): 235–46. A series of paperback anthologies made sick jokes readily available to the general public. See *Sick Jokes, Grim Cartoons & Bloody Marys* (New York: Citadel, 1958); *More Sick Jokes and Grimmer Cartoons* (New York: Citadel, 1959); and *Still More Sick Jokes and Even Grimmer Cartoons* (New York: Citadel, 1960). The combined contents of these three books were then reissued as Max Rezwin, ed. *The Best of Sick Jokes* (New York: Pocket Books, 1962). It should also be noted that sick or black humor is also an important part of literature. One critic has gone so far as to claim that Black Humorists have restored the American novel to relevance. See Douglas M. David, *The World of Black Humor* (New York: E. P. Dutton, 1967), 22. For further references to the considerable scholarship devoted to black humor, see Lutz Röhrich, *Der Witz* (Stuttgart: J. B. Metzler, 1977), 313.

14. For additional sick Jesus texts, see Sutton-Smith, "'Shut Up and Keep Digging,'" 20–21, and Abrahams, "Ghastly Commands," 245–46.

15. I collected this joke from my colleague, Professor Sherwood Washburn, in the mid-1970s. Professor Washburn is a distinguished physical anthropologist. The point of this joke about racism is that sickle-cell anemia is a disease that occurs almost exclusively among blacks in Africa and the New World. The sickle-cell trait appears to be genetically transmitted

and seems to be positively correlated with resistance to malaria. Thus originally it may have been a useful adaptive feature. All of the other good news/bad news joke texts were collected in Berkeley, California, in 1978–1979. The majority have to do with medical malpractice, unnecessary surgery, and the like. It is certainly appropriate for sick humor to treat illness and hospital care.

16. This is a common sick joke. Sutton-Smith, "'Shut Up and Keep Digging,'" 15, reports: "Son, will you quit kicking your sister." "Oh, that's all right. She's already dead." Similarly, Roger Abrahams remembered a joke current in his childhood in Philadelphia (circa 1942): "This boy was walking down the street kicking a baby. A policeman walked up to him and said, 'What are you doing there?' 'I'm kicking the baby down the street.' 'You're what?' 'Oh, it's all right, he's dead.'" See Abrahams, "Ghastly Commands," 239–40. In other versions, a nurse brings the baby in to the new father and either drops it several times or throws it across the room saying, "April Fool. Born Dead." (cf. Sutton-Smith, 17–18.)

17. Sutton-Smith, "'Shut Up and Keep Digging,'" 22.

18. Abrahams, "Ghastly Commands," 242. A version from the University of California, Berkeley, Folklore Archives collected in Grass Valley, California, in 1958 is: "As funny as a truckload of dead babies."

19. This is clearly an updated revision of an older elephant joke from the 1960s: "How do you make an elephant float?" "Two scoops of elephant in root beer (or ginger ale)."

20. For this interpretation of the elephant joke cycle, see Roger D. Abrahams and Alan Dundes, "On Elephantasy and Elephanticide," *Psychoanalytic Review* 56 (1969): 225–41. Reprinted in Alan Dundes, *Analytic Essays in Folklore* (The Hague: Mouton, 1975), 192–205. See also Chapter 4 of this book.

21. For evidence pointing to the use of the frog as a symbol of the white stereotype of the black, see Alan Dundes, "Jokes and Covert Language Attitudes: The Curious Case of the Wide-Mouth Frog," *Language in Society* 6 (1977): 141–47. See Chapter 5 of this book.

22. I remember hearing (and telling) this joke in the early 1950s in New Haven, Connecticut. No doubt its popularity among college undergraduates had something to do with its theme of apparent parental rejection. College freshmen, while enjoying their independence from home and family, may also feel cast out and perhaps inadequate to face the new challenging environment of college life. There is a wish to return to the safety of the protective home (symbolized by the rosy-cheeked mother), even though to do so would be an admission of failure (to cope successfully in the outside world).

23. Other cultures also have folklore about dead babies. However, usually this folklore is in the form of legends about ghostly dead children who return to earth to haunt their relatives. (Sometimes the infants have died before having been baptized.) For examples of such folklore, see Finnish folklorist Juha Pentikainen's comprehensive monograph, *The Nordic Dead-Child Tradition: Nordic Dead-Child Beings, A Study in Comparative Religion*, FFC 202 (Helsinki: Academia Scientiarum Fennica, 1968). These narratives may also reflect guilt about actual or wished-for infanticide, but they are generally devoid of humor. In American folklore, by contrast, it is jokes, not supernatural legends or memorates, that treat dead babies.

24. One representative articulation of the anti-baby tendency in American culture is Lance Morrow's essay, "Wondering if Children Are Necessary," which appeared in *Time*, March 5, 1979, 42, 47. Morrow suggests that the increase of child abuse may be related to the same movement. Teenage alcoholism, drug use, and suicide may also be in part a consequence of real or imagined parental rejection and resentment of children. In that context, the dead baby jokes told by adolescents may also be about themselves vis-à-vis their parents.

25. There is evidence suggesting the increasing popularity of dead baby jokes. A paperback anthology published in July 1979 has seven texts of dead baby jokes (plus versions of "sickle-cell anemia," "the fellow in the next bed wants to buy your boots," "it's blind," "it was dead anyway," and "we wanted to wait until the children died," etc.). See Larry Wilde, *The Official Book of Sick Jokes* (Los Angeles: Pinnacle Books, 1979). Dead baby jokes may be spreading to Europe. My daughter Alison collected texts in Paris during the summer of 1979 from two Scottish teen-age girls. One such text is: **What's pink and screams? A peeled baby in a bag of salt.**

CHAPTER 2   *Game of the Name:*
A Quadriplegic Sick Joke Cycle

1. For a discussion of gallows humor, see A. J. Obrdlik, "Gallows Humor: A Sociological Phenomenon," *American Journal of Sociology* 47 (1942): 709–16; Elfriede Moser-Rath, "Galgenhumor wörtlich genommen," *Schweizerisches Archiv für Volkskunde* 68/69 (1972–1973): 423–32. Executioners feel anxiety too, though presumably not as much as their victims. But this may explain why contemporary Germans tell jokes about Auschwitz. See Alan Dundes and Thomas Hauschild, "Auschwitz Jokes," *Western Folklore* 42 (1983): 249–60. See also Chapter 3 of this book.

2. The reference to Homer was cited by Max Rezwin in his *The Best of Sick Jokes* (New York: Permabooks, 1962), 11. Making fun of handicapped

or deformed individuals has been reported in many cultures. Laura Bohannan (who writes as Elenore Smith Bowen) singled out this feature for the title of her novel, *Return to Laughter*. In this fictionalized account of her fieldwork in Nigeria, she indicates disgust at her informants' pleasure in such humor. One informant told her, "There's nothing funnier than yelling 'Snake!' at a blind man." Her response: "Their laughter at suffering was merely one symbol of the gulf between their world and mine." The gulf is not as great as Bohannan would have us believe. See Elenore Smith Bowen, *Return to Laughter* (Garden City, NY: Doubleday, 1964), 228, 231.

3. *The Iliad of Homer*, Richard Lattimore, trans. (Chicago: University of Chicago Press, 1951), 82–83, Book Two, lines 243–70.

4. See, for example, C. J. S. Thompson, *The Mystery and Lore of Monsters, with accounts of some Giants, Dwarfs and Prodigies* (New Hyde Park, NY: University Books, 1968).

5. For an account of Little Willies, see Alan Dundes, "The Dead Baby Joke Cycle," *Western Folklore*, 38 (1979): 146–48. See also Chapter 1 of this book. For a sampling of some 90 texts, see Leopold Fechtner, *American Wit and Gags* (New York: Vantage, 1969), 196–207.

6. For discussions of these cycles, see Brian Sutton-Smith, "'Shut Up and Keep Digging': The Cruel Joke Series," *Midwest Folklore* 10 (1960): 11–22; Roger D. Abrahams, "Ghastly Commands: The Cruel Joke Revisited," *Midwest Folklore* 11 (1961–1962): 235–46; Alan Dundes, "The Dead Baby Joke Cycle," *Western Folklore* 38 (1979): 145–57; Mac E. Barrick, "The Helen Keller Joke Cycle," *Journal of American Folklore* 93 (1980): 441–49. Typical anthologies of texts include: Rezwin, *The Best of Sick Jokes;* Larry Wilde, *The Official Book of Sick Jokes* (Los Angeles: Pinnacle Books, 1979); and Max Hodes, *The Official Sick Joke Book* (London: Macdonald Futura, 1980).

7. Sutton-Smith, "'Shut Up and Keep Digging,'" 18. For other versions, see Rezwin, *The Best of Sick Jokes*, 19; Wilde, *Official Book of Sick Jokes*, 8; and Barrick, "Helen Keller," 445.

8. This joke depends on the difficulty encountered by native speakers of Japanese when they attempt to articulate the /l/ phoneme in English. There are other jokes that play on this same phonological alternation: for example, "What is the sound made by a Japanese camera? 'Crik.'"

9. All the texts reported in this chapter were collected from oral tradition by members of my 1983 fall semester folklore class at the University of California, Berkeley. The interaction between oral tradition and popular culture can profitably be gauged by tracing the increasing extent to which these jokes have been included in popular joke anthologies.

In *Truly Tasteless Jokes* (New York: Ballantine, 1982) by Blanche Knott (obviously a nom de plume), a short section is devoted to the handicapped. Only three jokes of the cycle reported here were included, e.g., Stew and Eileen (p. 57). The sequel, *Truly Tasteless Jokes Two*, published in 1983, contained four—Bob, Skip, Matt, and Art (p.41). In another 1983 sequel, *Truly Tasteless Jokes Three*, we find Patty, Sandy, and Russell (pp. 45–46). By 1984, we find an entire book devoted to the punning name tradition. Sean Kelly's *A Book Called Bob* (New York: Warner Books, 1984) contains 109 texts, including those reported here. For an additional 33 examples of what are termed "torso jokes," see Reinhold Aman, "Kakologia: A Chronicle of Nasty Riddles and Naughty Wordplays," *Maledicta* 7 (1983): 305–307.

CHAPTER 3   *Auschwitz Jokes*

1. Terrence Des Pres, *The Survivor: An Anatomy of Life in the Death Camps* (New York: Pocket Books, 1977).

2. See Antonin J. Obrdlik, "'Gallows Humor'—A Sociological Phenomenon," *American Journal of Sociology* 47 (1942): 709–16; Elfriede Moser-Rath, "Galgenhumor wörtlich genommen," *Schweizerisches Archiv für Volkskunde* 68/69 (1972–1973): 423–32.

3. For an early discussion of self-hate, see Kurt Lewin, "Self Hatred Among Jews," *Contemporary Jewish Record* 4 (1941): 219–32.

4. Unless otherwise indicated, all texts were collected by Thomas Hauschild in West Berlin during the summer of 1982 from informants ranging in age from twenty-six to sixty years.

5. We thank folklorist Utz Jeggle in Tübingen for sending us this text.

6. We are grateful to folklorist Bengt af Klinterg in Stockholm for providing all the Swedish texts cited in this essay. He indicated that such *"judevitsar"* (jokes about Jews) were popular among teenagers in the early 1970s.

7. See Alan Dundes, "Life is Like a Chicken Coop Ladder: A Study of German National Character Through Folklore," *Journal of Psychoanalytic Anthropology* 4 (1981): 265–364.

8. Texts 8, 9, and 10 were collected directly in English translation from Dr. Vera Bendt in Berlin in April 1982. We are indebted to Dr. Bendt for calling our attention to the Auschwitz joke cycle in the first place.

9. This text was also sent to us by Utz Jeggle from Tübingen. Oven jokes are also found in the United States and Sweden. A text collected from

a Jewish young man from Los Angeles in 1981: What's the difference between a Jew and a pizza? A pizza doesn't scream when it is put in the oven.
The Swedish version: What is the difference between a Jew and a bun?
The Jew screams when he is pushed into the oven. Another Swedish text
asks: What was Hitler's worst shock? When he got the gas bill. In an English
text collected in Leeds in 1973, we find the same theme: How do you
get a Jew in a telephone (booth)? Throw a ha'penny in. How do you get him
out? Shout gas. See Sandra McCosh, *Children's Humour* (London: Granada,
1976), 227, 723. For a brief discussion of the idea that a German "urge
towards self-obliteration may be defended against by, for example, ascrib-
ing it to the Jew—that is, it is the Jew who craves death, not I"—see
Stanley Rosenman, "The American Nazi and the Wandering Jew," *American Journal of Psychoanalysis* 39 (1979): 363–68 (esp. 364–65).

10. For a sample of the discussion of the impact of Turkish workers in Germany, see "Die Türkei und die Türken in Deutschland," which constitutes
the entire issue of *Der Burger im Staat* 32 (3) (September 1982): 165–200.
For several representative texts of anti-Turkish jokes, see Richard Albrecht, "Was ist der Unterschied zwischen Türken und Juden? (Anti-)
Türkenwitze in der Bundesrepublik Deutschland 1982: Versuch über ein
gesellschaltliches Dunkelfeld," *Zeitschrift für Volkskunde* 78 (1982): 220–29.
Only three texts out of two dozen actually recorded are reported.

11. This text is cited in Albrecht, "'Was ist der Unterschied . . . ,'" 220, and
it also appeared in "Nutten und Bastarde erschlagen wir," *Der Spiegel* 27,
July 5, 1982, where it was reported as a wall graffito. This suggests just
how widespread this particular joke is in contemporary Germany.

12. We are indebted to anthropologist Uli Linke for reminding us of the
prevalence of this metaphor. Folklorist Lutz Röhrich claims that the idiom
is older than Nazism and Auschwitz, deriving originally from the language of chemists and physicists. See his *Lexikon der sprichwörtlichen Reden-
sarten* (Freiburg: Herder, 1977), 1108. For the anti-Semitic implications
of the expression, see Peter Schütt, "Der Mohr hat seine Schuldigkeit
getan . . . Gibt es Rassismus in der Bundesrepublik," *Eine Streitschrift*
(Dortmund: Weltkreis Verlag, 1981), 25. For a more general discussion
of anti-Semitism in modern Germany, see also Alphons Silbermann, *Sind
wir Anti-Semiten?* (Köln: Verlag wissenschaft und politik, 1982).

13. See Peter Hamm, ed., *Aussichten* (München: Biederstein Verlag, 1966),
263. We thank professor Wolfgang Mieder of the University of Vermont
for calling our attention to this poetic allusion to Auschwitz jokes.

14. This text was reported by Albrecht, "'Was ist der Unterschied. . . .'"

15. See Alan Dundes and Thomas Hauschild, "Auschwitz Jokes," *Western
Folklore* 42 (1983): 249–60.

16. See Albrecht, "'Was ist der Unterschied. . . .'" Albrecht advocates self-censorship and reported only three out of two dozen texts actually recorded.

17. For the UCLA graduate student letter, see "The Postal Connection," *The California Folklore Newsletter* 1, no. 1 (Spring 1984), 4; for the U.C. Berkeley undergraduate letter, see S. E. Bingham, "Darkness and Light," *The Daily Californian* 15, no. 172 (July 6, 1984), 4. *Both* argued that such jokes should be ignored by scholars: "What a useless pastime and excuse for scholarship to collect these horrific anti-Semitic so-called jokes."

18. See Silbermann, *Sind wir Anti-Semiten?* For a review of his study, see "Holocaust mindert nicht den Judenhass," *Süddeutsche Zeitung* 15 (January 19, 1984), 44.

19. Schütt, "Der Mohr hat seine," 75. The authors of the postscript to Auschwitz Jokes have noted such graffiti in Berlin, Cologne, Frankfurt, and Koblenz between 1982 and 1984. A general reference to this type of graffiti is contained in "Nutten und Bastarde," 38.

20. Quoted from John Nielsen, "Rising Racism on the Continent: Immigrants Face Economic Hardship and Increasing Prejudice," *Time*, February 6, 1984, 40–41.

21. A more extensive discussion of this problem may be found in Hamida Bosmajian, *Metaphors of Evil: Contemporary German Literature and the Shadow of Nazism* (Iowa City: University of Iowa Press, 1979), xii.

22. See "Rechtsradikale: Gegner 1," *Der Spiegel*, December 12, 1983, 31–32.

23. See "Neonazis: Drastische Gegenwart," *Der Spiegel*, February 13, 1984, 57–61.

24. Unless otherwise indicated, the texts included in this essay were collected by Uli Linke in January 1983, in Cologne, Aachen, and Koblenz from male informants in their early twenties. However, we are greatly indebted to folklorist Jess Nierenberg, who generously shared his collection of such jokes with us. Jokes from Nierenberg are numbered 21b, 22, 27, 28, 30, and 33.

25. This text appears in Rainer Wehse, "Warum sind die Ostfriesen so gelb im Gesicht?" *Die Witze der 11–14 jährigen—Texte und Analysen*. Artes Populares: Studia Ethnographica Et Folkloristica, 6 (Frankfurt a.M., 1983), p. 17, no. 51.

26. For other versions of this joke, see Dundes and Hauschild, "Auschwitz Jokes," 251–52.

27. For an extended discussion of the possible anal-erotic factors underlying the Nazi efforts to "eliminate" *dirty* Jews, see Dundes, "Life is Like a Chicken Coop Ladder," 119–31.

28. Cited from Timothy Garton Ash, "Jokes: Explore the Gulf Between Communist Ideology and Reality," *Los Angeles Herald Examiner*, October 23, 1983, Section F, 1, 4.

29. For further consideration of projection, see Alan Dundes, "Projection in Folklore: A Plea for Psychoanalytic Semiotics," in *Interpreting Folklore* (Bloomington: Indiana University Press, 1980), 33–61.

30. This text was collected in 1974 in Fremont, California, from a German male in his late forties. It was reported directly in English translation.

31. We are indebted to sociologist Christie Davies at the University of Reading in England for making this text available to us.

CHAPTER 4 *On Elephantasy and Elephanticide: The Effect of Time and Place*

1. For a sample of the considerable humor literature, see Norman Kiell, *Psychoanalysis, Psychology and Literature: A Bibliography* (Madison: University of Wisconsin Press, 1963), 139–42.

2. For reports of the elephant cycle, see Alan Dundes, "The Elephant Joking Question," *Tennessee Folklore Society Bulletin* 29 (1963): 40–42; Roger D. Abrahams, "The Bigger They Are, the Harder They Fall," *Tennessee Folklore Society Bulletin* 29 (1963): 94–102; Jan Harold Brunvand, "Have You Heard the Elephant (Joke)?" *Western Folklore* 23 (1964): 198–99; Mac E. Barrick, "The Shaggy Elephant Riddle," *Southern Folklore Quarterly* 28 (1964): 266–90; Ed Cray and Marilyn Eisenberg Herzog, "The Absurd Elephant: A Recent Riddle Fad," *Western Folklore* 26 (1967): 27–36. Elephant jokes were widely diffused via the mass media: see "Elephants by the Trunk," *Time*, August 2, 1963, 41; "Beastly Riddles Are Big," *Seventeen*, August 1963, 228–29; Jerome Beatty, Jr., "Tradewinds," *Saturday Review*, August 3, 1963, 7; Eugene Gilbert, "Elephants Lead the Herd of Teener Jokes," AP Newsfeature, November 14, 1963. (Many of these are mentioned in Barrick, above.) There were a number of joke folios that emerged filled with these jokes, some authentic, some ersatz: *The Elephant Book* (Los Angeles: Price, Stern, Sloan, 1963); a sequel, *Elephants, Grapes & Pickles* (Los Angeles: Price, Stern, Sloan, 1964); Marcie Hans and Lynn Babcock, *There's an Elephant in My Sandwich* (New York: Citadel Press, 1963); Robert Blake, *101 Elephant Jokes* (New York: Pyramid Books, 1964).

3. Freud's most extended statement of the psychology of wit is contained in his monograph, *Wit and Its Relation to the Unconscious*, most recently translated by James Strachey as *Jokes and Their Relation to the Unconscious*

(London, 1960). The most important works of his followers are found in Kiell, *Psychoanalysis, Psychology and Literature.*

4. Ernst Kris, *Psychoanalytic Explorations in Art* (New York: International Universities Press, 1952), 205.

5. Freud emphasized this element of formal control duping the superego through economy of means in *Wit and Its Relation to the Unconscious.* For an insightful discussion of children's joking techniques, see Martha Wolfenstein, *Children's Humor: A Psychological Analysis* (Bloomington: Indiana University Press, 1978). See also Sandra McCosh, *Children's Humour* (London: Granada, 1979).

6. For a discussion of the totality of regression in the state of submission in regard to the Negro slave in the United States, see Stanley M. Elkins, *Slavery* (Chicago: University of Chicago Press, 1959; New York: Grosset and Dunlap paper reprint, 1963), 81–139. For the way in which this suppression caused an effect on black folklore in the depiction of the hero in childish trickster form, see Roger D. Abrahams, *Deep Down in the Jungle . . .:Negro Narrative Folklore from the Streets of Philadelphia* (Hatboro, PA: Folklore Associates, 1964), 65–69.

7. Abrahams, *Deep Down*, 136–47.

8. *Over Sixteen* (New York: Elgart, 1951), 19.

9. This is a variant of an old joke usually told about a nurse or nurse's aide working in a hospital. Legman cites a 1928 text in which a rabbi earns more than a priest "because he gets all the tips," in "Rationale of the Dirty Joke," *Neurotica* 9 (Winter 1952):59.

10. This text was reported in Dundes, "Elephant Joking Question," 41. With few exceptions, all of the texts in this article were collected in the vicinities of Austin, Texas, and Berkeley, California. Some seem to be unique, although most were collected in both places and were in all likelihood equally popular throughout the United States. Few texts that emerged in our collecting experience or in print are not susceptible to the analysis pattern suggested here.

11. Sigmund Freud, *A General Introduction to Psychoanalysis* (New York: Permabooks, 1953), 162.

12. For sample texts, see Abrahams, "The Bigger They Are," 99.

13. Abrahams, "The Bigger They Are," 100. The use of voice qualifiers in castration humor is common. For example, the use of a high-pitched falsetto occurs in the emphasized portions of the following punch lines: "Operator, I've been *cut off*!" "Hey, there's sharks in *these waters*." "Watch out for the barbed wire fence!" "What barbed wire *fence*?" For an excellent

account of castration humor, see G. Legman's "Rationale of the Dirty Joke," 49–64.

14. The "adult" status of the elephant is also revealed by the answer to the question, "How do you talk to an elephant?" The answer — "Use big words" — reflects a child's-eye view of adult vocabulary, and in fact a child might well try to use "big words" when speaking to adults.

15. We are indebted to John Greenway for pointing out that the introduction of the ballet slippers may have been a result of the reissue of Walt Disney's movie "Fantasia" around the time of the currency of this cycle.

16. The attribution of greater sexual appetite and competence to an enemy appears to be a fairly general phenomenon. See Robert Seidenberg, "The Sexual Basis of Social Prejudice," *Psychoanalytic Review*, 39 (1952): 90–95. For representative texts of white jokes about black sexuality, see D. J. Bennett, "The Psychological Meaning of Anti-Negro Jokes," *Fact*, 1, no. 2 (1964): 53–59. For a literary reference in which black genital superiority is couched in elephantine imagery, see John Steinbeck, *The Grapes of Wrath* (New York: Modern Library, 1939), 14.

17. From the white's point of view, the absurdity of the elephant's trying to conceal his true nature and color by wearing human shoes of a certain color might be analogous to what some whites think is the rationale underlying the black's attempts to adopt certain status symbols of white culture and dress. But while the black might prefer not to be recognizable on the basis of color, he cannot possibly conceal his color, no matter what he wears or owns. As an elephant is indubitably an elephant no matter what color his sneakers or toenails are, so also the black's identity is unmistakable. The white stereotype of black values may, in this light, illuminate the text: "Why did the elephant sit on the marshmallow? *Because he didn't want to fall in the cocoa.*" This could express the white conviction that the elephant (black) would prefer to sit precariously on the small *white* "safe" marshmallow rather than fall *down* to be immersed in the larger mass of *brown* cocoa. It is worth remarking that the wordplay on "color" in the elephant joke cycle, if the present black/elephant hypothesis is correct, is reminiscent of a type of punning wit commonly found in dreams. Further, the "grape-banana-plum" riddle cycle that followed hard on the heels of the elephant jokes were equally castratory and used color descriptions even more emphatically. For texts, see Barrick, "Shaggy Elephant Riddle."

18. This text and several of the other racial color riddles cited here were reported in Abrahams, "The Bigger They Are."

19. As Mac E. Barrick has pointed out in "You Can Tell a Joke With Vigah If It's About a Niggah," *Keystone Folklore Quarterly*, 9 (1964): 166–68,

the successor to this type of "nigger" riddle is a whole series of narrative jokes using, often ironically, the Southern stereotype of the black, but with an ambivalent point of view in regard to the attitude toward the black.

20. An interesting corroboration of this hypothesis comes from clinical data contributed by psychiatrist L. Bryce Boyer. He reports: "I one time had a patient in analysis who spent some interviews around the theme of racial problems, then found himself telling elephant jokes, then resumed the talk about racial problems. His own conflicts at that period dealt specifically with castration fears and fantasies of retribution against his father and authority figures. He clearly equated Negroes and elephants with his father and specifically spoke of the Negro's alleged huge genitals and the elephant's trunk while also talking of childhood memories of seeing his father's penis, the size of which was most impressive to him" (from personal correspondence).

CHAPTER 5   *The Curious Case of the Wide-Mouth Frog: Jokes and Covert Language Attitudes*

1. This text was collected from Lisa Payne, a student at Thornton Junior High School in Fremont, California, in June 1976.

2. This version was collected from Holly C. Dorst, who first heard it in Rock Island, Illinois in 1971. (I am indebted to folklorist John Dorst for collecting the joke from his wife.)

3. Raven McDavid, "Some Social Differences in Pronunciation," *Language Learning* 4 (1953): 107.

4. Hans Kurath and Raven McDavid, *The Pronunciation of English in the Atlantic States* (Ann Arbor: University of Michigan Press, 1961), 113.

5. This text was collected from Beckie Olson, a student at Thornton Junior High School in Fremont, California, in May 1976. I also thank folklorist Steve Kassovic for reminding me of an older joke that uses the same range of punch lines as the wide-mouth frog joke. In the older joke, the punch line is uttered by a woman, after a man tells her that just as the size of a man's nose indicates the size of his phallus, so the size of a woman's mouth indicates the size of her vagina.

6. This would seem to parallel the case of the elephant in the elephant joke cycle. The superphallic elephant made a number of attempts to conceal himself by changing color. **"Why do elephants wear green tennis shoes?" "To hide in the tall grass." "Why do elephants paint their toenails red?" "To hide in cherry trees."** Part of the white stereotype of the black man includes

the idea that the black would like to change his color, i.e., to white. Whites' label of blacks as "colored" supports the interpretation. In any case, the absurdity of an elephant's trying to disguise his nature by wearing green tennis shoes or painting his toenails red is analogous to the wide-mouth frog's altering its speech pattern. The elephant remains an elephant just as the frog remains a frog.

7. Katherine George, "The Civilized West Looks at Primitive Africa: 1400–1800, A Study in Ethnocentrism," *Isis* 49 (1958): 62–72.

8. Raven McDavid, "Dialect Differences and Inter-group Tensions," *Studies in Linguistics* 9 (1951): 27–33.

9. I am greatly indebted to Dell Hymes for assistance in spelling out the important features of the phonological symbolism of "wide-mouth frog" and for other invaluable editorial suggestions.

10. McDavid, "Some Social Differences," 107, 109, 114.

11. Carroll E. Reed, *Dialects of American English* (Cleveland and New York: The World Publishing Company, 1967), 32.

12. Robert Toll, *Blacking Up: The Minstrel Show in Nineteenth-Century America* (New York: Oxford University Press, 1974), 254.

13. Roald Dahl, *Charlie and the Chocolate Factory* (New York: Alfred A. Knopf, 1964), 72–76.

14. To support the present interpretation linking frogs and blacks symbolically, I note a song sung by one of the principal "Muppet" characters in the popular educational television series for children, "Sesame Street." Kermit, who is a frog, sings, "It's not so easy being green," which most viewers understand to refer to the difficulties of being "colored," i.e., black, in a white society. The didactic television song is, of course, a conscious attempt to fight racism. (In addition, folksingers Peter, Paul, and Mary sing, "I'm in Love with a Big Blue Frog. . . .") In contrast, the wide-mouth frog joke is an unconscious attempt to indulge in racism. Consider, for example, the implications of the view that a wide-mouth frog parent is so ignorant that it doesn't know what to feed its babies. Doesn't part of the white stereotype include the belief that many (lower-class) black parents provide inadequate care for their small children?

CHAPTER 6 *The Jewish American Princess and the Jewish American Mother in American Jokelore*

1. Compare Irving Howe, "The Nature of Jewish Laughter," *American Mercury* 72 (1961): 211–19 and Salcia Landmann, *Jüdische Witze* (München:

Deutscher Taschenbuch Verlag, 1963) and *Jüdische Witze: Nachlese 1960–1976* (München: Deutscher Taschenbuch Verlag, 1977).

2. William Novak and Moshe Waldoks, *The Big Book of Jewish Humor* (New York: Harper & Row, 1981), 268.

3. Howard J. Ehrlich, "Observations on Ethnic and Intergroup Humor," *Ethnicity* 6 (1979): 396.

4. Beverly Gray Bienstock, "The Changing Image of the American Jewish Mother," in *Changing Images of the Family,* Virginia Tufte and Barbara Myerhoff, eds. (New Haven and London: Yale University Press, 1979), 184; Charlotte Baum, Paula Hyman, and Sonya Michel, *The Jewish Woman in America* (New York: New American Library, 1977), 237.

5. Sara Reguer, "The Jewish Mother and the 'Jewish American Princess': Fact or Fiction?" *USA Today* 108, no. 2412 (September 1979): 41.

6. Zena Smith Blau, "In Defense of the Jewish Mother," *Midstream* 13, no. 2 (February 1967): 43.

7. Mark Zborowski and Elizabeth Herzog, *Life Is with People: The Culture of the Shtetl* (New York: Schocken, 1962), 293.

8. Compare Martin Grotjahn, "Jewish Jokes and Their Relation to Masochism," *Journal of the Hillside Hospital* 10 (1961): 186; Samuel Irving Bellman, "The 'Jewish Mother' Syndrome," *Congress Bi-Weekly* 32 (17) (December 27, 1965): 3; Ehrlich, "Observations," 396 (sweaters); and Simon R. Pollack, *Jewish Wit for All Occasions* (New York: A. & W. Visual Library, 1979), 187.

9. Compare Blanche Knott, *Truly Tasteless Jokes* (New York: Ballantine, 1982), 21.

10. David Boroff, "The Over-Protective Jewish Mother," *Congress Weekly* 24 (27) (November 4, 1959), 7.

11. Compare Pollack, *Jewish Wit,* 113.

12. Gerry Blumenfeld, *Some of My Best Jokes Are Jewish* (New York: Paperback Library, 1969), 65–66.

13. Ibid., 80.

14. Compare Larry Wilde, *The Last Official Jewish Joke Book* (New York: Pinnacle Books, 1980), 32.

15. Knott, *Truly Tasteless Jokes,* 21. This joke could also be interpreted as reflecting the stinginess element of the stereotypic Jew.

16. Blau, 45.

17. Bernard Rosenberg and Gilbert Shapiro, "Marginality and Jewish Humor," *Midstream* 4 (1958): 80. For other versions, see Wilde, *Last Official Jewish Joke Book,* 42, and Novak and Waldoks, *Big Book,* 71.

18. Blanche Knott, *Truly Tasteless Jokes Two* (New York: Ballantine Books, 1983), 9.

19. Compare Jacqueline A. Mintz, "The Myth of the Jewish Mother in Three Jewish, American, Female Writers," *The Centennial Review* 22 (1978): 346, for a version; for a brief discussion of the tale's distribution, see Alexander Scheiber, "A Tale of the Mother's Heart," *Journal of American Folklore* 68 (1955): 72, 86, 89.

20. For another text set in Bloomingdale's, see Larry Wilde, *More The Official Jewish/Irish Joke Book* (New York: Pinnacle Books, 1979), 43; Novak and Waldoks, *Big Books*, 274.

21. Compare Larry Wilde, *The Official Jewish/Irish Joke Book* (New York: Pinnacle Books, 1974), 37.

22. Bienstock, "Changing Image," 175–76.

23. Jules Zanger, "On Not Making It in America," *American Studies* 17 (1) (1976): 41.

24. Bienstock, "Changing Image," 186.

25. Baum, Hyman, and Michel, *Jewish Woman in America*, 241.

26. Erika Duncan, "The Hungry Jewish Mother," in *The Lost Tradition: Mothers and Daughters in Literature*, Cathy N. Davidson and E. M. Broner, eds. (New York: Frederick Ungar), 231.

27. Zanger, "On Not Making It," 42.

28. Larry Wilde, *Official Book of John Jokes* (New York: Bantam, 1985), 62.

29. Compare Illana Hitner Klevansky, *The Kugel Book* (Johannesburg: Jonathan Ball, 1982); Alan Levine, *Unreal Humour of the Kugel & Bagel or Are Kugel's Children Born with Designer Genes?* (Hillbrow: Kugel & Bagel Promotions Ltd., 1983).

30. Compare Wilde, *Last Official Jewish Joke Book*, 18.

31. Julie Baumgold, "The Persistence of the Jewish American Princess," *New York* 4 (12) (March 22, 1971), 28.

32. Mintz, "Myth of the Jewish Mother," 352.

33. Debbi Lukatsky and Sandy Barnett Toback, *The Jewish American Princess Handbook* (Arlington Hts, IL: Turnbull & Willoughby Books, 1982), 69; Knott, *Truly Tasteless Jokes*, 22; Julius Alvin, *Totally Gross Jokes* (New York: Zebra Books, 1983), 15.

34. Knott, *Truly Tasteless Jokes Two*, 18; Maude Thickett, *Outrageously Offensive Jokes*, II (New York: Pocket Books, 1984), 68 (without reference to J.A.P.).

35. Lukatsky and Toback, *Jewish American Princess Handbook*, 76; Maude Thickett, *Outrageously Offensive Jokes* (New York: Pocket Books, 1983), 44.

36. Blau, "Defense of the Jewish Mother," 44.

37. Knott, *Truly Tasteless Jokes*, 21; Alvin, *Totally Gross Jokes*, 14.

38. Thickett, *Outrageously Offensive Jokes*, 46.

39. Compare Thickett, *Outrageously Offensive Jokes*, 43; Knott, *Truly Tasteless Jokes Two*, 23.

40. Compare Knott, *Truly Tasteless Jokes Two*, 25.

41. Lukatsky and Toback, *Jewish American Princess Handbook*, 57.

42. Larry Wilde, *The Official Jewish/Irish Joke Book* (New York: Pinnacle Books, 1974), 99; Leslie Tonner, *Nothing but the Best: The Luck of the Jewish Princess* (New York: Ballantine Books, 1975), 70; Lukatsky and Toback, *Jewish American Princess Handbook*, 110. This would imply that single Jewish girls do indulge in sexual activity.

43. Tonner, *Nothing but the Best*, 56; Larry Wilde, *The Last Official Jewish Joke Book* (New York: Pinnacle Books, 1980), 48.

44. Anon., *Race Riots: An Anthology of Ethnic Insults* (New York: Kanrom, 1966), [8]; Lukatsky and Toback, *Jewish American Princess Handbook*, 86.

45. Wilde, *Last Official Jewish Joke Book*, 60; Knott, *Truly Tasteless Jokes*, 19; Knott, *Truly Tasteless Jokes Two*, 10.

46. Thickett, *Outrageously Offensive Jokes*, 49; Wilde, *Official Book of John Jokes*, 65.

47. Compare Wilde, *Last Official Jewish Joke Book*, 22.

48. Knott, *Truly Tasteless Jokes Two*, 57.

49. Lukatsky and Toback, *Jewish American Princess Handbook*, 68; Knott, *Truly Tasteless Jokes Two*, 23; Thickett, *Outrageously Offensive Jokes*, 47.

50. Blanche Knott, *Truly Tasteless Jokes Three* (New York: Ballantine Books, 1983), 20.

51. Compare Samuel S. Janus, "The Great Jewish-American Comedians' Identity Crisis," *American Journal of Psychoanalysis* 40 (1980): 264.

52. Knott, *Truly Tasteless Jokes Two*, 27.

53. Compare Thickett, *Outrageously Offensive Jokes*, II, 90.

54. Compare Thickett, *Outrageously Offensive Jokes*, 45; Knott, *Truly Tasteless Jokes Two*, 26.

55. Knott, *Truly Tasteless Jokes Two*, 23; Thickett, *Outrageously Offensive Jokes*, 44.

56. Knott, *Truly Tasteless Jokes Three*, 18.

57. Thickett, *Outrageously Offensive Jokes*, II, 51. Compare Julius Alvin, *Utterly Gross Jokes* (New York: Zebra Books, 1984), 24: "Why is a tampon like a J.A.P.? Because they're both stuck up cunts."

58. Compare Knott, *Truly Tasteless Jokes*, 22; Wilde, *Official Book of John Jokes*, 64.

59. Compare Wilde, *Official Book of John Jokes*, 68.

60. Compare Knott, *Truly Tasteless Jokes Two*, 23; Julius Alvin, *Gross Jokes* (New York: Zebra Books, 1983), 14.

61. Knott, *Truly Tasteless Jokes Two*, 27; Wilde, *Official Book of John Jokes*, 64.

62. Alvin, *Totally Gross Jokes*, 13.

63. Ibid.

64. Compare Knott, *Truly Tasteless Jokes*, 22.

65. For another version, see Thickett, *Outrageously Offensive Jokes*, 49.

66. Compare Wilde, *Official Book of John Jokes*, 5.

67. Anna Sequoia, *The Official J.A.P. Handbook* (New York: New American Library, 1982), 8–9. In South Africa, the Prince is called a "Bagel," according to Levine, *Unreal Humor of the Kugel & Bagel*.

68. Anon., *Race Riots*, [8]; Wilde, *Official Jewish/Irish Joke Book*, 89.

69. Anna Sequoia and Patty Brown, *The Official J.A.P. Paper Doll Book* (New York: New American Library), 1983.

70. Patricia Erens, "Gangsters, Vampires, and J.A.P.s: The Jew Surfaces in American Movies," *Journal of Popular Film* 4 (1975): 213–17.

71. Tonner, *Nothing but the Best*.

72. Sequoia, *Official J.A.P. Handbook*, and Sequoia and Brown, *The Official J.A.P. Paper Doll Book*.

73. Lisa Birnbach, ed., *The Official Preppy Handbook* (New York: Workman Publishing, 1980).

74. For discussion of the J.A.M. and J.A.P. in American literature, see Baumgold, "Persistence of the Jewish American Princess"; Zanger, "On Not Making It"; Baum, Hyman, and Michel, *Jewish Woman in America*; Mintz, *Myth of the Jewish Mother*; and Bienstock, "Changing Image."

75. Alan Dundes, "Many Hands Make Light Work or Caught in the Act of Screwing in Light Bulbs," *Western Folklore* 40 (1981): 263–64; Novak and Waldoks, *Big Book*, 126; Knott, *Truly Tasteless Jokes*, 22.

76. Wilde, *Last Official Jewish Joke Book*, 32; Dundes, "Many Hands Make Light Work," 264; compare Knott, *Truly Tasteless Jokes*, 23.

77. Baum, Hyman, and Michel, *Jewish Woman in America*, 244; compare Blau, "In Defense of the Jewish Mother," 43.

78. Tamar Pelleg-Sani, "Personality Traits of the 'Jewish Mother': Realities Behind the Myths." Ph.D. dissertation, Psychology Department, United States International University, 1984.

79. Compare Baumgold, "Persistence of the Jewish American Princess"; Reguer, "Jewish Mother."

80. Martha Wolfenstein, "Two Types of Jewish Mothers," in *Childhood in Contemporary Cultures*, Margaret Mead and Martha Wolfenstein, eds. (Chicago: University of Chicago Press, 1963), 425.

81. Ibid., 426.

82. Ibid., 427.

83. Ruth Benedict, "Child Rearing in Certain European Countries," *American Journal of Orthopsychiatry* 19 (1949); compare Blau, "In Defense of the Jewish Mother," 43.

84. Tonner, *Nothing but the Best*, 12.

85. Compare Kurt Lewin, "Self-Hatred Among Jews," *Contemporary Jewish Record* 4 (1941); Sol Liptzin, "The Vogue of Jewish Self-Hatred," *Congress Weekly* 24 (11) (March 18, 1957); Rosenberg and Shapiro, "Marginality."

86. Joseph Dorinson, "Jewish Humor: Mechanism for Defense, Weapon for Cultural Affirmation," *Journal of Psychohistory* 8 (1981): 450.

87. Grotjahn, "Jewish Jokes," 184.

88. Dan Ben-Amos, "The 'Myth' of Jewish Humor," *Western Folklore* 32 (1973): 123.

89. Ibid., 125.

90. Naomi Katz and Eli Katz, "Tradition and Adaptation in American Jewish Humor," *Journal of American Folklore* 84 (1971): 219.

91. Stanley Brandes, "Jewish-American Dialect Jokes and Jewish-American Identity," *Jewish Social Studies* 45 (1983): 239.

92. Katz and Katz, "Tradition and Adaptation," 220.

93. Compare Heda Jason, "The Jewish Joke: The Problem of Definition," *Southern Folklore Quarterly* 31 (1967): 48–54.

94. Sequoia, *Official J.A.P. Handbook*, 10.

95. Ibid., 22.

96. Reguer, "Jewish Mother," 42.

97. Knott, *Truly Tasteless Jokes Two*, 112; Wilde, *Official Book of John Jokes*, 64.

98. Ehrlich, "Ethnic and Intergroup Humor," 393.

99. Baum, Hyman, and Michel, *Jewish Woman in America*, 239.

100. Ibid., 241.

101. Ibid., 238.

CHAPTER 7 *97 Reasons Why Cucumbers Are Better Than Men*

1. Compare Evan Esar, *The Humor of Humor* (New York: Bramhall House, 1952).

2. For a generous sampling of some 230 texts of this genre, see Leopold Fechtner, *American Wit and Gags* (New York: Vantage Press, 1969), 102–12.

3. Ibid., 93–101.

4. Gershon Legman, *Rationale of the Dirty Joke: An Analysis of Sexual Humor* (New York: Grove Press, 1968), 326.

5. Ibid., 331.

6. Compare Alan Dundes and Carl R. Pagter, *Urban Folklore from the Paperwork Empire* (Austin: American Folklore Society, 1975).

7. Lisa Rahfeldt, *Cucumbers Are Better Than Men Because. . .* (Watertown, MA: Ivory Tower Publishing, 1982).

8. M. L. Brooks, Donne E. Hanberry, Ivor Matz, Tom Westover, and Craig Westover, *Why Cucumbers Are Better Than Men* (New York: M. Evans and Company, 1983).

9. Compare Legman, *Rationale of the Dirty Joke*, 83–91.

10. Havelock Ellis, "Auto-Eroticism: A Study of the Spontaneous Manifestations of the Sexual Impulse," in Manfred F. DeMartino, ed., *Human Autoerotic Practices: Studies on Masturbation* (New York: Human Sciences Press, 1979), 191.

11. Betty Dodson, "Masturbation as Meditation," in Manfred F. DeMartino, ed., *Human Autoerotic Practices: Studies on Masturbation* (New York: Human Sciences Press, 1979), 173.

12. Legman, *Rationale of the Dirty Joke*, 209.

13. Alfred C. Kinsey, Wardell B. Pomeroy, and Clyde E. Martin, *Sexual Behavior in the Human Male* (Philadelphia: W.B. Saunders Company, 1948), 674.

CHAPTER 8 *Slurs International: Folk Comparisons of Ethnicity and National Character*

1. This chapter was originally a paper presented as part of the Charles Phelps Taft Interdisciplinary Forum on the Nature of Humor held at the University of Cincinnati on April 29, 1975.

2. A particularly useful listing of many sources is J. C. H. Duijker and N. H. Fridja, *National Character and National Stereotypes* (Amsterdam: North-Holland, 1960). For a cogent introduction to the study of national character, see Alex Inkeles and Daniel J. Levinson, "National Character: The Study of Modal Personality and Sociocultural Systems," in Gardner Lindzey and Elliot Aronson, eds., *The Handbook of Social Psychology*, 2d ed., 4 (Reading, MA: Addison-Wesley, 1969), 418–506. For recent scholarship, consult the *Revue de Psychologie des Peuples*, which began publication in 1945, or the *Journal of Cross-Cultural Psychology*, which started in 1970. For a brief discussion of national character in folk narrative, see Max Lüthi, *Märchen* (fünfte auflage) (Stuttgart: J. B. Metzlersche Verlagsbuchhandlung, 1974), 96–99.

3. Wilhelm Wackernagel, "Die Spottnamen der Völker," *Zeitschrift für Deutsches Alterthum*, 6 (1848): 254–61.

4. Otto von Reinsberg-Düringsfeld, *Internationale Titulaturen*, 2 vols. (Leipzig: Hermann Fries, 1863). Although Reinsberg-Düringsfeld's coverage of materials from the United States is extremely scanty, it mentions one slur against an American city. Cincinnati was called "Porkopolis" because of its eminence as a center for the breeding of hogs. Other Americanisms include "Nutmegs" for the inhabitants of Connecticut and "Muskrats" for the people of Delaware. See *Internationale Titulaturen*, 2, 111.

5. Henri Gaidoz and Paul Sébillot, *Blason Populaire de la France* (Paris: Librarie Léopold Cerf, 1884). The non-French materials may be found on pp. 321–78. Folklorists may be interested to know that Indiana University has acquired the Henri Gaidoz collection, which consists of more than 200 filing boxes filled with congress programs, folklore memorabilia, and especially numerous offprints sent by their authors to Gaidoz. The Gaidoz collection is housed in the Special Collections section of the Indiana University Library, and will be a boon to scholars interested in French and nineteenth-century folklore studies.

6. A. A. Roback, *A Dictionary of International Slurs (Ethnophaulisms)* (Cambridge: Sci-Art Publishers, 1944). For one of the few subsequent uses of the term, see Erdon B. Palmore, "Ethnophaulisms and Ethnocentrism," *American Journal of Sociology* 67 (1962): 442–45. The term is not used by Wm. Hugh Jansen in "A Culture's Stereotypes and Their Expression in Folk Clichés," *Southwestern Journal of Anthropology* 13 (1957): 184–200, or by Ed Cray in "Ethnic and Place Names as Derisive Adjectives," *Western Folklore* 21 (1962): 27–34.

7. Archer Taylor, *The Proverb* (Hatboro: Folklore Associates, 1962), 99.

8. I acknowledge my debt to Julia Anna Roth and her unpublished M.A. in Folklore thesis, submitted at the University of California, Berkeley,

in 1970. Entitled "The Multi-Nationality Joke: A Study of *Blason Popu-laire*," it was based on a collection of texts from informants living at International House in Berkeley. This text may be found on p. 63. For a Scandinavian version in which it is the Swedes who are waiting to be introduced, see Donald S. Connery, *The Scandinavians* (New York: Simon & Schuster, 1966), 18.

9. This text is taken from another thesis. See Carol Scholten, "Modern German Ethnic Humor: Jokes of German University Students about Fellow Germans, Frenchmen, Russians, and Americans," unpublished M.A. in Folklore thesis, University of California, Berkeley, 1971, p. 32. Texts in this paper not specifically acknowledged may be found in the Folklore Archives, University of California, Berkeley.

10. Antti Aarne and Stith Thompson, *The Types of the Folktale* (Helsinki: Academia Scientiarum Fennica, 1961), type 1626.

11. Roback, *Dictionary*, 192.

12. Ibid., 177. See also 195.

13. Ibid., 152.

14. See Carsten Bregenhøj, *Jyde, Fynbo og Sjaellaender* (Copenhagen: Dansk Folkemindesamling og Nordisk Institut for Folkedigtning, 1969). Roth, "Multi-Nationality Jokes," 32–41, has an extended discussion based upon numerous texts of the three individuals jumping out of an airplane. For the pig/goat in the cave, see pp. 42–43.

15. Roback, *Dictionary*, 240.

16. See John C. Brigham, "Ethnic Stereotypes," *Psychological Bulletin* 76 (1971): 15–38. Lippmann's definition is discussed on p. 15.

17. E. Terry Prothro and Levon H. Melikian, "Studies in Stereotypes: V. Familiarity and the Kernel of Truth Hypothesis," *Journal of Social Psychology* 41 (1955): 3–10.

18. For a brief consideration of this form, see Roger D. Abrahams and Joseph C. Hickerson, "Cross-Fertilization Riddles," *Western Folklore* 23 (1964): 253–57.

19. I have examined these particular stereotype traits in a detailed consideration of the Jew and the Pole in American folklore. See Alan Dundes, "A Study of Ethnic Slurs: The Jew and the Polack in the United States," *Journal of American Folklore* 84 (1971): 186–202. See also Chapter 9 in this book.

20. Scholten, "Modern German Ethnic Humor," 34.

21. Roback, *Dictionary*, 172.

22. Roth, "Multi-National Joke," 62.

23. Reported in L. M. Boyd, "The Grab Bag," *San Francisco Sunday Examiner & Chronicle, Sunday Punch*, January 13, 1974.

24. Vincent Stuckey Lean, "Comparisons with Other Nations," in *Lean's Collectanea*, vol. 1 (Bristol: J. W. Arrowsmith, 1902), 22; Roback, *Dictionary*, 158.

25. Roback, *Dictionary*, 158. It is difficult to say whether this proverb has more validity than Madariaga's categorical statement, "It is therefore to be expected that the Spaniard will excel in conception, the Frenchman in formation, and the Englishman in execution." See Salvador de Madariaga, *Englishmen, Frenchmen, Spaniards: An Essay in Comparative Psychology* (London: Oxford University Press, 1928), 127.

26. Roback, *Dictionary*, 242–43. For a Scandinavian version, see Connery, *Scandinavians*, 18.

27. Roback, *Dictionary*, 211.

28. Ibid., 237, 238.

29. Ibid., 165.

30. Ibid., 165, 238.

31. Lean, "Comparison with Other Nations," 24.

32. Reinsberg-Düringsfeld, *Internationale Titulaturen*, 4.

33. Roback, *Dictionary*, 237.

34. Scholten, "Modern German Ethnic Humor," 46.

35. Sometimes this particular multinational text is printed up on cards. Perhaps the written or printed form has led to a somewhat longer list of national participants than is the case with purely orally transmitted versions. For a sample printed version, see Alan Dundes and Carl R. Pagter, *Urban Folklore from the Paperwork Empire* (Austin: American Folklore Society, 1975), 61.

36. I reported both this text and the immediately preceding one in "A Study of Ethnic Slurs," 191.

37. Petr Beckmann, *Whispered Anecdotes* (Boulder: The Golem Press, 1969), 77.

38. Alan Dundes, "Laughter Behind the Iron Curtain: A Sample of Rumanian Political Jokes," *Ukrainian Quarterly* 27 (1971): 54. See Chapter 13.

39. Mariana D. Birnbaum, "On the Language of Prejudice," *Western Folklore* 30 (1971): 247–68.

40. Ibid., 256.

41. William Buchanan and Hadley Cantril, *How Nations See Each Other: A Study in Public Opinion* (Urbana: University of Illinois Press, 1953), 45.

42. Ibid., 50.

43. Ibid., 57.

44. Ibid., v.

CHAPTER 9   *The Jew and the Polack in the United States: A Study of Ethnic Slurs*

1. For samples of this extensive literature, see Georges A. Heuse, *La psychologie ethnique* (Paris: Librairie Philosophique J. Vrin, 1953); Paul Griéger, *La caractérologie ethnique* (Paris: Presses Universitaires de France, 1961); Don Martindale, ed., "National Character in the Perspective of the Social Science," *Annals of the American Academy of Political and Social Science* 370 (1967): 1–163; and especially the valuable bibliographical survey of J. C. H. Duijker and N. H. Fridja, *National Character and National Stereotypes* (Amsterdam: North Holland, 1960).

2. See the discussion by W. Edgar Vinacke, "Stereotypes as Social Concepts," *Journal of Social Psychology* 46 (1957): 229–43.

3. Representative are Daniel Katz and Kenneth W. Braly, "Verbal Stereotypes and Racial Prejudice," in *Readings in Social Psychology*, 3rd ed., Eleanor E. Maccoby, Theodore M. Newcomb, and Eugene L. Hartley, eds. (New York: Holt, 1958), 40–46; and G. Saenger and S. Flowerman, "Stereotypes and Prejudicial Attitudes," *Human Relations* 7 (1954): 217–38.

4. For Chinese examples, see Wolfram Eberhard, "Chinese Regional Stereotypes," *Asian Survey* 5 (1965): 596–608; for Turkish examples, see Wm. Hugh Jansen, "A Culture's Stereotypes and Their Expression in Folk Clichés," *Southwestern Journal of Anthropology* 13 (1959): 184–200. For additional discussion of the relationship between jokes and stereotypes, see Walter P. Zenner, "Joking and Ethnic Stereotyping," *Anthropological Quarterly* 43 (1970): 93–113.

5. Vinacke, "Stereotypes as Social Concepts," 232.

6. See the interesting study of children's rhymes by Nathan Hurvitz, "Jews and Jewishness in the Street Rhymes of American Children," *Jewish Social Studies* 16 (1954): 135–50.

7. E. Terry Prothro and Levon H. Melikian, "Studies in Stereotypes: V. Familiarity and the Kernel of Truth Hypothesis," *Journal of Social Psychology* 41 (1955): 3–10. For further consideration of cross-cultural stereotypes, see E. Terry Prothro, "Cross-Cultural Patterns of National Stereotypes,"

Journal of Social Psychology 40 (1954): 53–59; W. Buchanan and H. Cantril, *How Nations See Each Other* (Urbana: University of Illinois Press, 1953); and Wallace E. Lambert and Otto Klineberg, *Children's Views of Foreign Peoples: A Cross-National Study* (New York: Appleton-Century-Crofts, 1967).

8. Wm. Hugh Jansen, "The Esoteric-Exoteric Factor in Folklore," *Fabula* 2 (1959): 205–11, reprinted in Alan Dundes, ed., *The Study of Folklore* (Englewood Cliffs: Prentice-Hall, 1965), 43–51. An earlier delineation of the theoretical possibilities of stereotypes of "self" and "other" may be found in Oliver Wendell Holmes, *The Autocrat of the Breakfast-Table* (New York: Heritage Press, 1955), 47.

9. The classic study, Henri Gaidoz and Paul Sebillot, *Blason populaire de la France* (Paris: Librarie Leopold Cerf, 1884), is primarily concerned with slurs about different regions of France. One section, however—pp. 332–78—is devoted to foreigners.

10. The term proposed by A. A. Roback in *A Dictionary of International Slurs (Ethnophaulisms)* (Cambridge, MA: Sci-Art Publishers, 1944) has received little acceptance. However, see Erdon B. Palmore, "Ethnophaulisms and Ethnocentrism," *American Journal of Sociology* 67 (1962): 442–45.

11. For other anti-Hungarian proverbs, see Roback, *Dictionary*, 81.

12. For additional place name slurs found in the United States, see Ed Cray, "Ethnic and Place Names as Derisive Adjectives," *Western Folklore* 21 (1962): 27–34; and the various additions to his list, such as George Monteiro, "And Still More Ethnic and Place Names as Derisive Adjectives," *Western Folklore* 27 (1968): 51.

13. Dundes, *The Study of Folklore*, 2.

14. See Jansen, "The Esoteric-Exoteric Factor."

15. For alternative theories of the origin of "wop," see Roback, *Dictionary*, 70, and Palmore, "Ethnophaulisms," 44.

16. For other examples, see Roback, *Dictionary*, and Donald C. Simmons, "Anti-Italian-American Riddles in New England," *Journal of American Folklore* 79 (1966): 475–78.

17. For other considerations of the generic Jew in American folklore, see Roback, *Dictionary*, and Hurvitz, "Jews and Jewishness," and especially Rodolf Glanz, *The Jew in the Old American Folklore* (New York: Waldon Press, 1961).

18. This particular text is reported in a similar form by Bernard Rosenberg and Gilbert Shapiro, "Marginality and Jewish Humor," *Midstream* 4 (1958): 70–80, which also contains an enlightening discussion of such themes as the impossibility of the true conversion of a Jew to Christianity.

19. See Roback, *Dictionary*, 46–47.

20. See H. A. Wolff, C. E. Smith, and H. A. Murray, "The Psychology of Humor: A Study of Responses to Race-Disparagement Jokes." *Journal of Abnormal and Social Psychology* 28 (1934): 341–65.

21. See Roger L. Welsh, "American Numskull Tales: The Polack Joke," *Western Folklore* 26 (1967): 183–86; and such popular booklets as the anonymous *Race Riots: An Anthology of Ethnic Insults* (New York: Kanrom, 1966) and E. Zewbskewiecz, J. Kuligowski, and H. Krulka, *It's Fun to be a Polack* (Glendale, CA: Collectors Publications, 1965). Parallels for many of the texts cited in this paper may be found in these collections. For more recent treatments, see Mac E. Barrick, "Racial Riddles and the Polack Joke," *Keystone Folklore Quarterly* 15 (1970): 3–15; Jan Harold Brunvand, "Some Thoughts on the Ethnic-Regional Riddle Jokes," *Indiana Folklore* 3 (1970): 128–42; and especially the comprehensive listing in William M. Clements, *The Types of the Polack Joke*, Folklore Forum, A Bibliographical and Special Series, Number 3 (November, 1969).

22. See Simmons, "Anti Italian-American Riddles," 476.

23. See Roback, *Dictionary*, 110–11, where, for example, there is a Silesian slur referring to a Polish clothing pattern as being a "loud" design, implying a lack of taste. The lack of taste in clothing design and color seems to be part of the Polack stereotype in the United States also.

24. Roback, *Dictionary*, 110, reports the German idiom, *einen Polnischen machen*, meaning to blow one's nose into the hand.

25. See also Simmons, "Anti-Italian American Riddles."

26. See Roger D. Abrahams and Alan Dundes, "On Elephantasy and Elephanticide," in Chapter 4 of this book.

CHAPTER 10 *Polish Pope Jokes*

1. A newspaper article entitled "Pope Seen as Curb on Jokes: U.S. Poles Hope the Laugh's Over" by David Behrens appeared in the *Los Angeles Times*, November 25, 1978, Part II, 11. The article notes that the news of the Pope's election "triggered another brief but barbed round of Polish jokes," but not a single text is cited. The media, reluctant enough to treat ethnic slurs generally, would be unlikely to risk offending its Catholic audiences.

2. See, for example, William M. Clements, *The Types of the Polack Joke*, Folklore Forum Bibliographic and Special Series no. 3, rev. ed. (Bloomington: Folklore Institute, 1973), and Alan Dundes, "A Study of Ethnic Slurs: The Jew and the Polack in the United States," *Journal of American*

Folklore 84 (1971): 186–203. Popular paperback anthologies of Polish jokes also attest to the vitality of the cycle, although many of the jokes in these anthologies have obviously been adapted — for example, by adding Polish names to the protagonists to permit them to be included. Typical are Pat Macklin and Manny Erdman, *Polish Jokes* (n.p.: Patman Publications, 1976), and Larry Wilde, *The Last Official Polish Joke Book* (Los Angeles: Pinnacle Books, 1977).

3. Michael Novak, "The Sting of Polish Jokes," *Newsweek*, April 12, 1976, 13.

4. See Dundes, "A Study of Ethnic Slurs," 201. For further discussion of the general issues raised by ethnic slurs, see Alan Dundes, "Slurs International: Folk Comparisons of Ethnicity and National Character," *Southern Folklore Quarterly* 39 (1975): 15–38, and Chapter 9 of this book.

5. Clements, *Types of the Polack Joke*, 10. Clements indicates that the joke dates from 1969.

6. I received this text from Professor Marcello Truzzi, Department of Sociology, Eastern Michigan University, Ypsilanti, Michigan, in a letter dated November 3, 1978.

CHAPTER 11   *Many Hands Make Light Work, or Caught in the Act of Screwing in Light Bulbs*

1. William M. Clements, *The Types of the Polack Joke, Folklore Forum* Bibliographic and Special Series No. 3 (Bloomington: Folklore Institute, 1973), 27, E7.6.6, "The Number of Polacks Needed to Screw in a Light Bulb."

2. For a discussion of this trait and others in the Polack joke cycle, see Alan Dundes, "A Study of Ethnic Slurs: The Jew and the Polack in the United States," *Journal of American Folklore* 84 (1971): 186–203. See Chapter 9 of this book.

3. I have previously suggested that the American jokes about Polacks had antecedents in a German ethnic slur tradition about Poles. See Dundes, "Study of Ethnic Slurs," 200–201.

4. Judith B. Kerman, "The Light-Bulb Jokes: Americans Look at Social Action Processes," *Journal of American Folklore* 93 (1980): 454–58; Matt Freedman and Paul Hoffman, *How Many Zen Buddhists Does It Take to Screw in a Light Bulb?* (New York: St. Martin's Press, 1980). Kerman's original manuscript had "Many Hands Make Light Work" as a subtitle, but presumably editorial intervention eliminated it. I have gratefully borrowed it.

5. Most of the texts were collected in Berkeley, California, in 1979 and 1980. I acknowledge valuable assistance in supplying additional texts from: Swedish folklorist Bengt af Klintberg (who forwarded to me a set of light bulb jokes he had received from a friend in New York City); Berkeley linguist Nancy Levidow; and my daughter Alison, who collected texts from classmates at Harvard. Each of the groups named in the light bulb jokes could be the subject of a separate study. For example, Californians, as a group are featured in analogous jokes — "How many Californians does it take to water a plant? Two. One to pour the Perrier (mineral water) and one to massage the leaves."

CHAPTER 12 *Misunderstanding Humor: An American Stereotype of the Englishman*

1. See, for example, H. J. Eysenck, "National Differences in 'Sense of Humor,' Three Experimental and Statistical Studies," *Journal of Personality* 13 (1944/45): 37–54.

2. W. Carew Hazlitt, *Studies in Jocular Literature* (London: Elliot Stock, 1890), 92.

3. For a further consideration of this pattern, see Alan Dundes, "The Binary Structure of 'Unsuccessful Repetition,' in Lithuanian Folk Tales," *Western Folklore* 21 (1962): 165–74. The pattern occurs cross-culturally. The American Indian Bungling Host tale type (Motif J 2425) is an obvious example. For a consideration of more than 200 versions of this tale, see Mac Jean Faber, "The Tale of the Bungling Host: A Historic-Geographic Analysis," M.A. in Anthropology, San Francisco State University, 1970.

4. Hazlitt, *Studies in Jocular Literature*, 92–93.

5. Ibid., 93.

6. Charles C. Bombaugh, *Facts and Fancies for the Curious from the Harvest-Fields of Literature* (Philadelphia: J. P. Lippincott, 1905), 356–61. Earlier editions of this rarely cited but nonetheless interesting compilation of folklore do not contain the marred anecdote discussion. None appear, for instance, in Bombaugh, *Gleanings from the Harvest-Fields of Literature, Science and Art* (Baltimore: T. N. Kurtz, 1860). It is very likely that it was Hazlitt's notice of the form in 1890 which stimulated interest in it.

7. Evan Esar, *The Humor of Humor* (New York: Bramhall House, 1952), 262.

8. Norman Moss, *What's the Difference? An American-British/British-American Dictionary* (London: Arrow Books, 1978), 217. The tin-can distinction goes back to the turn of the century. See E. Azalia Hackley, "English in England," *The Colored American Magazine* 15 (1909): 175.

9. I collected this joke in Berkeley in 1971 from an informant who claimed he had first heard it in the 1930s.

10. This was collected by Sharon Gay Smith from Weldon H. Smith, age 48, in 1964. Mr Smith had heard the joke in Montgomery, Alabama circa 1954.

11. This joke was collected by Mary Gill from Charlotte Kursh, age 53, in 1965. Mrs. Kursh heard the story from her mother circa 1920 in the Cambridge, Massachusetts area. The same joke is found in Bombaugh, *Facts and Fancies*, 358–59, but without reference to an Englishman. [Venetia Newall, editor of *International Folklore Review*, reports: "An English friend of mine remembers the almost identical joke told when he was a boy in the 1930s by his father (born in 1888), although in this case the butt is an American. 'An Englishman invites a recently arrived American neighbor to lunch, but when the butler brings the main course—boiled tongue—into the dining room, it slips from the serving-dish to the floor. "Just a lapsus linguae," says the English host, to the great amusement of the gathered (English) guests. The American, who has missed the point, is determined not to be outdone, so he gives a lunch party, for which he orders the most expensive joint of beef. He tells his butler deliberately to let it fall, and then repeats the Englishman's comment. Nobody is amused.'"] In the marred anecdote tradition, it is frequently a folk metaphor that is misunderstood. In a letter to *Time Magazine*, we find, for instance, a version of "the old joke about the male robin who, upon finding a brown egg in his nest, inquired of his wife regarding this phenomenon. She replied that she had done it for a lark. The joke was retold later by a Briton who told it intact except for the tag line, which became: 'I did it for a sparrow.'" See G. L. Andrews, "The Bird," *Time*, January 12, 1970, 2, 4.

12. This toast was collected by Terry Viall from John W. Viall, age 63, in Salinas, California, in 1974. Mr. Viall remembers learning the joke around 1922 in Oshkosh, Wisconsin, from his mother, who had in turn learned it from her grandfather, who had immigrated from County Cork, Ireland. This would make the joke more than a century old at least.

13. I am indebted to Professor Doug McKay of the Department of Foreign Languages, University of Colorado, Colorado Springs, who learned the text in Colorado Springs in 1976. Gershon Legman's note on the limerick traces it back to a version published in *Anthropophyteia* in 1911. He remarks that he found the Tupper-topper as repeated by an Englishman appeared first in 1943. See G. Legman, *The Limerick* (New York: Bell Publishing Company, 1979), 20 (No. 97), 378.

14. This was collected by Linda Perotti from D. Steve Clare in 1968, who had heard the joke in Berkeley the same year.

15. See, for example, the joke quoted editorially in Footnote 11.

16. I am indebted to my daughter Alison for calling my attention to these examples of Anglo-French and Franco-English reciprocal stereotypes. The reciprocal traits of American exaggeration and British understatement have been noticed by many observers. Henry W. Nevinson, in his *Farewell to America* (London: J. and E. Bumpus, 1926), 11, included the following lines (which appeared first in *The Nation* in 1922): "Good-bye to the land where grotesque exaggeration is called humour, and people gape in bewilderment at irony, as a bullock gapes at a dog straying in his field!" Margaret Mead also drew attention to the understatement-overstatement distinction in her essay, "The Application of Anthropological Techniques to Cross-National Communication," in Alan Dundes, ed., *Every Man His Way: Readings in Cultural Anthropology* (Englewood Cliffs, NJ: Prentice-Hall, 1968), 524. The American delight in exaggeration and the English pleasure in understatement are manifested in the results of some experimental research in comparative humor. Eysenck, though without offering any explanation whatsoever for the data presented, remarked that in a study of English and American subjects' responses to a common corpus of jokes, "the item on which the English and Americans differed most" was the following:
Prison visitor: How long are you here for?
Convict: Thirty years.
Visitor: Ah well, here's another day nearly gone.
This item, Eysenck reported, was liked much better by the English than by the Americans. The item with the biggest difference between the two nations was the following, for which the Americans expressed a preference:
The speaker, who had arrived in a crabby frame of mind, looked around and beckoned the chairman.
"I would like to have a glass of water on my table, please," he said.
"To drink?" was the chairman's idiotic question.
"Oh, no," was the sarcastic retort: "When I've been speaking half an hour I do a high dive."
See Eysenck, "National Differences," 51, n.2.

17. For a useful anthology of selections from these and other writers, see Allan Nevins, ed., *America Through British Eyes* (New York: Oxford University Press, 1948). There have been numerous attempts to ascertain the English view of Americans, such as Fred Vanderschmidt, *What the English Think of Us* (New York: R. M. McBride, 1948). Often the English commented on the Americans' use or abuse of the English language. According to one report, for example, Andrew Lang reacted to American humorist George Ade's "Fables in Slang" in a characteristic way. One of the protagonists of Ade's stories entered an Italian restaurant that author Ade described as a spaghetti-joint. Lang's response was that he did not know

spaghetti had any joints. See Brander Matthews, "American English and British English," *Scribner's Magazine* 68 (1920): 622.

18. Mead, "Application of Anthropological Techniques," 530.

19. Ibid., 526, 529.

20. For more about projective inversion, see Alan Dundes, *Interpreting Folklore* (Bloomington: Indiana University Press, 1980), 51–56.

21. Compare Gertrude Hanchett, "A Multiple Scale of Attitudes Toward the British," *Journal of Social Psychology* 31 (1950): 203–204.

22. Esar, *Humor of Humor*, 262.

CHAPTER 13 *Laughter Behind the Iron Curtain: A Sample of Rumanian Political Jokes*

1. For a much more substantial sampling of Rumanian political jokes, see C. Banc and Alan Dundes, *First Prize: Fifteen Years! An Annotated Collection of Rumanian Political Jokes* (Rutherford, NJ: Fairleigh Dickinson University Press, 1986). This collection of more than 300 jokes also demonstrates that the same jokes are told throughout Eastern Europe and the Soviet Union.